Tim O'Brien

Twayne's United States Authors Series

Frank Day, Editor

Clemson University

TUSAS 691

Tim O'Brien
Jerry Bauer

Tim O'Brien

Tobey C. Herzog

Wabash College

Twayne Publishers
An Imprint of Simon & Schuster Macmillan
New York

Prentice Hall International
London • Mexico City • New Delhi • Singapore • Sydney • Toronto

Twayne's United States Authors Series No. 691

Tim O'Brien
Tobey C. Herzog

Twayne Publishers
An Imprint of Simon & Schuster Macmillan
1633 Broadway
New York, NY 10019

Library of Congress Cataloging-in-Publication Data

Herzog, Tobey C.
    Tim O'Brien / Tobey C. Herzog.
        p. cm. — (Twayne's United States authors series ; TUSAS 691)
    Includes bibliographical references and index.
    ISBN 0-8057-7825-X (hardcover : alk. paper)
    1. O'Brien, Tim, 1946–   —Criticism and interpretation.
2. Vietnamese Conflict, 1961–1975—Literature and the conflict.
I. Title. II. Series.
PS3565.B75Z69 1997
813'.54—dc21   97-25478
                                                                                   CIP

10 9 8 7 6 5 4 3 2

Printed in the United States of America

This book is dedicated to
my wife, Peggy
my sons, Rob and Joe

Contents

Preface

This critical study of Tim O'Brien's life and books (not his short stories) arises from my experiences teaching O'Brien's nonfiction and fiction in a variety of literature classes at Wabash College, from my scholarship on American literature emerging from the Vietnam experience, and from my sincere belief that O'Brien is one of America's best contemporary writers.[1] My interest in O'Brien also emerges from some intriguing parallels and differences in the lives of two baby boomers. Both of us were born in October 1946 in small Midwestern towns. Our fathers were World War II veterans, and we had similar childhoods—sports, war games, and Fourth of July parades. Graduating from high school in 1964, we attended small liberal arts colleges, also in the Midwest. Soon after college graduation, we received draft notices and faced decisions at a time when the national debate about America's involvement in Viet Nam raged. O'Brien's difficult decision not to resist the draft but to enter the army in August 1968 still haunts him to this day and is perhaps the defining moment of his life; my decision to enter the army in February 1969 was routine. We each served a tour of duty in Viet Nam (1969–1970)—he as a foot soldier in a combat unit; I as a clerk in a personnel support unit. After our discharges from the army in 1970, we entered Ph.D. programs: he in government and I in British literature. His interest in writing about the Vietnam War or, as he notes, in exposing its "brutality, injustice, and stupidity" and in telling stories began almost immediately after his return from Viet Nam. My interest in teaching about the Vietnam experience did not surface until 1979 as I struggled with ways to help my students and me understand America's involvement with the country of Viet Nam, the tumultuous war, and its aftermath. Our paths led us in different directions—O'Brien's to fame and numerous literary awards for his short stories and books; mine to a rather obscure life teaching at a small college in a small Midwestern community.

Our paths have crossed on a few occasions. I first became aware of Tim O'Brien in 1979 as I was preparing to teach my first literature course devoted to Vietnam War narratives. As I was having a difficult time selecting quality books about the war for my undergraduate students, I was thrilled to discover O'Brien's *Going After Cacciato*. It was much more than a war story; it was a sophisticated, complex, play-ful, and mysterious tale that transcended the battlefield and dealt with universal issues of artistic creation, courage, fear, chaos, and self-understanding. Over the next 15 years, I discovered that these features are hallmarks of O'Brien's fiction. Our paths crossed once again in November 1994 when O'Brien visited the Wabash campus, and this book project became a possibility. At Wabash, O'Brien's willingness to talk about his life and approaches to writing, as well as his eagerness to teach his audiences about storytelling, convinced me that his own words should be an important part of any critical study of his life and works. Consequently, my lengthy interview with Tim O'Brien during two days in July 1995 became an essential beginning for this project.

Because our conversations revealed how closely O'Brien's life and works are intertwined, I organized the first chapter of this book around O'Brien's roles as son, soldier, and author. Through this interview, I also confirmed my own sense of the key themes, principles of storytelling, and artistic goals that underlie all of his works and that are helpful start-ing points for a critical study of his six books. Additional information gathered from numerous interviews O'Brien has given throughout his career has validated these initial plans and perceptions. As a result, this book gives voice to reviewers, scholars, and Tim O'Brien—son, soldier, and author. This book also allows me to comment on his works from the perspective of a teacher and a reader interested in the wide-ranging body of literature emerging from "Vietnam" (the war and ongoing expe-rience) and "Viet Nam" (the country).

O'Brien's place among authors and soldier-authors writing about the Vietnam experience is firmly established. His war autobiography, *If I Die in a Combat Zone* (1973), and his novels *Going After Cacciato* (1978) and *The Things They Carried* (1990) have received universal praise and are widely read in high school and college classrooms. But as O'Brien is quick to point out, just as these three books are much more than war stories, so he is more than a "war writer." His remaining novels, *Northern Lights* (1975), *The Nuclear Age* (1985), and *In the Lake of the Woods* (1994), move from the battlefields of Viet Nam to the towns, cities, mountains, woods, and lakes of the United States where, in O'Brien's words, "the war of the living" occurs. Within these settings, O'Brien examines many of the same themes found in his war narratives: virtue, courage, evil, mortality, human relationships, quests for control, difficult choices, commitment, and the personal and global politics of life. And in all of his books, O'Brien explores the hearts and minds of his characters as they grapple with difficult decisions and external forces affecting their lives.

As a character in *Going After Cacciato* observes, "Things may be viewed from many angles. From down below, or from inside out you often discover entirely new understandings." O'Brien as a soldier, author, and even a character in his own stories has spent considerable time writing about people, relationships, war, and various themes from different angles, both within and across his works. Because of this continuity of subject matter and narrative techniques, together his works become a body of integrated stories as he uses his characteristic techniques of repetition (iteration) and multiple perspectives (angles) to develop these tales. For example, he explores his recurring fight-or-flight theme from various angles, including his own choices as well as those of fictional characters deciding sometimes whether to commit themselves to war or at other times whether to commit themselves to a meaningful life. The outcomes of these narrative angles of reality are elegantly crafted stories that readers find, for the most part, ambiguous, thought-provoking, ambitious, playful, and moving. In exploring the mysteries of the human heart and mind, O'Brien reveals the power of story-truth (shaped by the imagination) as opposed to mere happening-truth (recalled events). Most of all, his stories fit O'Brien's own definition of a "true war story": "a true war story if truly told makes the stomach believe."

In the chapters to come, I examine important events in the life of son, soldier, and author O'Brien that significantly influence the content, tone, and structure of his books. I also examine key overarching themes, such as the relationship of memory and imagination, individuals' quests for control in their lives, father-son relationships, and the politics of life. Finally, I analyze the intricate structures of his works that enhance the content, mystery, and power of his writing. Across his six books, we detect this author developing his skills as a writer and repeatedly returning to issues that he cares about. We discover this observer of human nature probing the mysteries of people's souls and psyches. We also appreciate the teacher O'Brien instructing his readers on the art of storytelling.

Acknowledgments

I particularly want to thank Tim O'Brien for encouraging me to complete this project and granting a two-day interview that provided a wealth of information. Several other individuals made this project much easier by contributing time, talents, information, friendship, and advice. Professor Catherine Calloway at Arkansas State University, in willingly sharing her O'Brien bibliography with me, provided invaluable aid and friendship. Marilyn Knapp Litt used her Internet skills to secure useful articles and reviews that are an important part of this book. Professor Frank Day served as a helpful editor. Wabash College summer interns Gabe Sowder and Jason Sloat contributed their research skills and insights as undergraduate English majors. Most of all, I wish to thank Wabash students in my Vietnam tutorials and modern war literature classes who have contributed needed encouragement, as well as helpful questions and viewpoints related to O'Brien's writings.

I also wish to thank the following who have kindly given permission for the use of copyrighted material:

Excerpts from *Going After Cacciato* by Tim O'Brien. Copyright © 1975, 1976, 1977, 1978 by Tim O'Brien. Used by permission of Delacorte Press/Seymour Lawrence, a division of Bantam Doubleday Dell Publishing Group, Inc.

Excerpts from *If I Die in a Combat Zone* by Tim O'Brien. Copyright © 1973 by Tim O'Brien. Used by permission of Delacorte Press/Seymour Lawrence, a division of Bantam Doubleday Dell Publishing Group, Inc.

Excerpts from *The Things They Carried*. Copyright © 1990 by Tim O'Brien. Reprinted by permission of Houghton Mifflin Co./Seymour Lawrence. All rights reserved.

Excerpts from *In the Lake of the Woods*. Copyright © 1994 by Tim O'Brien. Reprinted by permission of Houghton Mifflin Co. All rights reserved.

Excerpts from *Northern Lights* by Tim O'Brien. Copyright © 1975 by Tim O'Brien and published by Delacorte Press/Seymour Lawrence. Reprinted by permission of the author.

Chronology

1946   William Timothy O'Brien Jr. is born 1 October to William T. (insurance salesman) and Ava E. Schultz O'Brien (elementary school teacher) in Austin, Minnesota.

1956   Family moves to Worthington, Minnesota.

1964   Matriculates at Macalaster College in St. Paul, Minnesota.

1967   In summer, studies in Prague, Czechoslovakia; writes unpublished novel as course project.

1968   Graduates summa cum laude and Phi Beta Kappa with B.A. in political science from Macalaster. Served as student-body president during senior year.

1968   Drafted into the U.S. Army in August 1968.

1969–1970   Completes 13-month tour of duty with 46th Infantry, 198th Infantry Brigade at LZ Gator in Quang Ngai Province, Viet Nam, as rifleman, RTO, and clerk. Awarded Combat Infantry Badge, Purple Heart, and Bronze Star. Honorably discharged with rank of sergeant.

1970–1976   Ph.D. graduate student in government at Harvard University. Dissertation on "Case Studies in American Military Interventions" unfinished.

1971–1972   Summer intern at *Washington Post*.

1973–1974   During leave of absence from Harvard, serves as national affairs reporter for the *Washington Post*. Covers general politics, Senate hearings, and first oil boycott.

1973   *If I Die in a Combat Zone* is published.

1973   Marries Ann Weller, an editorial assistant at Little, Brown publishing house (divorced 1995).

1975   *Northern Lights* is published.

1976   Wins O. Henry Memorial Award for short story from *Going After Cacciato*.

1978   *Going After Cacciato* is published, and second short story
        from this novel wins O. Henry Award.

1979   *Going After Cacciato* wins 1978 National Book Award.

1985   *The Nuclear Age* is published.

1986–1990   Publishes short fiction in *Harper's Magazine*, *McCall's*,
            Esquire, *Playboy*, *Granta*, *Quarterly*, *Gentleman's Quar-
            terly*.

1989   Short story "The Things They Carried" wins National
        Magazine Award in Fiction.

1990   *The Things They Carried* is published. Selected by *New
        York Times* as one of the year's ten best works of fiction
        and receives the *Chicago Tribune*'s Heartland Prize.
        Finalist for Pulitzer Prize.

1991   Wins Melcher Award for *The Things They Carried*.

1992   Wins *Prix du Meilleur Livre Étranger* award in France
        for *The Things They Carried*.

1994   In February returns to Viet Nam for the first time since
        tour of duty.

1994   *In the Lake of the Woods* is published. Named by *Time*
        magazine as best work of fiction published in 1994.

1995   *In the Lake of the Woods* receives James Fenimore Cooper
        Prize for best novel based on a historical theme.

1996   Publishes short story, "Faith," in *New Yorker,* which is
        part of a novel-in-progress.

Chapter One
Angles of Life and Art:
Son, Soldier, and Author

I begin this chapter introducing Tim O'Brien's life and works with a pertinent anecdote. Almost 25 years to the day after Seymour Hersh broke the story in the *New York Times* (13 November 1969) about the massacre at My Lai (4), South Viet Nam, Tim O'Brien visited Wabash College in Crawfordsville, Indiana. He was in the midst of his book tour for *In the Lake of the Woods,* which coincidentally also examines events at My Lai. But instead of lecturing on his latest novel, O'Brien began his evening address to an audience of students, faculty, and townspeople, including some Vietnam veterans, with a personal war story. He recalled his choice to enter the army despite his strongly held belief that the war in Vietnam was wrong: "[C]ertain blood for uncertain reasons."

O'Brien first described his summer of 1968, the time immediately after his graduation from college and subsequent receipt of a draft notice. He recounted his growing moral dilemma: whether to avoid induction by fleeing to Canada or serve his country by entering the army. The conflict culminated in his trip to the Rainy River, which forms part of the border between Minnesota and Canada, where O'Brien would decide his future. O'Brien continued his story with such detail and emotion that the listeners who were unfamiliar with his novels became hooked—emotionally drawn into Tim O'Brien's life. Those of us in the audience who were familiar with the chapter entitled "On the Rainy River" in his novel *The Things They Carried* were uneasy. Would O'Brien be honest with this group and tell them that the details of this so-called personal story were simply not factual?

"On the Rainy River" is a fictional story with a fictional narrator who happens to be named Tim O'Brien. At the end of his storytelling, O'Brien paused as the Wabash audience nodded knowingly at story's end: Tim O'Brien had decided to enter the army and to fight—and not to flee across the river into Canada. But then O'Brien confessed: The story was made up. True, the real Tim O'Brien did ponder fleeing to Canada in the summer of 1968, and the thoughts and fears of the real

Tim O'Brien did mirror those of his fictional counterpart. Yet the incidents on the Rainy River simply did not occur.

Such blurring of the line between fiction and reality, or story-truth and happening-truth (O'Brien's terms), is common for O'Brien. He has often told these literary lies in college classes, public readings, interviews, and even his own books.[1] Another example appears in a 1989 interview, in which O'Brien maintains that a character in *The Things They Carried*, Norman Bowker, and certain events are real, but soon after he confesses that "everything is made up."[2] O'Brien's assertion of a purportedly factual story or piece of information later contradicted by his confession of its fictive nature is his method for effectively introducing listeners to the complex intermingling of facts, history, fiction, truth, lies, memory, and imagination underlying all of his writing. Nevertheless, one reviewer labels this tension between fact and fiction in O'Brien's writing and his public persona as "disingenuous game playing."[3]

Furthermore, if the reactions of some of the Wabash audience are any indication, this teaching exercise and approach to writing also disappoint some listeners who want to hear "real" war stories and learn the facts about the "real" Tim O'Brien. Yet O'Brien is quick to point out publicly that the facts of his life and the historical accuracy of characters and events in his books—all happening-truths—are not important. According to the author, the focus should be on the emotional truths— story-truths—in his short stories and books. Moreover, as O'Brien privately admits, understanding the who, what, and why of the real son, soldier, and author is not an easy task; it is a quest that O'Brien himself is still struggling to complete and may never fulfill. This journey is also one on which he claims not to want a lot of company. For he would suggest that just as mystery and ambiguity are fundamental elements in his books, so similar uncertainty is an inevitable and desired aspect of his public and private life. Appropriately, one of the intriguing features of O'Brien's life is that this author, who relishes life's enigmas and uncertainty, has spent so much of his personal and professional life dealing with a war characterized by considerable confusion and doubt.

Yet readers' interest in separating fact from fiction—in replacing mystery with knowledge—in O'Brien's life and in his books is inevitable and at times invited by the author. First, O'Brien is perhaps one of the most accessible contemporary writers with regard to granting interviews; talking with newspaper and magazine reviewers; and sharing with audiences parts of his life and most of his views on writing during his numerous readings, lectures, classroom discussions, and writers' workshops. The very accommodating O'Brien seems genuinely interested in having people like him. Second, a decorated Vietnam combat veteran, O'Brien includes in his books (fiction and nonfiction) some real people and events from his war experiences. Such a blend of fact and fiction leads to unavoidable questions about his life and the autobiographical nature of his books and short stories. Nor does he restrict himself to using only his war experiences as raw material for his writing. For example, in a 1994 magazine article for the *New York Times Magazine,* O'Brien mixes personal narrative about a trip to Viet Nam in February 1994 with personal confession about his subsequent mental state and the traumatic breakup of a relationship with a Harvard graduate student a few months after their return from this trip. Furthermore, the structure, content, and confessional tone in this magazine article conspicuously parallel similar elements in *Lake of the Woods,* which was about to be published when the magazine article appeared and which O'Brien admits is his most personal novel.

Are knowing the links between a writer's life and work of value to readers? Is it helpful in understanding O'Brien's writing to know that this Vietnam veteran and author who carries the guilt of his military service in Viet Nam nevertheless keeps his army dress uniform—with medals—hanging in his closet and has a map of Viet Nam fastened to an apartment wall? Commenting on his films in a 1995 interview on the television program *60 Minutes,* American film director Rob Reiner observes that " 'if you're working with something honest, you will always tap into your own experience.' " The fictional narrator Tim O'Brien in *The Things They Carried* comments that "the thing about remembering is that you don't forget. You take your material where you find it, which is in your life, at the intersection of past and present."[4] And in discussing key themes in his books, author Tim O'Brien observes that "everything that I am doing flows out of the life I have led."[5] The point is that for readers fully to appreciate O'Brien's books, they should be familiar with a few details about his life and views about writing because he incorporates these elements, often transformed, into his writing. Furthermore, O'Brien might praise his readers for seeking such factual information since even he admits to searching for facts about events in his life. Thus, in preparing for his return trip to Viet Nam in February 1994, O'Brien spent considerable time at the National Archives in Washington, D.C., reviewing records of his military unit's activities in Viet Nam during 1969 and 1970, especially its operations in the My Lai area. In explaining to an interviewer why he undertook this research,

O'Brien comments, "It seems to me that this is an important thing for someone to do—to find the soil that literature grows out of. I had forgotten, as we all do, a great deal of my own history. And to recover some of that history, some of that ground—to see it freshly, to see it anew—invigorated me as a writer."[6]

The facts that follow about O'Brien's life as a son, soldier, and author are additional bits of that soil gathered from interviews, published biographical data, and O'Brien's own works—fiction and nonfiction. Although establishing a starting point for readers of his books, this brief biography does not necessarily present the truths about Tim O'Brien. Nor, as O'Brien warns, should this information be used to support a pop-psychology analysis of his life or a facile reading of his works as products of his own psychic therapy. O'Brien believes that just as uncertainty and mystery abound in his writing, so some ambiguity should still mark portions of his own life and its relationship to his writing. But, as he also admits, the threads of his personal life in his writing "are not only numerous, but they're also incredibly important in my work: the father theme, the theme of heroism, the theme of history and war, the theme of loneliness and alienation, the theme of the importance of imagination in our lives as a way to escape and to change the world. There's also the theme of magic which runs through all of my work" (Herzog, Interview). All of these influences mark the life and writing of Tim O'Brien—son, soldier, and author.

Life

Son

As O'Brien recounts in *If I Die in a Combat Zone,* his war autobiography, he "grew out of one war and into another."[7] The chapter titled "Pro Patria" provides selected information about O'Brien's traditional childhood and adolescence in a small town in southern Minnesota, including incidents that one might also find with different settings in other Vietnam war autobiographies, such as Ron Kovic's *Born on the Fourth of July* and Philip Caputo's *Rumor of War.* Specifically, O'Brien's brief vignette examines his all-American, small-town upbringing in Worthington, Minnesota (baseball, girls, typical high school events), and the influence of politics and war on his coming of age.

His parents were both World War II veterans; he and friends played war games with military surplus equipment on the local golf course; Fourth of July celebrations involved fireworks, parades, and patriotic speeches by members of the VFW and the American Legion; he learned of war, both the Second World War and Korea, from stories told by veterans at the courthouse and from a parade honoring a POW from the Korean War; and he began to get involved in politics in a superficial way—attending Democratic party meetings or a candidates' forum sponsored by the League of Women Voters. According to O'Brien's written account, this part of his life, lived in a community that was and still is "a place for wage earners . . . not very spirited people, not very thoughtful people" (*Die,* 21), ended in an insignificant way: "One day in May the high school held graduation ceremonies. Then I went away to college, and the town did not miss me much" (*Die,* 24). From this written account, readers sense the origins of the prominent place war holds in this writer's life and works, and they also sense the beginnings of a political activism amidst the political and intellectual constriction that O'Brien experienced growing up on the prairies of Minnesota. Nevertheless, compared to these brief details in *If I Die,* the facts emerging from his personal interviews present a much more complex and fascinating portrait of O'Brien's life up to the present.

William Timothy O'Brien Jr., named after his father, who was a native of Brooklyn, was born 1 October 1946 in Austin, Minnesota, located in the southeastern part of the state. Prior to his entering fourth grade, O'Brien and his family moved to Worthington, Minnesota. This town of about 10,000 people in southwest Minnesota near the Iowa border is the self-proclaimed "Turkey Capital of the U.S." with its annual Turkey Day parade in September. The town also has a community college and is situated on the banks of Lake Okabena, which will become a prominent setting in one of his novels. Supporting the middle-class O'Brien family were O'Brien's father, who sold insurance, and his mother, Ava E. Schultz O'Brien, who taught second grade. O'Brien's parents had married in 1944 after meeting in Norfolk, Virginia, where the senior O'Brien was in the navy and Ava O'Brien was a Wave working in a hospitality suite. Tim O'Brien is the oldest of three children. His sister, Kathleen, one year younger, lives in Austin, Texas, where she edits medical texts, and his brother, Greg, 10 years younger, works in sales in Minneapolis.

On the surface, the author's life through high school seems stereotypical of someone growing up during the '50s and early '60s in a middle-class family residing in a small Midwestern community. In Worthington, O'Brien enjoyed baseball, particularly playing shortstop on the local little league team and being coached by his father. At the local country club father and son played golf, a game O'Brien occasionally still plays. Tim spent Saturday mornings in front of the television watching cowboy movies starring Gene Autry, Roy Rogers, the Lone Ranger, and Lash LaRue. "Those guys were heroes of mine, imaginary heroes. . . . They were the kind of hero who knew right from wrong and was willing to act on it to the point of risking his life" (Herzog, Interview). The young O'Brien also had real-life heroes, sports figures such as Ted Williams and Bill Skowron. And—not unusual for the son of a World War II veteran—O'Brien grew up admiring his father's war decorations and listening to numerous war stories (which focused more on the humorous aspects of military life) from his father, who served on a destroyer off the coasts of Okinawa and Iwo Jima during the two major Pacific campaigns. Mixed together, these and stories from other veterans, plots suggested by comic books and movies (*Pork Chop Hill* and Audie Murphy's *To Hell and Back*), and outfits from the local military surplus store became the grist for war games and fantasies that O'Brien created as a kid on the local golf course. Thus, history merged with fiction to influence the activities of these games, and the games also reflected O'Brien's imagined notion of his heroism at that time, "Tim the Hero." "I was the American hero and there were Germans and Japanese to be killed out on that golf course. . . . When the time came [to go off to war] I would be physically brave and morally brave" (Herzog, Interview).

But beneath the surface, other features of O'Brien's family life in Austin and Worthington suggest a somewhat different childhood from that of his friends. These distinct features have significantly influenced his development as a writer. One involves the role of books and language in his youth. He grew up in a family that valued books. An avid reader and a member of the Worthington library board, his father brought stacks of books into the home from the time O'Brien was very young until he left for college. At a young age, O'Brien enthusiastically read *Grimm's Fairy Tales,* and from ages six to nine he also read many books in the children's series called *Wonder Books,* with titles such as *Timmy Is a Big Boy Now* (his favorite) and *Larry of the Little League.* This last book, because of O'Brien's own interest in baseball, caught his attention at age 10 or 11 and became the stimulus for his first piece of fiction, "Timmy of the Little League," written at this time. O'Brien also read *Tom Sawyer* and *Huckleberry Finn,* with Huck later becoming an important imaginary hero for the teen-aged O'Brien: Huck's efforts to escape the narrow-minded social conventions of a small town in Missouri mirrored O'Brien's growing desire to escape a small town in Minnesota (Herzog, Interview).

Related to his and his family's interests in books was Ava O'Brien's involvement in reading, language, and the quality of O'Brien's school essays: As an elementary schoolteacher, "she cared about where the commas, apostrophes, and dashes go, things that in the long run make a huge difference to a writer. Without a command of the code, which is English grammar, you cannot fulfill yourself as a writer. You can't make full use of the English repertoire" (Herzog, Interview).

In addition to the importance of reading and language in this family, conversations about significant issues, ideas, and current events regularly occurred at the dinner table. The stimuli for these discussions would usually be movies, television programs, books, and magazine articles, with the talk moving from a particular program or article to general discussion. For example, O'Brien recalls that when he was in high school during the Cold War in the early 1960s, family conversations regularly focused on threats of nuclear destruction. An article on the hydrogen bomb might lead to an exchange on the imminent threat of nuclear war and the potential impact on Worthington of radioactive fallout from a nuclear attack on the Midwest.

Politics was also a popular topic of conversation, especially during the Kennedy presidency, with Kennedy becoming one of O'Brien's high school heroes: "I actually went to Minneapolis to a speech he gave. . . . I really admired his politics. I'm not so sure that I'd be such a fan today. But back then, notions like the Peace Corps meant a lot to me. His seeming elegance of style meant a lot to me, the way he carried himself, his wit, his intelligence. All those qualities impressed me and still do" (Herzog, Interview). Another subject of "heated" conversation was religion. O'Brien's father was a "lapsed Catholic," and his Methodist mother was a "staunch defender of meat and potatoes Midwestern religion" (Herzog, Interview). O'Brien's father scoffed at religion of all sorts (and still does), particularly the trappings of Catholicism and the Pope's positions on social issues. Perhaps as evidence of Ava O'Brien's power in the family, the O'Brien children, until they went away to college, regularly attended the Methodist Church. Their father occasionally accompanied them but did so "kicking and screaming" (Herzog, Interview).

As O'Brien describes his family's keen interest in books and their frequent conversations on political and social issues, he hints that such family activities and concerns distinguished his somewhat liberal middle-class family from the rest of conservative Worthington, but not in any particularly dramatic fashion. Growing up in such a family environment did, however, ultimately influence his perspective on the virtues and limitations of life and people in the Midwest in general and Worthington in particular—views he speaks about today. In noting these people's virtues, he lists the "independence of spirit" and a belief in the "human individual." The limitations, on the other hand, emerge from a smugness and self-centeredness typified by some of Worthington's residents: "a peculiar sort of ingrown smugness . . . a kind of smugness with respect to personal virtue. A kind of smugness that takes delight in ignorance in some way. Those high-falutin' Easterners, those crass Westerners, those redneck Southerners" (McNerney, Interview, 22).

O'Brien's evolving desire to escape this environment came from his sense that living in such a place required "not making waves," "not speaking one's mind," and "toeing the prairie line" (Herzog, Interview). According to O'Brien, Worthington was the sort of town that would send young men off to a war (Vietnam) "but not know the first damn thing about the war. It is my country right or wrong, a kind of pride in ignorance in a strange way" (Herzog, Interview). Yet consistent with O'Brien's desire not to break completely from his past, the author still regularly returns to Worthington to visit his parents and to play in an annual golf tournament.

Another feature of O'Brien's early life continues to affect his life and works: the sometimes difficult and always complex relationship O'Brien has always had with his father. In describing this tie, O'Brien notes how his father had a "dominantly affirmative as opposed to dominantly negative" influence on his growing up (Herzog, Interview). William O'Brien supported his son by playing ball with him, teaching him to play golf, and taking him on trips. Furthermore, when describing his father's personal traits, O'Brien emphasizes that the senior O'Brien was a model for him, particularly the father's capacity to devour books and understand what he was reading. His judgments about literature also impressed the young O'Brien and still do to this day. These literary assessments are "ordinarily pretty black and white, but they are firm; they are heartfelt, not wishy-washy" (Herzog, Interview). In describing his father, O'Brien cites traits similar to those he uses in characterizing his boyhood political hero John F. Kennedy: intelligence, wit, grace in public—"an extremely stylish guy, a charming man" (Herzog, Interview).

On the other hand, problems also developed in this father-son relationship, especially while O'Brien was in junior high and high school. O'Brien's father was "an alcoholic, bad alcoholic, institutionalized a couple of times; his alcoholism hurt me deeply. That is, it changed his personality so radically that it made him very, very hard to be with" (Herzog, Interview). Dinners were an especially difficult time for O'Brien. His father would sometimes begin drinking after work and "by the time dinner came around he would be sullen and way inside himself and the man that I loved and adored, the charming, stylish guy had vanished" (Herzog, Interview). On these occasions, William would taunt and tease young Tim—about his weight and his disgusted response to his father's drinking: "[H]e could feel my disgust at his drinking and would turn it on me in a funny way. 'What's wrong? What's wrong with you?' " (Herzog, Interview).[8] But the teasing also occurred when his father was sober and lasted until O'Brien left for college. "I felt that I was never good enough for him, could never please him no matter what I accomplished. And to this day I still don't understand what it was that didn't please him. I wanted desperately to win his love, affection, and esteem and never seemed to be able to do it, no matter what I did in the world" (Herzog, Interview).

Contributing to this uneasy relationship between father and son and to O'Brien's feelings of rejection were a few times when William O'Brien—institutionalized for his alcoholism—would vanish from his son's life. Wondering whether his father would be cured and return home, the young O'Brien experienced both fear and hope. He longed for some radical change in his father's behavior that never happened. These absences also created moments of self-consciousness for O'Brien. For example, he describes an occasion when his father, who was O'Brien's little league coach, was institutionalized at midseason. O'Brien felt awkward. He was unsure whether the other players knew the reasons for his father's disappearance. He was also uneasy about the players' opinions of him and his father, and he hesitated to tell the team the truth about the situation.

As a way of escaping these periods of confusion and loneliness, O'Brien turned to magic, first through reading library books about magic and then through practicing the art with purchased magic tricks: "It was a form of escape, of trying to change that world, that mad world, a little bit—of making miracles happen, a way of earning applause" (Herzog, Interview). From age 10 on, O'Brien practiced earnestly to perfect his talents in this area. On three trips to New York City with his father, who was attending insurance conventions, O'Brien visited Lou Tannen's magic store, which at the time was a mecca for famous magicians. O'Brien always returned to Worthington with an expensive magic trick—his father's treat. With these devices and others purchased locally, O'Brien performed at junior high convocations, talent shows, and birthday parties where he was paid just enough to acquire more tricks. He maintained this keen interest in magic for six or seven years, but it waned during his last two years of high school and ended with his departure for college.

Upon arriving at Macalaster College in St. Paul, Minnesota, in the fall of 1964, O'Brien's life changed dramatically; a self-styled "awakening" occurred during the next four years. Gone was the loneliness of junior high school occasioned by his father's alcoholism and absences, "the nadir of [O'Brien's] life" (Herzog, Interview); gone was an undistinguished high school career—a second-tier social life because he was not good enough to play varsity athletics and grades that were a cut below the best; and gone were the social restrictions O'Brien had felt living in Worthington and the emotional pressures of living with his father. Although Macalaster was O'Brien's second choice for college (he wanted to go to the University of Chicago but was either not accepted or not awarded a scholarship), it turned out to be a place where, with his newfound freedom, he flourished intellectually and politically.

As a political science major who took many courses in philosophy and some in English, he studied hard, learned a great deal, and received outstanding grades. He particularly remembers the strong impression that his English classes, teachers, and specific authors made upon him, especially those in American colonial literature (Hawthorne) and modern American and British literature (Joyce, Faulkner, Hemingway, and Dos Passos). "I was excited about literature in a way that I hadn't been prior to taking these courses. I had read a lot as a kid and was interested in books in general. But then I liked them for the story and for what they would do to me emotionally. But the technical aspects of fiction excited me in college for the first time. I have a feeling that had I not taken those courses and not had the great instructors, I wouldn't be a novelist today" (Herzog, Interview).

While in college, he also became fascinated with many of the political and epistemological issues that have prominent places in his works. Macalaster stimulated his interest in writing in another way: giving him an opportunity in the summer of 1967 to study in Prague, Czechoslovakia, as part of the Student Project for Amenity Among Nations (SPAAN). Instead of doing a customary research project in political science or economics, O'Brien chose to fulfill the program's requirements by writing a novel: "a weird spy novel with heavy political overtones and an overlay of cold war politics. . . . It was a terrible piece of work, one which I hope someday I can recover from the Macalaster offices" (Herzog, Interview).

Another aspect of O'Brien's intellectual arousal during these undergraduate years was an emerging political activism at a time when student politics, according to O'Brien, really mattered. O'Brien describes Macalaster during the years of 1964 through 1968 in the following way: "It wasn't a radical school. That is to say, it wasn't full of Communists and SDS types [Students for a Democratic Society]. But it was an extremely politically conscious school, partly because of the Walter Mondale (former student) and Hubert Humphrey (former professor) connections to the school and partly because some of the professors at the school were well known in Minnesota politics" (Herzog, Interview). O'Brien describes his political outlook during this period as "an old-fashioned liberal attitude; change is effected through legitimate political means: caucuses, elections, etc." (Herzog, Interview). As a result, he had no sympathy for the violent means for change being advocated and used by students and movements on other college campuses.

As student-body president during his senior year, O'Brien turned his attention to issues of student and academic life. On the Macalaster campus, debate raged over the college administration's role of in loco parentis involving visitation rights, coeducational dormitories, and alcohol policies. O'Brien argued that students should not be treated as wards but as human beings, especially if they were old enough to be sent off to war. Thus he advocated eliminating mandatory curfews for women, acknowledging the rights of 21-year-olds to possess alcohol in college dormitories, and loosening rules regulating male guests in women's living units. He also pushed for reforms in grading policies at Macalaster and for the establishment of libraries in living units.

As a Macalaster student and student leader, O'Brien also concentrated his restrained political activism on the Vietnam War, a war that even at this time he believed was "ill-conceived and wrong" (Herzog, Interview). In opposing the war, he took part in a few small peace vigils and campus debates that took place both inside and outside the classroom. But the large-scale and sometimes violent student protests that were already occurring on other American campuses and that would become widespread in 1969, 1970, and 1971 were absent at Macalaster, a fact that O'Brien appreciates today. As part of his limited antiwar activism, O'Brien participated in Eugene McCarthy's 1968 presidential campaign by doing house-to-house campaigning on weekends. O'Brien supported McCarthy simply because at that time this senator was the only candidate who had taken a political stand against the war. "I remember right after he announced for the presidency he visited Macalaster's fieldhouse, and it was jammed with supporters. It was a heady occasion. I was full of hope. I was a children's crusader in my soul. I wanted that war ended so badly. But I wanted it ended through legitimate political means" (Herzog, Interview). Instead of seeing his wish come true, however, O'Brien was just beginning his long-lasting association with the Vietnam War. This involvement moved to a new level as O'Brien graduated Phi Beta Kappa and summa cum laude with a B.A. degree in political science. Two weeks later, O'Brien received his draft notice.

Soldier

"The summer of 1968, the summer I turned into a soldier, was a good time for talking about war and peace" (*Die,* 25). With these words, O'Brien attempts in a brief chapter of his war autobiography to describe that fateful summer after graduating and receiving a call to military service. As described in "Beginning," O'Brien's summer was filled with games of golf and pool, along with internal debates and conversations with friends about the reasons for and against going to war. It was a summer spent hoping for miracles—an end to the war. In addition, it was a summer of "pounding the typewriter. I did it all summer. . . . That horrible summer made me a writer. . . . It was just stuff—bitter, bitter stuff, and it's probably full of self-pity. But that was the beginning."[9]

To this day, mystery and uncertainty mark the milieus and characters of O'Brien's novels and even his own life, but out of this summer of 1968 one incontrovertible certainty emerges in his life as a son, soldier, and author—O'Brien's guilt and shame for having entered the military and having fought in the Vietnam War. As O'Brien admits, he was not then nor is he now a pacifist; instead, he believes that certain wars are justified, such as World War II and possibly Korea. In the summer of 1968, however, he vehemently opposed Vietnam and analogous wars (the Spanish-American War, the Crimean War, and the Boer War)—and he still does. Citing political and humanistic grounds, he believes that a legitimate war requires "some sort of just cause," not a war fought to impose one country's will on the "legitimate aspirations and desires of another nation" (Herzog, Interview). He also notes that from his perspective, a wide range of moral, legal, philosophical, historical, and factual ambiguities clouded the issues and complicated America's entry into Viet Nam: "You don't kill people and you don't die when everything is so ambiguous. There's not some sense of consensus on the side of rectitude for that war" (Herzog, Interview).

By the summer of 1968, O'Brien's only contact with the Vietnam War had been through infrequent war protests on the Macalaster campus, national political debates, and, of course, media accounts. At the time, O'Brien did not know any Vietnam veterans. To this day, he does not recall any specific conversations about the war during that summer or earlier with his family, although he is sure that it was a topic of dinnertime conversation. He does remember that "in general both my mom and dad were skeptical of the war. . . . [T]he degree of their skepticism I just don't know about. I know that once I was drafted they were damn skeptical of the war. Once I was over there, they wanted that war over" (Herzog, Interview).

Spending most of the summer in "a kind of fog" that alternated among moments of self-pity, denial, and fantasy, O'Brien hoped for some sort of a miracle that would abort his moral dilemma—either an end to the war or a phone call from the local draft board notifying him that he simply was not soldier material. Another facet of this emotional state was O'Brien's occasional feeling that his induction into the army was inevitable. With his graduate program at Harvard due to begin in the fall, O'Brien might have secured from his local draft board a graduate-school deferment from military service. Inexplicably, he chose not to pursue this option, and since he had no religious or moral grounds for opposing war in general, he did not pursue a deferment as a conscientious objector.

Moreover, unlike many of his contemporaries trying to avoid being sent to Viet Nam, he did not seriously consider joining a military reserve unit. He believed that getting into the reserves was impossible because the units were full; more important, he thought that such a route to avoiding the war was a "cop-out." Instead, foreshadowing the responses of several major characters in his novels to similar war-related dilemmas, he turned to imagination and fantasy as a way of dealing with his situation. "I would fantasize that I was going to Canada, crossing the Rainy River. I'd fantasize getting into my car and just driving away. . . . They were elaborate fantasies; they were waking fantasies. I would imagine what I would have to pack. What documents I would have to bring. What clothes I would bring along. Where I would leave the car. The note I would leave for my parents. I mean they were elaborate heuristic exercises" (Herzog, Interview).

The fantasies soon ended. In spite of his heartfelt opposition to this particular war, O'Brien entered the military on 14 August 1968 ("by a sort of sleepwalking default": *Die,* 31), and his guilt over this decision began. Today, friends, family, and the public still attempt to assuage his guilt by citing O'Brien's confusion at the time, his service to his country, his conduct as a good soldier, the inevitability of going off to war, and the overwhelming agreement now within his country that the Vietnam War was wrong. O'Brien, however, adamantly refuses to embrace any justification for his act of acquiescence. Rather, his decision to go to war torments him to this day.

His pronouncement of personal guilt and cowardice related to this act is buttressed by the fact that he regards himself differently from the way he views several of his fellow soldier-authors, for example Caputo and Kovic, who developed an opposition to the war only while in Viet Nam or after their return. O'Brien argues that he, unlike these other soldier-authors, is particularly culpable because he entered the military as a "guilt" (his word), knowing that the war in Viet Nam was "ill-conceived and morally wrong" (Herzog, Interview). He did the wrong thing in not following his conscience. But O'Brien is quick to point out that certainly not every soldier who went off to war committed a shameful and cowardly act. He believes that everyone had to follow his or her own conscience. "In my case I committed an act of unpardonable cowardice and evil. I went to a war that I believed was wrong and participated in it actively. I pulled the trigger. I was there. And by being there I am guilty" (Herzog, Interview). So why did O'Brien enter the army in the summer of 1968—obligation, upbringing, or the need for love? Whatever the case, this defining event in his life, a "flee-or-fight" decision, is one that author Tim O'Brien considers repeatedly from different angles in both his fictional and nonfictional writing.

Once O'Brien entered the army, the start of basic training at Fort Lewis, Washington, heightened the reality of his situation. "It [basic training] was god-awful. In some ways my memories of basic training are more horrific than my memories of Vietnam" (Herzog, Interview). Because of his college education, his opinions about the war, and his lack of interest in being a soldier, O'Brien felt different from many of his fellow draftees. The humiliation, regimentation of behavior and attitude, and physical stress—prominent parts of shaping new recruits in this training—led O'Brien to despise the entire training period. He particu-

larly hated the drill sergeants who conducted the physical and psychological training, especially one identified as Blyton in *If I Die*.

As the eight weeks of basic training progressed, O'Brien felt increasingly depressed. Adding to this psychological turmoil was his uncertainty about where he would be assigned after basic training—infantry
school or some occupation that made use of his education and talents.
His soul mate and confidant during this uneasy time was Erik Hansen,
another draftee who, like O'Brien, was a college graduate, had grown
up in Minnesota, and also strongly opposed the Vietnam War. The two
shared their feelings, their arguments for and against leaving the army,
and their guilt over being in the army.[10] Unlike O'Brien, Hansen
decided in basic training to enlist for an additional year to guarantee
that he would not be assigned to an infantry unit in Viet Nam. O'Brien
hated the idea of spending more time in the army than was necessary;
therefore, he gambled on the outcome of his assignment. He lost.

He was assigned to an advanced individual training (AIT) unit in the
infantry at Fort Lewis and later received the inevitable orders for Viet
Nam. Hansen, on the other hand, became a transportation clerk,
although he was eventually assigned to Viet Nam. Without the physical
and psychological harassment of basic training, O'Brien's 12 weeks in
advanced infantry training proved uneventful. But his unrelenting guilt
over being in the army forced him into one more decision about whether
to flee the military or to fight in Vietnam. In his chapter titled "Escape"
in *If I Die*, O'Brien describes this moral dilemma during AIT and its resolution. With his last-minute refusal to cross the Canadian border and
fly to Sweden, this reluctant soldier found himself arriving in Viet Nam
in February 1969 and beginning a tour of duty highlighted by his decorated service to his combat unit, including a Purple Heart, Bronze Star
for Valor, and the prized Combat Infantry Badge (CIB).

After landing in Cam Ranh Bay, South Viet Nam—not as the typical
innocent soldier out to prove his manhood, courage, and patriotism but
as an atypical, guilt-ridden soldier—Private First Class O'Brien soon
traveled to Chu Lai for the customary in-country training ("Now or
Never Training") given to both combat and noncombat personnel. After
seven days, O'Brien was assigned to Firebase LZ Gator (seven miles
south of Chu Lai and home to around 800 soldiers) with Third Platoon,
Alpha Company, Fifth Battalion of the 46th Infantry, 198th Infantry
Brigade, American Division—a rather ominous assignment given the
unit's area of operations in Quang Ngai Province, a heavily mined area
that was home to a significant population of Communist sympathizers

and Vietcong. At this point, the lonely and displaced O'Brien began to take stock of his new surroundings and his feelings—the faint smell of mildew, the dawn breaking (an unusual sight for the late-sleeping civilian O'Brien), his fear and sense of imminent doom, and his first introduction to the war: "I remember at night watching from a distance the gunships putting down sheets of red flame on the Batangan Peninsula and thinking 'My God, I'm going to be out there at some point soon' " (Herzog, Interview).

In Alpha Company, O'Brien, nicknamed "College Joe," served as a rifleman for about two months, during which time he was wounded and received a Purple Heart. In April, by default, he took over as a radio-telephone operator (RTO), first carrying the portable radio for the platoon's commanding officer, then for his company commander (named Captain Johansen in *If I Die*), and later for Johansen's replacement. Since the RTO is a conduit for information, such a job seems a fortunate assignment for a future storyteller. On one hand, O'Brien heard unfiltered war stories and orders coming over the airwaves; on the other hand, he relayed outgoing stories about the unit's activities, some factual and some invented. The job was dangerous, however, since the radio's antenna became a convenient marker for snipers targeting a unit's commanding officer. O'Brien continued in this job for five months until late August when he received a combat soldier's dream assignment—a job in the rear as a clerk in battalion headquarters at Firebase LZ Gator.

A few incidents from O'Brien's time in combat are particularly significant. The first incident involved O'Brien's actions in combat that led to his receiving a Bronze Star for Valor. It is an event that O'Brien neither refers to in his writing nor particularly wishes to discuss in interviews. According to O'Brien, neither the action nor the award was a big deal: "[Bronze Stars] were given out like a dime a dozen. I'd say half the guys [in his unit] must have gotten Bronze Stars" (Herzog, Interview). Nonetheless, O'Brien received his medal for rescuing a wounded member of his platoon in the midst of hostile fire. Although O'Brien did not even know the fellow soldier's name, the rescue was not an unthinking "John Wayne" act of bravery. On the contrary, it was a calculated, thinking action by a very scared soldier: "Partly, I was calculating the odds. What are the odds that I'm going to get shot. . . . There was a slight calculation, but the odds seemed pretty slim that I was going to get hurt. They were slim, and it was over in twenty seconds" (Herzog, Interview). O'Brien also emphasizes that his time in combat was characterized by limited contact with the enemy: "In a year, I only saw the living enemy once. All I saw were flashes from the foliage and the results, the bodies."[11]

Other notable incidents from O'Brien's tour included combat activities in 1969 around Pinkville, which contains the subhamlet of My Lai (4). This area is one that O'Brien frequently uses as a setting in his war narratives and one that he revisited in February 1994. When questioned about his memories of this place, O'Brien describes the physical condition of Pinkville, especially the villages of My Lai and My Khe one year after the infamous massacres in 1968, and the emotional state of the Vietnamese inhabitants. He recalls scarred and mangled villages resulting from repeated American attacks; land dotted with Vietcong land mines that took a heavy toll on American soldiers; and inhabitants' sorrow, grief, and outward hostility toward the American soldiers brought on by years of bombs, napalm attacks, artillery fire, physical dislocation, and killing prior to and during the My Lai massacre. He also describes his unit's terror at undertaking operations in Pinkville, where sniper fire, exploding mines, and short firefights were routine; where the loyalties of the inhabitants were ambiguous; and where mystery shrouded recent events, including the massacres at My Lai and My Khe.

> The land just blew us to smithereens. We were afraid of the physical place, the way kids are afraid of closets after dark. The bogey-man feel of that place still haunts me. I still dream about the physical place. I don't dream about events that occurred, but I dream stories that happened in that hell—devastation and ghosts, the ghosts being the ghosts of My Lai. But they are not just from My Lai; the ghosts are from what happened prior to my getting there in terms of the bombing of the place, the wreckage of this area, the dislocation of all the villagers. . . . It was a place where evil had occurred, conspicuously had occurred. (Herzog, Interview)

O'Brien's experiences in Pinkville contributed immensely to his battlefield vow to return to the United States and crusade in his books against the Vietnam War: "I haven't kept many promises. That one I did keep" (Herzog, Interview).

After extending by one month the normal 12-month Vietnam tour of duty so he could receive an early release from the army upon his return to the United States, O'Brien completed the final 5 months of his 13-month obligation working as a clerk in a relatively secure rear area. Sergeant O'Brien then returned to the United States in March 1970 in typical fashion for American soldiers coming back from the war. He arrived as an individual soldier rather than with other members of his unit. For O'Brien this journey involved a flight on a commercial jet from Viet Nam to Japan to Tacoma, discharge from the army, and another flight to Minneapolis—all within the space of a few days. Once in Minneapolis, there were no welcome-home parades, no ticker tape, and no parties. He simply received a visit from his parents and brother, who asked few questions about his war experiences; O'Brien offered few details. After a brief stint working for the Metropolitan Council of Minneapolis doing research on urban planning, O'Brien turned his postwar spring and summer into a vacation of reading and traveling before departing for graduate school.

While living in Minneapolis, O'Brien participated in a march (May 1970) protesting the Cambodian invasion and the shootings at Kent State. Although he sympathized with the protests of Vietnam Veterans Against the War (VVAW) occurring in Washington at this time, he did not join them in leaving their medals at the White House or at the Capitol steps: "I wasn't a joiner and, in a way, I regret it. That is, I wish I had taken a stand then in a way that was political" (Herzog, Interview). O'Brien was simply happy to be alive and ready to get on with his life at Harvard.

According to O'Brien, his self-described "easy" emotional adjustment to civilian life—without the nightmares, midnight sweats, or flashbacks experienced by some Vietnam veterans—occurred because he, unlike some other veterans, was not consumed with a newly acquired guilt and disillusionment about himself and the war. By the summer of 1970, O'Brien had grown accustomed to his guilt. He had experienced such feelings of guilt prior to his entry into the military. "They [other veterans] had fantasies of themselves as one thing and discovered later they're not. When one discovers years later or months later that one is wrong, there is bound to be a horrible aftershock. In my case, I didn't need to have that discovered. It [that the war was wrong and I was a coward] had been discovered prior to my going. In a way, however, it makes my sins worse than theirs" (Herzog, Interview).

In addition to carrying this idiosyncratic moral and political guilt over his participation in the war, the soldier O'Brien, like the soldiers in *The Things They Carried,* carried with him other intangibles from the war that later made their way into his writing. These included an abiding fascination with military experiences and the vivid memories and stories from his tour of duty. Perhaps foremost among these was his understanding of love: love of virtuous acts and a realization of how difficult they are to fulfill. He also came away with an undying appreciation for moral bravery, peace, and one's own possibilities for virtuous action: "A human being has a shining silver star, each of us, inside of us. I wrote about it. You are not aware that the possibility is there until it is actualized by circumstances that require its presence" (Herzog, Interview). Furthermore, O'Brien learned that even for the reluctant soldier, combat at times can be attractive: It offers camaraderie, danger, and adrenaline rushes and both builds and tests physical and mental endurance. And O'Brien learned hate—hatred for the war and for some of his fellow servicemen who were poor soldiers or who bullied the Vietnamese. Finally, as a soon-to-be author, O'Brien carried with him from his military experiences the events, dialogue, settings, sounds, smells, images, people, and resolve to write against the war that would become as important in his works as the themes, experiences, and emotions gathered from his life prior to that seminal event: "The war made me a writer."[12]

Author

Exploring O'Brien's role as an author involves examining key events in his life after his return from Viet Nam, incidents contributing to his development as a writer. Also important are his writing habits and goals, along with a few significant, recurring themes in his books. O'Brien's post-Vietnam summer ended with his enrollment as a doctoral student in government at Harvard University, an academic pursuit that was to be interrupted frequently by intense periods of personal writing and occasional departures for jobs in journalism. At no time prior to or during his military experience had O'Brien committed himself to writing as a full-time career. In fact, after being accepted at Harvard during the spring of 1968, O'Brien was determined to study political science in graduate school so that he could pursue a career in academe, foreign service, or politics.

But his upbringing and several events were to lead him gradually toward a career as a writer: his fascination with language instilled by his mother and his teachers; his lifelong exposure to books; during his Vietnam tour of duty and shortly after, the publication in Minnesota papers and *Playboy* of a few vignettes written in Viet Nam; and O'Brien's battlefield vow to write against the war. Therefore, when he arrived at Harvard in the fall of 1970, he knew that he wanted to be a writer, but he was not convinced of his commitment or his chances for success. At this juncture, he viewed earning a Ph.D. at Harvard as a sure path to a viable profession during a time when writing was still a pastime for him.

Conveniently, this graduate work, which according to O'Brien ended somewhere around 1976 or 1977 when he had passed his Ph.D. oral exams and simply disappeared from the program, contributed significantly to his development as a writer. For example, his research for his dissertation on "Case Studies in American Military Intervention," of which he finished about 50 pages, became an ongoing meaningful influence for his writing. Specifically, readings in political theory—Aquinas, Marsilius of Padua, Aristotle, Plato, Dante, Machiavelli, Locke, and Michael Walzer (*Just and Unjust Wars* and *Essays on Disobedience, War, and Citizenship*)—assumed an added significance with his military background, and they still buttress some of the philosophical discussions on courage, moral conduct, and just causes for war that appear in his novels.

Also contributing to his development as a writer during this period at Harvard were fortuitous summer internships (1971 and 1972) at the *Washington Post* and a stint in 1973–1974 as a full-time general assignment reporter on the *Post*'s national affairs desk.[13] In fact, O'Brien views his jobs at the *Post* as time very well spent, for he learned important lessons about the writing craft ("Newspaper stories are called stories for a reason": Herzog, Interview) and the discipline required to write every day. As a reporter, he learned to write stories with significant leads, to develop an efficiency and economy in his selection of language, to use active verbs in his sentences, and with the help of editors at the *Post* to become a better editor of his own writing (Herzog, Interview).

During this time at Harvard and the *Post*, O'Brien's marriage in 1973 to Anne Weller, an editorial assistant at Little, Brown publishing house, provided stability and support to his writing and academic pursuits. On the other hand, during these years his intermittent labors on various works (*If I Die*, finished in 1972; *Northern Lights*, written during O'Brien's off hours while at the *Post*; and *Cacciato*, written during 1975–1977) created havoc in his graduate studies. And yet, not until the publication and success of *Cacciato* in 1978 did O'Brien finally believe he was ready to give his undivided attention to writing.

Once fully committed to his writing career, O'Brien approached this activity with a tenacity indicative of his nature. In a 1979 interview he noted that "I work seven days a week, six to eight hours a day. On weekends, I may only work five to six hours. I'm slow, I need big chunks of time. It's very regularized."[14] During the 16 years after his success with

Going After Cacciato, O'Brien's absolute dedication of time to his writing and his almost obsessive concern with the craft of writing and editing have led to a slow but steady publication of numerous short stories and three novels (*The Nuclear Age* in 1985, *The Things They Carried* in 1990, and *In The Lake of the Woods* in 1994).

In a 1994 interview, O'Brien hinted, however, that this slow pace—one book about every four or five years—and his all-out commitment to writing had taken their toll on his psyche and personal life. Consequently, he stated that he would not write another novel but would instead probably focus on short stories: "I'm aware of the limits of my life now as we all are when we get older. I would prefer to be able to do 50 stories about different facets of the world as opposed to just three or four more books, which is all I probably would be able to finish" (McNerney, Interview, 25). In a July 1995 interview, O'Brien elaborated on this change in his writing interests, noting that his former dedication to the craft had almost totally disappeared: "I pretty much have quit, not entirely. I'm still trying, but I'm only trying whenever the mood hits me now, which is once a week for an hour. I didn't take a pledge not to write. . . . I felt like I couldn't. Part of me does want to, but not enough of me, yet" (Herzog, Interview).

O'Brien also admitted in his 1994 article for the *New York Times Magazine* that his personal life during the years since publication of *The Things They Carried* had been tumultuous and had adversely affected his writing: a lengthy separation from his wife ending in a 1995 divorce after 22 years of marriage; treatment for depression; the painful breakup of a lengthy relationship with a Harvard doctoral candidate; and the emotional return to Quang Ngai Province and My Lai in February 1994. In this article, which is part narrative and part confession, O'Brien wrote, "I'm on war time, which is the time we're all on at one point or another: when fathers die, when husbands ask for divorce, when women you love are fast asleep beside men you wish were you. . . . If there's a lesson in this, which there is not, it's very simple. You don't have to be in Nam to be in Nam" ("Vietnam," 55). And months later in our 1995 interview, he characterized his life as one still "in disarray, full of depression, personal anguish. That anguish has somehow got to vanish or there never will be that fire again [to write]" (Herzog, Interview).

Yet much more recently (1997), O'Brien appears to have recovered somewhat from this personal and professional malaise. As a positive sign of O'Brien's renewed enthusiasm for his writing, he returned to the lecture and reading circuit in 1996 and published a short story, "Faith," in

the *New Yorker* (February 1996). According to O'Brien, this story is part
of a novel he is currently writing, and in a letter he addresses his resur-
gent interest in this project: "Yes, 'Faith' is part of a novel-in-progress.
Who knows how the fire returned? Compulsion? Boredom? The lure of
what seemed a good story? Healing, maybe?" (letter from O'Brien to
the author, 17 January 1997).

Art

In addition to knowing something about the relationship of O'Brien's
life to his career as an author, readers should also know four interrelated
principles that have guided O'Brien's development as a writer. First,
writing well (important ideas and careful use of the language) and reading great authors are absolute requirements for O'Brien. Second, along
with thought-provoking subject matter, mystery and ambiguity in both
content and structure are the essence of good fiction: " [W]ith plot and
character, the depletion of mystery robs a story of the very quality that
brings us to pursue fiction in the first place."[15] Third, a cryptic phrase
from *In the Lake of the Woods,* "the angle shapes reality," provides insight
to his notions about fragmented structure, repetitive content, and multiple perspectives found in his works.[16] Finally, O'Brien believes his writing is characterized by a "strict realism." He dismisses critics' efforts to
label him a "surrealist" or a "magical realist" (because of the use of fantasy and imagination in his works) or to link him with such Latin American "fantasy fiction" writers as Jorge Luis Borges *(Labyrinths)* and
Gabriel García Márquez *(One Hundred Years of Solitude)*. Thus, in arguing
that the so-called surrealism found in *Going After Cacciato* is consistent
with his strict realism, O'Brien notes that "war is a surrealistic experience": "[I]n war, the rational faculty begins to diminish . . . and what
takes over is surrealism, the life of the imagination" (McCaffery, Interview, 135). Similarly, in commenting on his "bouncing around in time"
in his novels or his characters' propensity to engage in fantastic daydreams, O'Brien emphasizes that he is merely exploring the realities of
the human mind: "Time is scrambled in our memories and in our imaginations and in our dreams. . . . We don't remember events, most of us,
always in chronological order" (Herzog, Interview). He further notes
that flights into imagination, fantasy, and daydreams are integral elements of human lives as individuals escape the world, model the world,
or explore possibilities for their future actions. Such activities in
O'Brien's novels are not magical realism; they are real.

If O'Brien is a realist in his content, then he is also a perfectionist when it comes to presenting this content. Combining his emphasis on mystery and ambiguity of content and structure with his attention to the rhythm, clarity, and power of his writing, O'Brien labors to produce carefully crafted sentences often containing intentional ambiguity of content. Contributing to this style are the influence of O'Brien's mother and the training of teachers concerned with the proper use of the English language. The results are evident in the slow pace of his writing and in his exhaustive revision strategies. As several other critics, particularly Steven Kaplan, have noted and documented, O'Brien tenaciously revises his prose, whether for the first edition or for a later edition, to the point where he scrutinizes every word and mark of punctuation.[17] Consequently, the changes in subsequent editions of his books often have little to do with the further development of themes or ideas but relate to details of clarity and style—avoiding monotonous rhythm or eliminating the distracting repetition of words such as *and* or *the:* "If you were to go through my manuscripts and look at the changes I make in the final stages of editing a manuscript, editing the proofs, even making changes for the paperback edition of *In the Lake of the Woods,* you would see that every comma matters to me. The rhythm of every sentence matters to me; the look of the page matters, the blend of elements" (Herzog, Interview). Such attention to detail, as O'Brien readily admits, makes writing all of his books incredibly difficult.

In further assessing his approaches to writing, O'Brien cites the importance of learning his craft from strengths of great writers and developing a depth and breadth of subject matter that will engage a broad, thoughtful audience. Accordingly, O'Brien cites, among others, the following writers as influencing him: Shakespeare (themes, dramatic monologues, and deft use of flashbacks in such plays as *Hamlet, Macbeth, King Lear,* and *The Tempest*); Hemingway (clarity of sentences but a disturbing simplicity in his moral philosophy); Faulkner (the ambiguity, complexity, and mystery of content and structure at the heart of his stories); Fowles (the moral significance of his themes); Joyce (a master of language and story structure); and Conrad (despite his awkward sentences, a simple, direct, and clear storytelling by "one of the two or three greatest writers who ever lived": Herzog, Interview).

As he talks about these prominent writers, O'Brien indicates that his goal as a writer is to be "read by the centuries"—but not as a war writer. He bristles at this narrow label often pinned on him: "It's like calling Toni Morrison a black writer or Shakespeare a king writer" (Herzog,

Interview). Although much of his writing deals with war, he considers himself much more than a war writer and admits that "to a great extent Nam is the material of my life. Not to write about it would be to betray myself."[18]

For author O'Brien, the Vietnam War affords a familiar moral and physical terrain that engenders inherent intensity, conflict, and genuine emotions. As a writer, therefore, he does not have to work at creating these elements in a story but instead can explore deeper moral, political, and human issues that are timeless and not confined to the battlefield. The subject of war becomes a starting point for O'Brien's self-described quest for "everness" and "alwaysness" to his writing (Herzog, Interview). Consequently, his broad themes relate to his ultimate goal of having his works contribute to "understanding the war of the living" (McNerney, Interview, 24)—individuals' daily struggles with issues of conscience, despair, deteriorating relationships, evil, temptation, moral dilemmas, self-discovery, and, of course, mortality. And at the heart of an O'Brien story is the mystery that is related to these characters, outcomes, and truths and that is ultimately shared by readers and the author. This underlying focus of O'Brien's writing is what Catherine Calloway labels a postmodernist interest in the "problematic nature of reality, a process that engages both the protagonist and the reader."[19] Such an approach to life and art forces O'Brien's readers to live with uncertainty.

O'Brien does not, however, begin a new writing project with these questions, answers, or even themes firmly fixed in his mind; instead he begins with language. First, a sentence comes to him ("It was a bad time") that seems interesting enough to follow with another sentence ("Billy Boy Watkins was dead, and so was Frenchie Tucker") and a subsequent sentence leading eventually to a page containing a situation, scene, or possibility.[20] And if that page is intriguing, he continues with the next page: "I've learned over time not to do anything but trust the language, nothing but that. Not to force a theme into a book or to force a story into a book. Not to force characters into a book. Simply let the words carry me along. It's as if the words are a river. If the river is strong enough and has a sense of direction to it, you will follow it. And if nothing comes of the story after forty or fifty pages, I'll drop it eventually" (Herzog, Interview). As the chunk of writing progresses, questions related to the "aboutness" of the story and characters pique O'Brien's interest: Why was it a bad time? How did Billy Boy and Frenchie Tucker die?

Moreover, at the core of this interest is often the mystery of story and character, as well as unanswered queries about the human spirit and people's motivations for action. Hence, in delving into his characters' hearts and minds, O'Brien asks numerous questions. Why are these individuals the way they are? What has contributed to their personality, to their moral outlook on life, to their choices, to their desires? What baggage of life do they carry with them into events, moral dilemmas, and relationships (Herzog, Interview)? In pursuing these matters, O'Brien places his characters in stressful situations—military basic training, a misadventure in a snowstorm, a combat assault on a Vietnamese village, a war protest in the United States, or a heated political campaign for the U.S. Senate. He chronicles how the characters grapple with the situations and with their attendant efforts at understanding themselves. From O'Brien's perspective, the most absorbing main characters are "those who are befuddled by themselves. They don't live under the illusion of knowing themselves" (Herzog, Interview). Thus, his major characters Paul Perry, Paul Berlin, William Cowling, and John Wade become interesting studies, whereas such minor characters as Stink Harris and Sidney Martin from *Going After Cacciato* remain relatively insignificant because "they are too certain about their own lives, and, as a result, they are too certain about the choices they confront" (Herzog, Interview).

Like his characters, author O'Brien frequently cannot answer the questions about human motives and desires he has raised. Rather than forcing an answer, he simply lets the ambiguity develop in the story, building it into the structure, characters, and themes as he explores possibilities: "Like all things that are interesting to me, I don't want to be positive. To be positive explains itself, and the world doesn't usually explain itself. The world usually has mystery. . . . Too many writers want to solve their own mysteries. That's what kills books" (Herzog, Interview). In particular, readers of *Going After Cacciato, The Things They Carried,* and *In the Lake of the Woods* come to understand how O'Brien intentionally uses ambiguity of structure and content in these novels to enhance this uncertainty. Readers struggle to separate actuality from possibility, truth from lies, memory from imagination, author from character, and one perspective from another. Commenting on these features of O'Brien's writing, one critic uses the label "fabulation" and notes that O'Brien "persistently undermines belief and the suspension of belief in order to reach for more complex truths" (Ringnalda, 106).

In addition to utilizing the seemingly disordered structure, shifting viewpoints, and blurred distinctions between fact and fiction, O'Brien frequently disrupts the chronological flow of time in his works as he explores characters' minds, creates enigmas, and enhances the realism. For example, Paul Perry in *Northern Lights* and Paul Berlin in *Cacciato* mentally jump back and forth among present (experience), past (memories), and future time (imagination). Narrators such as William Cowling in *The Nuclear Age* and the fictional Tim O'Brien of *The Things They Carried* shift quickly among different times in their stories. The narrators may even merge past, present, and future while making it difficult for readers to determine the sequence of events or to separate categories of time.

This disruption and merging of time, according to O'Brien, mirrors the scrambling of time and fluidity of time naturally occurring in our minds as we bounce around within or among memories, fantasies, and dreams. Not to mimic such thought processes, he maintains, would be to impose an artificiality on his works that would destroy their realism. Such patterns of shifting time also contribute to the intentional uncertainty surrounding events and characters that, as his readers come to understand, is often left unresolved at the end of a story: What happened to John and Cathy Wade in *In the Lake of the Woods,* or why did Martha not date Lieutenant Jimmy Cross in the story "Love" *(Things)?* The answers, according to O'Brien, are as elusive to him as they are to his readers. The questions and possibilities are what matter.

O'Brien's abiding fascination with mystery and ambiguity of actions and characters leads to another key ingredient in his writing—the technique of incremental repetition, or iteration. In chapter 29 of *In the Lake of the Woods,* the narrator notes, "It is by the nature of the angle, sun to earth, that the seasons are made, and that the waters of the lake change color by the season, blue going to gray and then to white and then back again to blue. The water receives color. The water returns it. The angle shapes reality" (*Lake,* 288). The narrator goes on to note that "repetition itself is in the nature of the angle" (*Lake,* 287). In reading O'Brien's works individually or collectively, readers encounter situations and themes repeated within and across books and stories; usually, however, they are described or developed from different angles (perspectives) and with added details, for example, a protagonist's choice of fleeing or fighting in a war, the death of an American soldier, or a slaughter of water buffalo by American soldiers. As a result, works such as *If I Die in a Combat Zone* and *The Things They Carried,* with their collection of individual stories linked by recurring themes, characters, and situations, are each truly integrated works. More significant, for some of the same reasons, O'Brien's six books—when viewed as a whole—become an integrated collection of works. This pattern of repetition with variation within and across his books reflects O'Brien's own indecision about the characters, outcomes of actions, and life itself.

O'Brien, his narrators, his characters, and his readers view events, choices, and individuals from changing perspectives and with varying results. As observers and their angles of perspective change and as events transform, reality and truth also alter while postmodernist uncertainty increases: "The angle makes the dream (*Lake*, 286). As a result, events take their reality from participants' and witnesses' very different perceptions: "In any war story, but especially a true one, it's difficult to separate what happened from what seemed to happen. What seems to happen becomes its own happening and has to be told that way. The angles of vision are skewed" (*Things*, 78). For O'Brien, his books become a series of mirrors (a central metaphor in *In the Lake of the Woods*) reflecting images, events, and people from varying angles. Also, as one critic notes, "his stories become epistemological tools, multidimensional windows through which the war, the world, and the ways of telling a war story can be viewed from many different angles and visions."[21]

These altered perspectives—inward and outward—of people, events, and truth lead to a core of overarching topics in O'Brien's books. Careful readers will find these related themes recurring throughout his works but explored from different angles, developed in distinct ways, and concluded with diverse results. Therefore, to begin to appreciate the depth and craft of O'Brien's writing, readers should note the following motifs drawn from the author's experiences, readings, and observations of human nature. His goal as a writer is not to provide answers to questions connected to these topics but to force readers into examining them from contrasting angles and with new understandings. Consequently, O'Brien develops all of this subject matter within the context of the underlying goal for his writing, which is to explore the enigma and complexity of the human heart and mind without arriving at definitive answers: "Characters that don't work, I believe, are characters who are explained away by the author" (Herzog, Interview).

Memory and Imagination

For O'Brien, memory and imagination are avenues toward exploring possibilities, solving problems, making choices, and creating stories. Imagination also can be an avenue for escaping the real world, or it can be a danger: "Imagination was a killer" (*Things*, 11). Such views of these powers of the mind are grounded in O'Brien's own life and underlie all of his writing. As a boy on a golf course in Worthington, Minnesota, O'Brien used to visualize characteristics of courage important to him at that point in his life or to escape unpleasant moments at home. Later, imagination enabled him to sort through the possibilities and outcomes of not entering the army in the summer of 1968 or of not going to Viet Nam in February 1969. Once in Viet Nam, as described in *If I Die*, fantasy heightened his nighttime fears of an unseen enemy and his daytime fears of unseen land mines. More recently, O'Brien's inventiveness, fueled by memories of the people and events of his tour of duty, allowed him to predict what his return to Viet Nam in February 1994 would be like.

All of these real-life examples of memory and imagination working in harmony mirror the functioning of these powers in his career as an author. Remembrances furnish author O'Brien's daydreams with the raw materials for creation: "The memory-traffic feeds into a rotary up in your head, where it goes in circles for a while, then pretty soon imagination flows in and the traffic merges and shoots off down a thousand different streets" (*Things,* 38). Thus, O'Brien's recollections of thoughts and feelings associated with his draft notice are mentally revisited to produce "On The Rainy River" *(Things);* similarly, reminiscences of his uneasy relationship with his father and O'Brien's youthful fascination with magic are transformed into central themes in *In the Lake of the Woods.* For O'Brien, this role of memory in the creative process can also extend to the collective awareness of a nation, its history; thus, memories of the My Lai massacre recorded in books and government documents become the substance for O'Brien's imaginative formulation of the world of John Wade in O'Brien's *In the Lake of the Woods.*

O'Brien's interest in the connections between memory and imagination as they relate to literary invention also leads to another prominent feature of his books—their self-referential quality as the author, through narrators and characters, explores the craft of storytelling. Numerous critics have noted that O'Brien's books, particularly *Going After Cacciato, The Things They Carried,* and *In the Lake of the Woods,* become classic examples of metafiction. For example, Catherine Calloway, in writing about *The Things They Carried,* observes that this novel, as well as *Cacciato,* is "as much about the process of writing as it is the text of a literary work" (Calloway 1995, 51).[22] In fact, O'Brien would argue that all of his books deal with the art of telling and writing stories: "But for me one of the chief joys of writing fiction is one way or another to be self-referential" (Herzog, Interview). He does this by experimenting with and commenting on narrative voices, structure, concepts of storytelling, the nature of creating a work of art, the relationships between reality and fiction, the development of an author, and, as in his most recent novel, the role of author as magician. For this reason, readers of O'Brien's works are treated to a short course in creative writing.

Perhaps imagination functions most significantly in his books as a heuristic tool and as a means of arriving at truth, "exercising the imagination is the main way of finding truth" (Naparsteck, Interview, 10). As a result, imagination in O'Brien's work becomes a powerful guide; it helps an individual solve problems or determine a course of action in his or her own life. As O'Brien comments, humans do not always determine actions based on rational analysis. Instead, imagination becomes a way for people to explore potential outcomes of an action. They picture an action and analyze hypothetical pleasure, distress, satisfaction, resolution, or reactions from others; then they act accordingly (Herzog, Interview). In the sections of *If I Die* dealing with O'Brien's dilemma of whether to flee the war or fight, readers find the soldier's imagination functioning heuristically as O'Brien considers the possible outcomes of his potential decisions. By exploring the "what if" in his own life, as well as in the lives of his major characters, O'Brien illustrates the power of imagination to transform information and to influence behavior when individuals confront difficult situations or moral decisions.

Closely allied with this personal epistemological working of imagination is its role as a way for authors to arrive at elusive and ever-changing truths. The paradox of this role, of course, is that the "noble lies" created by a writer's imagination become vehicles for arriving at a higher level of truth: "Lies aren't always told just to lie; lies are sometimes told, and always told by good fiction writers, to get at the truth," which O'Brien labels "story-truth" (Herzog, Interview). This truth, portrayed by authors and felt by readers, contrasts with "happening-truth," which is lived by authors and characters. The latter contains the facts of an event, the surface details; the former presents the underlying truth of events, the pain and passion surrounding the experience: what is felt "in your [readers'] bowels, and in your gut, and in your heart, and in your throat" (Herzog, Interview).

O'Brien illustrates the distinctions by citing from *The Things They Carried* his story about the death of Curt Lemon and the reactions of his fellow soldiers. From *If I Die,* he describes the happening-truth on which this fictional story is based: O'Brien's very close friend Chip Merricks stepped on a booby-trapped artillery round and was blown into a bunch of bamboo. O'Brien did not see the event take place, but he did see the aftermath. In his fictional account of the event, O'Brien created a game of catch with a smoke grenade, the imagery of sunlight and shade, and the song "Lemon Tree" sung immediately after the event by Curt's friends as they remove pieces of his body from a tree. As an author, O'Brien invents these details to create the emotional story-truth related to this incident. According to O'Brien, the emotional truth in this case involves individuals' macabre responses to horror, especially in war. People will often inject seemingly inappropriate humor into an emotionally traumatic situation. Such a response becomes "a way for the comic to diffuse the horrible, or at least make it endurable" (Herzog, Interview). Author O'Brien's artistic goal for story-truth is stated by the fictional narrator Tim O'Brien in "Good Form": "I want you to feel what I felt. I want you to know why story-truth is truer sometimes than happening-truth" (*Things*, 203).

Order and Control

As O'Brien explores the hearts and minds of his major characters, they, through various tricks of the mind, often attempt to introduce order, control, and understanding into their chaotic existence. For example, they immerse themselves in the routines and surface details of daily life, such as eating meals or counting their steps during a military march, thus choking off thoughts of helplessness and confusion. Characters use memory to reconstruct sequences of events in their lives, thus establishing causal connections or gaining insight. They also employ imagination as a means of escaping immediate chaos by controlling feelings of bewilderment and defenselessness. Within O'Brien's books, combat soldiers most often face these moments of disorder and lack of control as they struggle to control their fate, fears, and sense of insignificance and mortality on a tumultuous battlefield.

Civilian life, too, presents similar situations and resulting tricks of the mind, a fact that Paul Perry, William Cowling, and John Wade discover as they search for order amidst disarray. As O'Brien observes, "The ability to manufacture order out of seeming chaos is important to our psychological well-being. Humans are causal animals. We have an impulse to order events, seek out causes and consequences" (McCaffery, Interview, 143). Nowhere is this observation better illustrated than in *Going After Cacciato*, where soldier-author Paul Berlin attempts to establish order in his life by determining, through memory, the correct sequence of events preceding his night of guard duty and by choosing, through imagination, the future course of his life.

At the same time, readers of this novel struggle to order the actual events that randomly surface in Berlin's memories and to control some-what this fictional world. To accomplish this task, they must separate the facts of Paul Berlin's existence from the fictional events created in his mind. As O'Brien constantly reminds his readers, control, or the lack of control, is a recurring topic influencing the structure of all of his works: "[O]ut of control, and maybe it always had been. One thing leading to the next, and pretty soon there was no guiding it, and things happened out of other things" (*Cacciato,* 219). O'Brien's interest in how his characters and readers handle this disorder and uncertainty allows him to explore from many different angles related themes of self-discovery, choice, courage, virtue, and love.

For a character in an O'Brien novel, establishing order and control in one's life requires an understanding of the self (Why am I the way I am?), the world (How does the world influence who I am and what I must decide?), and the possibilities for individual choice (What options do I have?). Such a quest might involve Paul Berlin's and William Cowling's simple desire to examine their fears or a character's quiet contem-plation of a relationship with a father. The latter occurs as Paul Perry seeks to understand how his father's views of life and of his sons have shaped Perry's behavior, his choices, and his own perspective on life. Or such a quest for control may occur on a grander scale and in a hostile and topsy-turvy environment as American soldiers attempt to grasp the purpose of the Vietnam War; the language, culture, and politics of the Vietnamese people; or soldiers' own roles in the chaos. Nevertheless, at the heart of such journeys toward understanding, in which some fail and others partially succeed (certainty ruins plots as well as character devel-opment), is O'Brien's fascination with the relationship between control and choice in his characters' lives. Do individuals have the responsibility and power to make meaningful and informed decisions (free will), thus establishing command over their lives? Or are these choices limited, pre-determined by forces outside the individual's purview (deterministic view)? As one might suspect, O'Brien presents evidence throughout his books to support both sides of the argument: causal behavior shaped by a character's upbringing, environment, or internal stresses; and inde-pendent actions undertaken after a character's careful consideration of possibilities, outcomes, and personal interest.

As O'Brien probes the processes and outcomes of choosing, he forces his characters and his readers to grapple with philosophical issues, moral questions, competing values, and above all the power of love, which O'Brien notes is the dominant principle in his life as well as in the lives of his characters: "Speaking just as a human being, it seems to me that in my own life, most of the important actions I have taken have been actions to win either the love of others or, to some degree, love for myself" (Herzog, Interview). Because of all these influences on selection, O'Brien and his characters confront many moral puzzles requiring more than contemplation. They require action. Should courageous actions be unthinking actions? For example, is a soldier's instinctive charge on an enemy position courageous? Should a person lie to another human being in order to preserve love? Should soldiers, to safeguard their lives, refuse a direct order from an officer to search an enemy tunnel before destroying it? Should a soldier flee the battlefield if he or she believes a war to be wrong? In choosing a course of action, should an individual place greater weight on the love of others or on the love of self? These and related questions of deciding between competing values lead to recurring situations and themes in O'Brien's books, whether in the context of O'Brien's own military experience or in fictional contexts, such as Viet Nam's battlefields, the Minnesota wilderness, antiwar protests, or a political campaign.

Underlying the complexity, uncertainty, and causality related to these issues, however, is O'Brien's firm belief that "ultimately the greatest gift of God is freedom of will" (Herzog, Interview). Therefore, at certain times—not always—and despite all the so-called determiners of human behavior, all individuals have, according to O'Brien, "the possibility of action, virtuous action, coming out of a desire for pure virtue, the world notwithstanding" (Herzog, Interview). Such a belief is reinforced by O'Brien's use of a brief passage from Dante's *Divine Comedy* (*Paradiso*, V, 19ff.) as the epigraph to *If I Die:* "The greatest gift which God in His bounty / bestowed in creating . . . / . . . was the freedom of the will" (Charles S. Singleton, translator). How his characters respond to these possibilities for virtuous action when facing difficult situations or the equal merits of competing values becomes a true measure of their courage or cowardice, virtue or evil. In portraying such fictional situations, O'Brien reminds readers that everyone lives with and responds to inevitable conflicts between good and evil, caring and apathy, courage and cowardice.

Fathers and Sons

As noted earlier in describing O'Brien's years in junior high school and high school, the young O'Brien occasionally had a difficult relationship with his father. At one moment, this man could be an admirable role model; at another time, he might be a hard-to-please, taunting parent. As a direct result of this complex association—or as a significant coincidence—relationships between fathers and sons and between quasi fathers and sons are prominent in every one of O'Brien's books. Some of these pairings are positive, such as Paul Berlin's and William Cowling's interactions with fathers who dispense wisdom, display love, and support their sons' actions. Other father-son relationships, such as Paul Perry's and John Wade's, are tumultuous and destructive for the sons as they struggle to gain acceptance and love from their fathers by doing everything possible to please them. Norman Bowker's link with his father in "Speaking of Courage" *(Things)* is a more ambiguous example. In this relationship based on mutual affection and a father's indirect expectations, Bowker feels the pressure of his father's apparent obsession with the war medals his son might win: " 'I'll tell you something, O'Brien. If I [Bowker] could have one wish, anything, I'd wish for my dad to write me a letter and say it's okay if I don't win any medals. That's all my old man talks about, nothing else. How he can't wait to see my goddamn medals' " *(Things, 39)*.

　　Suggested by Bowker's wish is the link among all these diverse father-son ties in O'Brien's works: a son's quest for a father's love by fulfilling his father's real or imagined expectations. In directly commenting on the Bowker passage and indirectly assessing his own relationship with his father, O'Brien says, "I don't know if it is just Americans—I doubt it—or just Midwestern Americans—I doubt it—but for the men I have known in my life, there is a kind of pressure, a fatherly pressure, over the shoulder to do well in the world. This pressure sometimes pushes you to do well in bad kinds of ways, that is, to charge a bunker and get your head blown off so as to impress your father with a medal. You know that the pressure is there, a way of winning love" (Herzog, Interview).

　　Obviously, such pressure to be loved by his father, his family, and his country contributed to O'Brien's decisions not to flee the military and may have played some part in his efforts to be a responsible soldier in Viet Nam. This "over-the-shoulder pressure," which is not restricted to soldiers, becomes a prominent force in the development of O'Brien's principal characters and the decisions they make. Some characters, such as a Paul Perry struggling to understand this pressure of expectation, advance beyond it. Other characters, such as John Wade, are incapable of escaping the external and self-imposed pressure, constantly seeking their father's approval and love even after the father has died.

O'Brien expands this pattern of father-son relationships by introducing two variations of this theme. The first occurs in war books where military officers become father figures for men in their units. As leaders, these officers control the lives and daily existence of the enlisted personnel. They dispense advice and wisdom, provide directions, and create expectations, realistic or unrealistic for their "sons." Some officers approach their task with a genuine concern for the welfare of their troops. Others become addicted to the power and blinded by their unit's mission. Within some of these battlefield associations are ideal father figures, such as Captain Johansen in *If I Die,* who combines characteristics of courage, wisdom, allegiance to mission, and—most of all—a compassion and love for his men. At the opposite end of the spectrum in the same book is Major Callicles, the autocratic, oracular father figure who lacks temperance and bullies his men into accepting his view of the world and his notions of courage. Other military figures assume paternal roles in *Going After Cacciato,* in which Lt. Sidney Martin and Lt. Corson also represent opposite ends of the spectrum in their relationships with their men. Although basically a good person, the former makes choices based on the goals of the mission rather than on the welfare of the individual soldiers under his command. In contrast, Corson chooses the welfare of his men over the demands of the mission, thus enjoying the affection of his troops but failing to achieve military objectives.

O'Brien's second adaptation of the father-son bond involves the characters Henry Berdahl in "On The Rainy River" and Claude Rasmussen in *In the Lake of the Woods.* Both elderly gentlemen befriend younger men working through difficult moments in their lives and provide the spoken and unspoken support, trust, and compassion that the younger men so desperately need. Through patience and appropriate questions, they also give the younger men opportunities to examine their futures and to resolve some of their turmoil through informed choices. In commenting on the roles that Berdahl and Rasmussen play, O'Brien notes that in some ways they go beyond the role of a father figure. They are an "idealized almost divine disembodied conscience. That is, they are reckoners of virtue, the watchers of our decisions and the choices we make or fail to make in our lives" (Herzog, Interview). Berdahl and Rasmussen become sympathetic observers and nurturers, roles that readers of O'Brien's works find missing in some of the other key father-son relationships.

Politics

The three overarching themes briefly introduced so far are often interrelated, and each spawns attendant themes. Such patterns of connection also hold for this last thematic thread among O'Brien's books. For an author who spent several years in a graduate program reading political theory, political perspectives offer more angles for examining reality— not a surprising outcome for O'Brien. Political philosophy overtly appears in *If I Die,* but in other works it also underlies moral and political choices involving individuals' obligations to their government, for example, Paul Berlin's decision not to flee his unit in *Going After Cacciato.* Of further interest to readers are the implicit ways in which O'Brien introduces politics into all of his works. In a 1989 interview, O'Brien comments that his four books up to this point are political: "I think anything I've ever written has that as its center theme, even more than issues of courage—how individual human lives are influenced by global forces beyond the horizon" (Naparsteck, Interview, 6). Such a comment is still true.

Throughout his books, the Vietnam War, the threat of a nuclear holocaust, or the arenas of state and national politics have an undeniable impact on the lives of O'Brien's main characters. These political forces, however, do not become the focus of the books. In fact, in the most controversial political arenas, such as the Vietnam War, O'Brien largely ignores the competing political ideologies of situation (the reason for and impact of U.S. or North Vietnamese government policies on the war and people). A quote from *Going After Cacciato* describing apolitical American soldiers perhaps suggests O'Brien's rationale for this approach: "There was no serious discussion. No beliefs. They fought the war, but no one took sides" (*Cacciato,* 240). Instead, the global forces are crucibles and catalysts, testing main characters and forcing them to react through self-analysis, reassessment of relationships, troublesome choices, personal politicization, or depoliticization. Characters must then deal with the consequences of their decisions. Thus, the Vietnam War requires Tim O'Brien (both the real and fictional characters) and Paul Berlin to determine whether to flee or fight based on their own values and not on underlying ideological issues. The threat of nuclear war forces Paul Perry to examine his relationship with his father; the same threat, along with the Vietnam War, influences William Cowling first to resist the draft and later to build a bomb shelter in his back yard because of the importance he places on safety, family, and love. Finally, in O'Brien's *In the Lake of the Woods,* the Vietnam War and a campaign for the U.S. Senate impinge upon John Wade's life at various points and in the process reveal weaknesses in his character. As the outside world affects an individual's world, the processes and outcomes of individual choices, not the global political forces themselves, become O'Brien's interest. The direct influence of these forces in everyday lives illustrates the nature of politics in the concrete, not in the abstract. O'Brien's stories do not present political lessons; they explore the responses of characters' hearts and minds to political forces.

O'Brien also introduces politics into his books in a third way, one involving responses to personal issues rather than to global politics. For O'Brien, the most important and pervasive way in which his writing is political is through his notion that "politics has to do with the adjudication of competing values" (Herzog, Interview). On a public level such adjudication occurs when a government makes policy decisions on budget items. For example, does it value budgetary restraint or food and health care for the poor? On a personal level, choices of competing values occur constantly in individuals' lives and thus become centerpieces of all O'Brien's novels. Therefore, on the surface an O'Brien story may seem apolitical, but under this very idiosyncratic definition, all of his writing is political. As an example, O'Brien cites his 1993 short story "Loon Point."[23] In the story, a married woman on a trip without her husband has a brief affair with a man who drowns soon afterward. The woman agonizes over how she should handle this secret affair. O'Brien notes, "That story is the most domestic story I have ever written, the most removed from the global world impinging. Nonetheless, it is political in my opinion because it involves the adjudication of values: On the one hand, I [the woman] wish I could be open about this. On the other hand, if I am open, I'm a known adulteress. On the other hand, I wish my husband cared enough to ask a question or two about what happened on my little journey" (Herzog, Interview). More often than not, individuals in O'Brien's books adjudicate competing values of courage, love, happiness, virtue, truth, expectations, acceptance, and responsibility. Their eventual choices and the processes for arriving at them connect this theme of politics with the other overarching themes of memory-imagination, order-control, and fathers-sons. Examining such political choices also falls within author O'Brien's principal goal in his stories of exploring the mystery and uncertainty of the human heart and mind from various angles. In the following chapters of this book, I explore these various angles, along with the mysteries and ambiguities of O'Brien's subject matter, characters, story form, and personal life.

Chapter Two

Origins of Theme and Craft: *If I Die in a Combat Zone* and *Northern Lights*

In Tim O'Brien's second novel, *Going After Cacciato,* Major Hgoc, a Viet-cong intelligence officer, gives the following advice to a squad of bewildered American soldiers who have unexpectedly fallen into an operations center located in a tunnel complex in South Viet Nam: " 'So you see,' said Li Van Hgoc as he brought down the periscope and locked it with a silver key, 'things may be viewed from many angles. From down below, or from inside out, you often discover entirely new understandings' " (*Cacciato,* 82). The major urges the Americans to pause in their quest to capture an AWOL soldier and to reflect on the war and their individual experiences, thus achieving perspective and understanding. Analogous to passages from *In The Lake of the Woods* suggesting that angles of perspective shape reality, the major's simple advice serves as a critical paradigm for readers of O'Brien's works and a writer's guide for O'Brien himself as he writes about war, his own experiences, human nature and relationships, and moral issues. Throughout his books, O'Brien follows this counsel using the technique of iteration, or incremental repetition ("I continue to use repetition in my work to this day, but not so that it's done just for its own sake": Naparsteck, Interview, 2), as he returns to events, choices, and issues from different perspectives and with additional information. Consequently, readers find that O'Brien has created a collection of integrated works in which he explores recurring core and attendant themes as son, soldier, author, and even a fictional character in his own stories. O'Brien's six books, therefore, can lead the author and his readers to "entirely new understandings" or, at the very least, intriguing clarifications of complicated issues. Along the way, O'Brien also uses this technique of repetition with variation (changing angles and additional information) to structure his stories, raise questions about the art of storytelling, and investigate fundamental relationships between memory and imagination, facts and truths.

In his first two books, *If I Die in a Combat Zone, Box Me Up and Ship Me Home* (nonfiction, 1973) and *Northern Lights* (fiction, 1975), readers find O'Brien's initial considerations of these key themes and the origins of his various narrative strategies for storytelling. Yet reviewers and scholars have largely ignored these early works. In the case of *Northern Lights,* such lack of interest might be explained by the inferior quality of the book when compared with his other novels. And the absence of initial interest in *If I Die* might be explained by its 1973 publication date (a time when many Americans wanted to forget the Vietnam War), by the proliferation of war novels and war autobiographies already published by 1973, or by confusion over the book's genre—nonfiction or fiction. Nevertheless, these two works, especially *If I Die,* introduce O'Brien's craft and subject matter. A useful analogy might be comparing the function of these first two works to the role of the first story, "The Things They Carried," within his novel by the same name. As a form of prologue, this short story introduces the themes—the tangible and intangible things soldiers carry with them during and after the war—that O'Brien examines throughout the rest of the book. Similarly, *If I Die* and *Northern Lights* together become essential literary maps for O'Brien's later work, as they establish the directions of form and content for his collection of integrated novels.

If I Die in a Combat Zone

The publication history for O'Brien's first book follows a pattern occurring frequently with all of his later books—except *Northern Lights*. Typically O'Brien publishes stories (fiction or nonfiction) in newspapers and magazines and then significantly rewrites them, combines them with other published materials, or adds them to unpublished material for publication in book form. In the case of *If I Die,* the process began while O'Brien was still in the army. During his tour of duty in Viet Nam, O'Brien kept an extensive personal journal that included "little anecdotes, four or five pages. Not stories but vignettes" of his feelings and experiences.[1] He, unlike Norman Mailer, had not gone off to war intending to write the ultimate war novel based on his military experiences; instead, O'Brien created these descriptive sketches of his experiences simply because he preferred writing them to composing cards and letters to his family, which tended to be "full of self-pity and terror" (Herzog, Interview).[2] While in Viet Nam, he sent a few of these vignettes home to be published in local newspapers *(Minneapolis Star and Tri-*

bune and *Worthington Daily Globe).* In the summer of 1970, after returning from the war, O'Brien published the nonfictional "Step Lightly" in *Playboy* (July 1970), and during his second year in graduate school, he published the nonfictional vignette "The Enemy at My Khe" in the *Washington Post* (20 August 1972). Also during this time in 1972, as a break from his graduate studies, O'Brien reworked the published nonfictional stories, combined them with unpublished material, and then "very quickly—I mean in a month or so—I stitched it [manuscript] together into a book [*If I Die*] and sent it off. After sending it off, I forgot about it" (Schroeder, Interview, 148).

Despite reservations of publisher Seymour Lawrence, who was disturbed by the "somber mood" of this book and felt it needed "more prostitutes and dope peddlers" (Caldwell 1990, 69), O'Brien's war autobiography was published in 1973. Its complete title, *If I Die in a Combat Zone, Box Me Up and Ship Me Home,* comes from a marching song sung by trainees in army basic training and advanced individual training (AIT). Obviously, O'Brien gambled by publishing a book at a time when America's combat role in Viet Nam had just ended and the American public was tired of the war and anxious to forget the entire experience. Also, as O'Brien notes, in contrast to the glut of books about "patriotic grunt experiences" in the Vietnam War, he intended his book to be about the "realities of war" in order to fulfill his battlefield vow of writing against armed conflict:

> I wanted to write a book about the infantryman's experience through the eyes of a soldier who acknowledged the obvious: that we were killing civilians more than we were killing the enemy. The war was aimless in the most basic ways, that is, aimless in the sense of nothing to aim at, no enemy to shoot, no target to kill. They [enemy] were among the people. As a consequence, the fire was put out in massive quantities against whole villages. I wanted to write a book that got at that so I could feel that I was doing something. (Herzog, Interview)

In the book, which is not a strict chronological narrative, O'Brien describes growing up in Worthington, Minnesota, details the fateful summer of 1968 when he received his draft notice, chronicles his progress through basic training and AIT, and devotes a significant portion of the book to his experiences in and observations about war. O'Brien spent most of his tour of duty (February 1969 into March 1970) as a radio-telephone operator (RTO) in the Americal Division with Third Platoon, Alpha Company, Fifth Battalion of the 46th Infantry, 198th Infantry Brigade at Landing Zone (LZ) Gator just south of Chu Lai. This area of Quang Ngai Province becomes the principal setting for the war episodes in his later books. In his series of nonfiction stories, O'Brien addresses various subjects, including his personal dilemmas as a reluctant draftee whose parents served in the military during World War II. He also explores the heart and mind of average combat soldiers, the actions of an American officer who becomes O'Brien's embodiment of courage, the absurd nature of the Vietnam War, and the fate of Vietnamese civilians caught in this conflict.

Reviewers and critics have been generally positive in their judgments of this first book, although they often are confused about its genre and label it in many ways, including "fiction," "nonfiction," "snapshots," "sketches," "journal," "parables," "semi-fictionalized story," and "autobiography." Ironically, even the paperback publisher was confused about the appropriate category by placing the letters "FIC" (fiction) on the spine of the 1979 Laurel Edition and "NF" (nonfiction) on the 1987 edition. But in interviews, O'Brien repeatedly describes the book as "mostly straight autobiography. All of the events in the book really happened; in one sense it is a kind of war memoir and was never intended to be fiction" (Schroeder, Interview, 136). Reviewers generally praise O'Brien's gripping subject matter and authentic style, although the critic for the *Times Literary Supplement* notes that the author "doesn't lay claim to any original ideas."[3] More typical of the notices is the following passage from the *New Statesman:* "In a style which is lucid, relaxed, razorsharp and consciously dispassionate, the wasteland of Vietnam unreels before us. Without fuss or rhetoric he [O'Brien] registers the arbitrary deaths and futile suffering of soldiers and citizens alike."[4]

At one point in his war autobiography, O'Brien seems to contribute his own critical assessment of *If I Die* by asking, "Can the foot soldier teach anything important about war, merely for having been there?" O'Brien is quick to answer, "I think not. He can tell war stories" (*Die,* 32). Despite such a decisive response, the value and purposes of these war stories remain central questions for O'Brien and his readers in this and his other works. In an interview, O'Brien notes that "storytelling is the essential human activity. The harder the situation, the more essential it is. In Viet Nam men were constantly telling one another stories about the war. Our unit lost a lot of guys around My Lai, but the stories they told stay around after them. I would be mad not to tell the stories I know" (Bruckner, C15).

To understand the value, purpose, and place within modern war literature of O'Brien's first book of war stories, we must consider age-old questions involving the role, content, truthfulness, and form of soldiers' and veterans' oral and written war stories. How and why do these combatants revisit their war experiences during and after a war? Do they exchange oral stories with other soldiers after battles in order to preserve memories or to cope with the horrors? Do they re-create experiences through memories or simple diary entries when away from the battlefield in order to control and shape the experiences? Or, like British World War I poet Wilfred Owen, do they consciously write literature while in combat? Having left the war, do these veterans suppress their experiences and stories? Do they transcribe their memories into a war memoir (revisit the war), or do they transform the recollections through imagination into creative pieces of art, literature, and music (re-create the war)? Finally, what purposes do these stories serve for the teller and the audience: therapy, entertainment, propaganda, education, or insight into the mind and soul of the storyteller?

What seems quite apparent is that every war produces an outpouring of published war stories for various purposes, in diverse forms, and by both inexperienced and experienced writers. For example, Chester Eisinger, in commenting on the stories of World War II American veterans, observes that "everyone—everyone and his brother, one is tempted to say—wrote a war novel. Some of these books were dull but a great many were competent. . . . Many were written by men who had not before published a novel and have not since."[5] If Eisinger had expanded his categories of first books to include nonfiction, such an observation would also be particularly true for veterans of the Vietnam War. For instance, Sandra Wittman's bibliography of writing about the Vietnam experience from 1954 to 1988 contains entries for 582 literary and adventure novels and 481 personal narratives and biographies, and the numbers in all of these categories have increased dramatically since 1988.[6]

As suggested by Wittman's citations, a particularly popular literary form for first-time writers of Vietnam War stories—including O'Brien—is that of the book-length war memoir or autobiography. Paul Fussell, World War II combat veteran and well-known literary critic, addresses some of the key issues of form, content, and authenticity related to one of these genres in his widely acclaimed study of British literature (memoir, fiction, and poetry) emanating from World War I. In *The Great War and Modern Memory,* Fussell pays particular attention to such noted British soldier-authors of World War I as Siegfried Sassoon, Robert Graves, and Edmund Blunden—for whom "remembering the war became something like a life work."[7] In discussing their literary achievements, Fussell notes that the war memoir is "a kind of fiction, differing from the 'first novel' (conventionally an account of crucial youthful experience told in the first person) only by continuous implicit attestations of veracity or appeals to documented historical fact" (Fussell, 310). Such a definition of war memoir connects with Phillipe Lejeune's definition of autobiography: "retrospective prose narrative written by a real person concerning his own existence, where the focus is his individual life, in particular the story of personality."[8]

Both Fussell and Lejeune differentiate memoir and autobiography from the traditional memoir (the recollections usually of a prominent person about other important people or about significant public events) and from the diary, or journal, which lacks the retrospective and shaping point of view of crafted narrative. Both critics emphasize the presence of artificial narrative structures (imaginative art), which give coherence, shape, and theme in re-creating rather than simply recording personal experience. Both emphasize the introspective nature of these forms and comment on the author's concern for truth: Lejeune through his "auto-biographical pact" between author and reader (Lejeune, 14) and Fussell through his "implicit attestations of veracity or appeals to documented historical fact" (Fussell, 310). Also linking the two critics' views is their sense that in one form or another confession is at the core of war memoir and autobiography. For Lejeune such disclosure comes from the narrator's focus on the "story of personality," whereas Fussell sees confession emerging from the inherent ironic vision present in war memoirs dealing inevitably with the collision between a soldier's initial innocence and later awareness of the nature of war: "Every war is ironic because every war is worse than expected" (Fussell, 7). Obviously, whether characters consciously confront this irony or simply analyze their battlefield actions, the situations of war often evoke literary confessions. These revelations come forth as participants explore the unconventional or unexpected acts of war as well as their own troubling thoughts and actions, all within the context of soldiers engaging in "heart-of-darkness" experiences. Such acknowledgments become an important part of war autobiography as the narrator employs literary truth telling and self-revelation as therapy, a request for forgiveness, an assertion of beliefs, a means for shocking the reader, a deconstruction or reconstruction of self-image, an invitation to judge the narrator, or a means for educating readers.

Within these general guidelines for the content and form of memoir and autobiography, developing an accurate label for *If I Die* can be problematic. As noted earlier, some reviewers consider O'Brien's book a journal because of its detailed description of military life. Other critics label it fiction because of O'Brien's extensive use of narrative devices to shape the material: fictional names, scene setting, and extensive dialogue. But *If I Die* also fits many of the criteria established by Fussell and Lejeune for war memoir and autobiography. Furthermore, at its most basic level, *If I Die,* although limited to a restricted period of the author's life, also follows somewhat the definition of traditional autobiography and thus contains subjects and structure suggested by the etymological roots of this word: *autos* (self); *bios* (life); *graphein* (to write).[9] For example, O'Brien focuses at various times on the confessional self-portrait of the conscious "I"; on the narrator's descriptions of his relationships with incidents and participants in war, mixed with commentary on society, politics, and human nature (the "we, they, and it" of life); and, to a limited degree, on the autobiographer's implicit concerns with the purpose, language, structure, significance, and effect of text emerging from a story about a life (the art of writing an autobiography).

Within this general critical framework of form and content, O'Brien's war autobiography finds a place alongside other notable first-person accounts of the Vietnam experience, such as Ronald J. Glasser's *365 Days* (1971), Ron Kovic's *Born on the Fourth of July* (1976), Philip Caputo's *A Rumor of War* (1977), Michael Herr's *Dispatches* (1977), Lynda Van Devanter's *Home Before Morning: The Story of an Army Nurse* (1983), Troung Nhu Tang's *Vietcong Memoir* (1985), Le Ly Hayslip's *When Heaven and Earth Changed Places: A Vietnamese Woman's Journey from War to Peace* (1989), and Tobias Wolff's *In Pharaoh's Army* (1994).[10] Most of these books focus predominantly on one of the tripartite categories within autobiography. For example, Kovic concentrates on I, and Caputo seems more interested in the we, they, and it incidents of war, with only an occasional foray into his own psyche. Among this collection of war autobiographies and memoirs, perhaps O'Brien's work, as its ranges over all three areas, seems closest to Herr's and Wolff's books in its movement from the personality of the I, to life involving the I, to issues related to writing and storytelling. With its collection of intertwined vignettes and nonfictional short stories, it is also closest to these works in form. Further, like the other two books, the form and content of *If I Die* illustrate Thomas Myers's description of the traditional American memoir, one containing elements of Fussell's underlying ironic vision: This memoir is "characterized more by wrenching personal development—the violent meeting of unexamined assumption and persistent historical lesson—than by smooth progressive evolution. As story, it is most often a chain of hard-won epiphanies rather than a serene symmetrical historical graph."[11] In addition, throughout his war autobiography, O'Brien arranges scenes—much like Herr in *Dispatches*—for dramatic effect rather than chronological accuracy. This latter feature, along with O'Brien's attention to setting, character, symbol, and dialogue, gives this work, like Herr's, a fictional aura. But *If I Die* is a much more crafted and controlled piece of writing when compared with the frenetic, jumbled, and fragmentary "illumination rounds" in Herr's book.

Of particular importance to readers of O'Brien's later works is the relationship of the form and content of *If I Die* to similar elements in his novels. Specifically, certain narrative strategies of this war autobiography anticipate O'Brien's techniques of iteration and multiple angles used in his other works, as well as the intertextuality of stories found in *The Things They Carried*. For example, as in this later piece of fiction with its 22 linked stories and commentary, O'Brien consciously connects the 23 nonfictional sections of *If I Die* with recurring themes and incidents presented from Tim O'Brien's various perspectives. The view is not that of a naive young soldier who loses his innocence once he enters the military and combat. Instead, readers see the war through O'Brien's own changing viewpoint: an author who feels guilty about his decision to go to war; a Vietnam veteran—neither cynic, patriot, nor apologist—who has carried on a typical love-hate relationship with the war and himself; a thoughtful person preoccupied with political and moral issues of bravery and fear; an insightful observer of human beings, relationships, and the ironies of war; and a budding novelist experimenting with a tightly crafted narrative style, dramatic heightening, and psychological probing in order to develop the writer's skills he will need later. Readers also encounter in this war autobiography the following themes that O'Brien will continue to consider from different standpoints in his later fiction.

To Flee or Fight

Out of the overarching subject of the quest for order and control in one's life found in all of O'Brien's works emerges the attendant theme of an individual's decision to flee or confront a difficult situation. With its potential political and moral ramifications, as well as its connection to personal attributes of courage and cowardice, such a decision becomes for O'Brien a defining moment, both in his personal life and later in the lives of several of his fictional characters. In *If I Die,* this choice involves the Vietnam War—whether O'Brien should fight in a war that he views as "wrong" (*Die,* 26) or avoid military service. This dilemma, as well as his related thoughts on cowardice, courage, and order in his life, becomes the basis for the confessional nature of the "auto" sections of this war autobiography—a focus on the "I" of *If I Die.* Whether it leads to a soldier's decision to fight or to depart intentionally from the war for personal reasons (often referred to as a "separate peace" in war literature), this moral quandary surfaces in many modern war stories, for example, those by Stephen Crane, Siegfried Sassoon, Ernest Hemingway, and Joseph Heller. But its presence in Vietnam war stories by Caputo, Herr, Kovic, O'Brien, and others is significant as more than a mere continuation of a traditional theme in war literature.

During and after the Vietnam War, the flee-or-fight question became a highly charged political, social, and moral issue—one that O'Brien has talked about quite eloquently in several interviews. This question, on both a personal and national level, eventually became a catalyst for some of the most divisive and traumatic defining moments of the Vietnam era in America. A member of the board administering the Clemency Program of 1974, Father Theodore Hesburg noted at a Notre Dame conference on Viet Nam (3 December 1993) that fewer than 2 percent of America's college graduates served in Viet Nam; the moral and political dilemma of whether to fight in an unpopular war, he observed, became particularly acute for those young Americans who had opportunities for educational and occupational deferments, along with extensive draft counseling. Certainly O'Brien, a 1968 Phi Beta Kappa graduate of Macalester College with acceptance into a graduate program at Harvard, fell into this category. Because of the widespread controversy surrounding the draft and O'Brien's emotional comments in interviews about his own draft status, not surprisingly this flee-or-fight question and its concomitant issues involving courage, cowardice, responsibility, embarrassment, and commitment appear in many of O'Brien's war stories.

Moreover, O'Brien, in typical fashion, views this personal dilemma from multiple perspectives throughout these works—reluctant civilians soon to be inducted into the army, draft resistors fleeing authorities, draftees in the midst of basic training, a confused soldier about to depart for Viet Nam after advanced infantry training, and combat soldiers in Viet Nam considering desertion. Some of these individuals are real people; others are fictional. A few are Tim O'Brien himself; others have either no connection to or perhaps a partial correlation with the author. Yet all must decide whether to run away from the war or to remain and fight, and it is left to author O'Brien to portray these inner debates, moral dilemmas, and psychological dramas that accompany the process of choosing.

As O'Brien describes his own situations in *If I Die* or those of characters in his novels, he does not always arrive at satisfactory closure for either the individuals in the stories or for his readers: "I wanted to use stories to alert readers to the complexity and ambiguity of a set of moral issues—but without preaching a moral lesson" (McCaffery, Interview, 149). Thus, within all these war stories, the moral issues related to fleeing or fighting are murky: Is it a display of courage, responsibility, and endurance to fight in Viet Nam, or is it an act of cowardice and irresponsibility to ignore convictions and fight in a war that one does not believe in? Do situations occur in which choosing to fight may actually result in abandoning one's principles? The answers to these questions are complicated, although O'Brien often seems ready to answer for himself, but not necessarily for his characters.

In *If I Die,* O'Brien presents the flee-or-fight quandary in three contexts: an American civilian pondering flight to Canada to avoid his induction into the military, draftees in army basic training discussing desertion, and a soldier during advanced infantry training planning his defection to Sweden. The first incident occurs during O'Brien's summer of 1968 after the author graduated from Macalaster College and received his induction notice. In between golf games and discussions about the war with friends during drives around Lake Okabena in Worthington, Minnesota, O'Brien debates whether to refuse induction and flee the war. The vignette titled "Beginning," the second story in the book, is important for two reasons. First, this real event previews O'Brien's later fictional story "On the Rainy River" in *The Things They Carried;* second, in this episode, O'Brien maps the moral terrain for this decision and others related to shunning the war. To support a decision to fight, O'Brien raises, with the help of Plato and Socrates, the argument of obligation to one's country, family, town, and teachers. He also cites the comfort argument, a desire to maintain a comfortable order in his life and avoid the inevitable upheaval if he were to flee the war: "It was not just that I valued order. I also feared its opposite—inevitable chaos, censure, embarrassment" (*Die,* 31). To support a decision to flee, O'Brien notes his opposition to the war (the argument of conscience): "I was persuaded then and I remain persuaded now, that the war was wrong" (*Die*, 26). Alternately hoping that the war will be over before his induction and trying to forget the situation, O'Brien resolves this physical and intellectual standoff through simple inaction. He enters the army: "But I submitted. All the soul searchings and midnight conversations and books and beliefs were voided by abstention, extinguished by forfeiture, for lack of oxygen, by a sort of sleepwalking default" (*Die*, 30–31).

The second flee-or-fight incident in O'Brien's war autobiography occurs in the fifth story labeled "Under the Mountain." Now a soldier in basic training at Fort Lewis, Washington, O'Brien questions his potential involvement with the Vietnam War, strives to maintain his independence from the other trainees who seem to relish playing at war, and struggles to keep his soul from being consumed by the military machine. Within the oppressive, regimented environment, O'Brien discovers a soul mate in Erik Hansen, another widely read draftee from Minnesota, and together they discuss their options for avoiding the war. Their conversations are important because Erik introduces into this debate additional arguments appearing in later books. First, Erik raises questions about whether his own desire to flee the army is motivated by moral opposition to the Vietnam War or by selfish reasons, the personal-safety argument: " 'I'm really afraid that all the hard, sober arguments I have against this war are nothing but an intellectual adjustment to my horror at the thought of bleeding to death in some rice paddy' " (*Die*, 44). He then cites Ezra Pound's poem "Hugh Selwyn Mauberly" to present the reality (social consequences) argument. The real reason people do not desert is their fear of "society's censure" of cowardice: " 'Fear of Weakness. Fear that to avoid war is to avoid manhood. We come to Fort Lewis afraid to admit we are not Achilles, that we are not brave, not heroes' " (*Die*, 45). Soon, however, the two soldiers fall into the mind-numbing routines of indoctrination and basic training; they forget the debate as O'Brien goes off to advanced infantry training and Erik, after enlisting for one additional year to avoid combat, prepares to become an army clerk.

The final occasion in *If I Die* for raising this question of departing the war occurs in the chapter labeled "Escape." The episode is a defining moment for Private O'Brien as he nears the end of his advanced infantry training at Fort Lewis and prepares for shipment to Viet Nam. As the realities of the battlefield loom closer and his efforts to avoid being sent to Viet Nam fail (conversations with a chaplain and battalion commander), O'Brien's concrete plans for defection replace abstract considerations. Embracing the conscience argument about a wrong war ("I think the war is wrong. I should not fight in it": *Die,* 63), he decides to desert the army by crossing the border into Canada and flying to Sweden, where many American deserters live. He elaborately plans the trip, saves enough money, compiles the proper documents, and writes letters for his family explaining his decision. Once again the weight of obligation, desire for order in his life, and a fear of society's censure prevent him from carrying out his scheme as he burns the letters to his family: "It was over. I simply couldn't bring myself to flee. Family, the home town, friends, history, tradition, fear, confusion, exile: I could not run. . . . I was a coward" (*Die,* 73).

With this self-inflicted judgment of "coward" for his failure to establish a separate peace, O'Brien seems to answer the question of courage and cowardice related to fighting in a war that one believes is wrong. But readers should be careful in too quickly accepting the narrator's judgment of himself as O'Brien's definitive response to this complicated moral issue. Later in the book, O'Brien documents his own tangled thoughts and feelings about courage within the battlefield environment. The issue of courage still haunts O'Brien the soldier more than any other concern, for as he states in the "Escape" story, he is also motivated in his actions by a "desire to prove myself a hero" (*Die,* 62). He later says, "I thought about courage off and on for the rest of my tour in Vietnam" (*Die,* 145). Within a philosophical discussion of battlefield courage titled "Wise Endurance," O'Brien the author intentionally complicates the issue of courage and cowardice as related to a separate peace. In cataloging various types of courage and describing his heroes, fictional and real, he implies that a young soldier's acknowledgment of obligation to his country, his family, and the war—for some people admirable principles—also is a type of courage and a sign of manhood. As described by Plato in the *Crito,* he also introduces Socrates' concept of wise endurance as a type of courage: "Proper courage is wise courage. It's acting wisely, acting wisely when fear would have a man act otherwise. It is the endurance of the soul in spite of fear—wisely" (*Die,* 137). Further, as O'Brien pointedly notes, "I had endured" (*Die,* 138). In the last chapter, O'Brien confesses that "[he] had compromised one principle and fulfilled another" and that he had learned "war is not all bad; it may not make a man of you, but it teaches you that manhood is not something to scoff" (*Die,* 204).

A cowardice of conscience or a courage of endurance—narrator O'Brien does not completely resolve these ambiguities and conflicts over his failure as a soldier to act upon the argument of conscience and flee the war. But, as noted earlier, this moral ambiguity seems to be the point of O'Brien's storytelling and the impetus for his many-angled considerations in later works. In addition, O'Brien's confessions related to this issue certainly fill multiple purposes. Such retrospective soul-searching may prove therapeutic for O'Brien as he confronts this significant issue and judges his response, if not definitively, at least with candor. His confessions also elucidate the complexity of moral issues within a context of war, suggest the motives behind his storytelling, and finally invite readers' judgments about individual conscience and obligation as related to the whole Vietnam experience. Such difficult judgments must emerge from readers' considerations of the controversial social, moral, and political quagmire of the Vietnam War as portrayed throughout this book. Readers will also have opportunities in O'Brien's subsequent works to reconsider these judgments.

The War Experience

Without question the special character of the Vietnam War becomes a significant subject in this war autobiography (as well as important background in O'Brien's later works). In attempting to describe the physical and psychological state of combat, O'Brien moves from an inward examination of his heart and mind as a participant in war to his outward look at the Vietnam War, the Vietnamese people, and the hearts and minds of other combat soldiers. He accomplishes this task through story and sketch from the perspective of an observer-participant. As O'Brien has noted, "The only way the horror of war can mean anything to us is through small detailed vignettes of episodes of evil."[12] Thus, O'Brien intersperses his confessional sections with these vignettes related to bios as the narrator becomes commentator revealing the routines of war, its absurdity, and its impact on combatants and civilians in Viet Nam. In these observation sections, O'Brien's role is often similar to Robert Graves's, the British World War I poet, as described by Paul Fussell: "As a memorist, Graves seems most interested not in accurate recall but in recovering moments when he most clearly perceives the knavery of knaves" (Fussell, 219). O'Brien's revelations about knavery seem restricted to the American military establishment, and most of the knaves are American soldiers.

Even so, O'Brien occasionally chronicles the brighter side of the human spirit, the compassion and brotherhood of the battlefield, in his portrait of the combat soldier's heart and mind. He also attempts to educate readers about several other subjects including life in the military from basic training through combat; functions of soldiers' battlefield language and stories; soldiers' routines and rituals; and the nature of ground combat in Viet Nam. Throughout these observations, O'Brien, unlike the traditional memorist who often focuses on prominent social and historical events, examines "simple, unprofound scraps of truth" and explores the character of common soldiers. Such material, shaped by the moral and artistic powers of O'Brien's authorial vision, leads to poignant insights about war and people: "Men die. Fear hurts and humiliates. It is hard to be brave. It is hard to know what bravery *is*. Dead human beings are heavy and awkward to carry, things smell different in Vietnam, soldiers are dreamers, drill sergeants are boors, some men thought the war was proper and others didn't care" (*Die,* 31).

From this list of observations, it is apparent that O'Brien's Vietnam War is similar to wars fought in other times and places. As a character in *Going After Cacciato* observes, " 'War kills and maims and rips up the land and makes orphans and widows. These are the things of war. Any war. . . . I'm saying that the *feel* of war is the same in Nam or Okinawa—the emotions are the same, the same fundamental stuff is seen and remembered' " (*Cacciato,* 176). Certainly O'Brien attempts to link soldiers in all of his war stories with other combatants—real and fictional—from other wars (a community of the battlefield) in terms of routines, rituals, events, and emotions. At the same time, he illustrates and dramatizes special features of a Vietnam experience that Walter Capps describes in the following way: "The Vietnam War did not mean what wars had meant before. Previous frameworks of interpretation did not count. Earlier criteria did not register. Former understanding did not fit."[13] In *If I Die,* O'Brien establishes for readers a conceptual and emotional framework for this war that will have relevance in his other war-related novels.

At the heart of this framework is the widely cited fact that unlike America's previous three major wars in the twentieth century, with their frequent large-scale battles and clearly defined front lines, the Vietnam war involved small units and lacked a definitive front and rear. Except for the rare large-scale battle with a North Vietnamese regiment or the street-to-street fighting in the battle for Hue during Tet of 1968, the ground war—O'Brien's war—revolved around small-scale firefights, night ambushes, booby traps, search-and-destroy missions, reconnaissance patrols, and helicopter assault combat missions. For American military strategists, the Vietnam War was to be a short war of attrition; the immensely superior U.S. military technology and firepower would ultimately wear down and wipe out the enemy. But "the splendid little war," a label first given the Spanish-American War of 1898 and used again in ironic fashion by Philip Caputo in *A Rumor of War*, turned into a political, social, and military quagmire for both the Americans and their South Vietnamese allies. From a military standpoint, it was a war in which Americans won most of the major battles but still lost the war. Front lines were nonexistent; the enemy was often unseen; enemy rocket attacks and ambushes could occur anywhere; and battlefield movements seemed more like a game of musical chairs as American soldiers continually captured, exited, and recaptured villages and Vietcong strongholds.

The common soldier in most wars has little understanding of overall military objectives and strategy. For American soldiers in Viet Nam, however, their frustration at an apparent lack of purpose, order, commitment, and progress in a limited war was particularly acute, especially as the war dragged on and support on the home front waned. Equally important, their understanding of the political issues, language, and people of both North and South Viet Nam was very limited or nonexistent. Also contributing to the American soldiers' frustrations were the brutality and impersonality of guerrilla warfare, a type of combat requiring participants' constant alertness and creating a high level of battle stress. The enemy's principal strategy was to cause havoc without being seen; consequently, tactics included small-scale night ambushes, snipers, numerous mines and deadly booby traps, and extensive mortar fire on American positions. The American soldiers' resulting sense of danger and helplessness often took its psychological toll.

Moreover, this war was fought against more than enemy soldiers. It was also waged against the elements (heat, rain, and cold); against the land (jungle, elephant grass, rice paddies, rain forests, mosquitoes, leeches, dust, and mud); and even against the civilian population. American soldiers, who for the most part did not understand the history of Viet Nam, the language, or the culture, often found themselves fighting an unseen enemy easily assimilated into towns, villages, and hamlets. As a result, American soldiers had difficulty instantaneously deciding whether Vietnamese civilians, including women and children, were friends, foes, innocent bystanders, indifferent observers, or active participants in the war. Rules of combat engagement for American soldiers were ambiguous at best. Was a farmer by day a Vietcong at night? Was a quiet village a support base for a Vietcong unit? Was any running

Vietnamese a fair target? Were the homes, villages, and farm animals of the Vietnamese appropriate targets for American soldiers carrying out their missions? The results of this confusion, ignorance, indifference, and racial hatred were often disastrous for both groups: innocent Vietnamese civilians killed by callous, angry, or confused American soldiers; compassionate Americans killed by innocent-looking civilians.

Further complicating the situation was the American military's method for determining battlefield success in a war of attrition—body counts. Since traditional methods for determining military victory, territory gained or lost, had little meaning within this contained and everchanging conflict, military planners and the U.S. media turned to body counts (number of killed and wounded on both sides) to gauge progress in the war and to give shape to this formless conflict. These figures were conveniently adjusted at every level of the chain of command within the American military. A frequent result of this policy was an absurd scoreboard mentality among American soldiers and officers. Taken together, these features of the Vietnam conflict engendered age-old war issues of courage, cowardice, guilt, moral dilemmas, brutality, absurdity, and darkness of the human spirit, but American soldiers viewed them within the special context of waging war under chaotic and ambiguous conditions. The resulting perspectives become centerpieces of works—including O'Brien's *If I Die* and his other war-related books—about the Vietnam experience by American soldier-authors.

In *If I Die,* O'Brien, the participant, observer, and guilt-ridden veteran, attempts to capture many of these features of the Vietnam experience through brief character sketches, narrative accounts, confession, and commentary. Such a motive suggests why O'Brien devotes lengthy sections to describing this war's monotony, night ambushes, aimless missions, phony ambushes, oppressive heat, technology gone awry, and numerous mines and booby traps. He also apprehends the war's special character in the following passage, which serves as a map for the war's physical and moral landscapes found in his later war-related novels:

> Patent absurdity. The troops are going home, and the war has not been won, even with a quarter of the United States fighting it. We slay one of them, hit a mine, kill another, hit another mine. It is funny. We walk through the mines, trying to catch the Viet Cong Forty-eighth Battalion like inexperienced hunters after a hummingbird. But Charlie finds us far more often than we find him. He is hidden among the mass of civilians, or in tunnels, or in jungles. . . . And each piece of ground left behind is his

from the moment we are gone on our next hunt. It is not a war fought for territory, nor for pieces of land that will be won and held. It is not a war fought to win the hearts of the Vietnamese nationals, not in the wake of contempt drawn on our faces and on theirs, not in the wake of a burning village, a trampled rice paddy, a battered detainee. (*Die,* 129–30)

Within this context of absurdity, confusion, ignorance, frustration, fear, and moral dilemmas, O'Brien moves from general commentary to specific details. In the process, he indirectly confronts one of the darkest and most highly publicized episodes of American involvement in this war—the My Lai massacre. He also directly explores the evil and moral ambiguities connected with atrocities committed by soldiers in war. Significantly, in *In the Lake of the Woods,* O'Brien will later revisit the events of My Lai and its political and moral ramifications. Certainly such incidents are not restricted to the Vietnam War but occur in all wars. Furthermore, examining soldier-on-soldier and soldier-on-civilian brutality is not unique to O'Brien's work but occurs in the best of modern war literature from Remarque's *All Quiet on the Western Front* to Mailer's *The Naked and the Dead.* War writers are fascinated with various forms of soldiers' "heart-of-darkness" journeys on the battlefield—spiritual and moral confrontations portrayed in Joseph Conrad's 1902 novella *Heart of Darkness.* In this book, Conrad selectively indicts European imperialism in late nineteenth-century Africa. His European characters, stripped of civilization's restraints, confront evil, primal emotions, chaos, and savagery. They face the literal and metaphysical darkness of the jungle, the horrors of conflict, and the unplumbed depths of the soul. Conrad's key questions become fundamental issues in modern war literature: What spiritual darkness (evil) lies in human hearts and minds? What can individuals do to hold off this darkness?

These same situations and weighty questions also become important to America's soldier-authors writing about the Vietnam War, including O'Brien. More to the point, for many of these writers such individual heart-of-darkness experiences assume an additional significance as they come to symbolize America's experience in Viet Nam and loss of innocence about the brutal and depraved nature of war. Undoubtedly, atrocities in Vietnam were committed by both sides, but incidents involving American soldiers become almost obligatory episodes in many American war narratives. Philip Caputo perhaps best articulates the moral conflicts underlying these heart-of-darkness experiences:

Out there [Viet Nam], lacking restraints, sanctioned to kill, confronted by a hostile country and a relentless enemy, we sank into a brutish state. The descent could be checked only by the net of man's inner moral values, the attribute that is called character. There were a few . . . who had no net and plunged all the way down, discovering in their bottom-most depths a capacity for malice they probably never suspected was there.[14]

Consequently, in his war autobiography and his novel *In the Lake of the Woods,* My Lai—a name that represents the place and the events—is particularly important to O'Brien, not only because of such attendant issues as virtue versus evil and courage versus cowardice but also because of O'Brien's personal connection to this area. On the morning of 16 March 1968, in My Lai (4) near the coast in Quang Ngai Province, Charlie Company of Task Force Barker, 11th Brigade of the Americal Division, entered the subhamlet and massacred somewhere between 347–500 Vietnamese civilian women, children, and old men. Later the American soldiers burned buildings and killed livestock. While this was occurring, Bravo Company of the same task force killed civilians in the hamlet of My Khe, located a few miles from My Lai. The incidents did not come to light until almost a year and a half later, and only one soldier, Lieutenant William L. Calley, was convicted for participating in the events.

Ironically, almost 13 months later, on 29 April 1969, Tim O'Brien's Alpha Company, also part of the Americal Division, entered this same area called Pinkville by American soldiers because of its pink coloring on American military maps indicating a "built-up area." For these soldiers, the color also signaled enemy territory. During this assault, O'Brien was wounded and later received a Purple Heart. On several later occasions, O'Brien's unit returned to this locale. In his chapters "Assault" and "My Lai in May," O'Brien describes the April events and subsequent combat assaults by helicopter into this area, which was one of the most heavily mined places in the war zone and feared by Alpha Company because of a high number of casualties sustained during an assault a few months earlier. This narrative of O'Brien's experiences in Pinkville becomes a confession, but not O'Brien's personal confession. It is a disclosure by combat soldiers in a hostile environment, soldiers who are frustrated by an unseen enemy and besieged by sniper fire, mortars, and enemy mines as villagers silently watch. O'Brien does not write this particular war story about Pinkville to justify the horrors committed one year earlier at My

Lai; he does, however, suggest that a complex relationship exists among the special features of guerrilla warfare in Viet Nam, the resulting physical and psychological trauma for American soldiers, and the subsequent outrages committed by these soldiers: freed from the restraints of civilization, decent human beings, along with immoral ones, as they had done in previous wars, release their frustration and savage emotions.

> Scraps of our friends were dropped in plastic body bags. Jet fighters were called in. The hamlet was leveled and napalm was used. I heard screams in the burning black rubble. I heard the enemy's AK-47 rifles crack out like impotent popguns against the jets. There were Viet Cong in that hamlet. And there were babies and children and people who just didn't give a damn in there too. But Chip and Tom were on the way to Graves Registration in Chu Lai, and they were dead, and it was hard to be filled with pity. (*Die*, 122)

In devoting significant portions of his war autobiography to these episodes in Pinkville, O'Brien, as he does with the flee-or-fight issue, introduces a situation fraught with complexity and moral ambiguities. He invites readers to place themselves in the position of the soldiers of Alpha Company and to imagine how they might react; is there a capacity for evil and inhumanity within all of us? O'Brien does not want readers to judge unthinkingly either the American soldiers or themselves but to ponder the possibilities. As O'Brien notes in an interview, "All stories have at their heart an essential moral function, which isn't only to put yourself in someone else's shoes, but to go beyond that and put yourself into someone else's moral framework. How would *you* behave in that world" (McNerney, Interview, 10)? As occurs with the compelling and complicated flee-or-fight issue, O'Brien returns in his later writing, through his imagination, to the moral ambiguities of the My Lai incident. Specifically, throughout *In the Lake of the Woods,* he explores the events, motivations, and moral fallout of the original My Lai massacre. He does so from different angles through the involvement of his fictional central character, a former army soldier in Calley's unit, and through real testimony and background information from the Department of the Army's investigations in 1970 and from the court-martial of Lieutenant Calley.

In dealing with the Pinkville episodes in *If I Die,* O'Brien indirectly raises two other themes emerging from his war experience and appearing in his other war-related works. The first of these is O'Brien's portrayal of the "other," or Vietnamese, in his war autobiography. According to O'Brien, not enough attention has been given by Americans to the plight of the Vietnamese during and after the war: "The devastation in terms of human lives that the war caused to the Vietnamese hasn't been faced by America. It's sort of been acknowledged in a general abstract sense, but not in a visceral sense" (Herzog, Interview). Yet as some critics argue and as O'Brien admits in interviews, only on rare occasions has he presented the Vietnamese viewpoint in his books and then only from a limited ethnocentric perspective. Such omissions and superficial portrayals mark many Vietnam War novels and memoirs by American authors, with the work of 1993 Pulitzer Prize recipient Robert Olen Butler *(A Good Scent from a Strange Mountain)* and novelist Susan Fromberg Schaeffer *(Buffalo Afternoon)* among the exceptions to this trend.[15] When the Vietnamese appear in *If I Die,* they are subjects of this American narrator's viewpoint and not given their own narrative voice. According to O'Brien, such a narrative strategy reinforces the point that American soldiers knew little about the Vietnamese.

Two brief exceptions to this narrative pattern do occur. In "Ambush" the first emerges from O'Brien's brief battlefield memory of a summer 1967 debate the author had about the war with a North Vietnamese student, actually an officer in the North Vietnamese Army, whom O'Brien met when he was studying in Prague, Czechoslovakia. Another Vietnamese viewpoint about the war is articulated in "Hearts and Minds" (the informal label given to the U.S. military's pacification program) in the form of a concise character sketch of a Vietnamese. A former Vietcong who became a scout for the Americans tried unsuccessfully to obtain a three-day leave from his American unit to visit his wife: " 'You [American officer] are here for one year. I've been in war for many billion years. Many billion years to go' " *(Die,* 186).

But for the most part the Vietnamese are presented in this war autobiography from O'Brien's and the American soldiers' perspectives as helpless victims of random or accidental shellings, human targets for shooting practice, wounded enemy soldiers, indifferent or hostile civilian observers, a phantom enemy, objects for solatium payments ("twenty dollars for each wounded villager; thirty-three dollars and ninety cents for each death": *Die,* 167), or stoic and noble inhabitants of a country that has been at war for ages: "The blind old farmer was showering one of the men [American soldiers]. A blustery and stupid soldier, blond hair and big belly, picked up a carton of milk and from fifteen feet away hurled it, for no reason, aiming at the old man and striking him flush in the face. . . . He was motionless, and finally he smiled. He picked up the bucket and with the ruins of goodness spread over him, perfect gore, he dunked into the well and came up with water, and he began showering the next soldier" (*Die*, 103).

The absence of a more significant Vietnamese presence in this and other of O'Brien's works (perhaps with the exception of Sarkin Aung Wan in *Going After Cacciato*) does not, according to O'Brien, suggest a conscious diminution on his part of the Vietnamese role in this war or an indifference to this people's plight. In fact, O'Brien argues that this absence in *If I Die* and in other books by Americans is one more indication of the nature of this war—American soldiers separated from the Vietnamese by race, culture, and language. And writers, despite their powers of imagination, often avoid writing about subjects they do not understand. O'Brien reinforces this observation in an interview: "I haven't attempted to present a Vietnamese viewpoint. Why haven't I? Because I don't know it. I don't know the life of the VC and the life of the Vietnamese. I know only a smattering about what Buddhism and Confucianism are. I know only a smattering of the culture. I don't know the language at all. I'm not going to deign to speak for people who can speak very well for themselves" (McNerney, Interview, 17).

The final issue in *If I Die* related to O'Brien's study of the war emerges from personal introspection and an observer's viewpoint as soldier-author O'Brien probes the heart and mind of the combat soldier. This theme, also dominating the pages of *Going After Cacciato, The Things They Carried,* and key sections in *In the Lake of the Woods,* is one that Stephen Crane, a literary influence on O'Brien, found missing from Civil War novels and memoirs: "I wonder that some of these fellows don't tell how they felt in those scraps! They spout eternally of what they did, but they are emotionless as rocks."[16] O'Brien also found this theme occasionally underemphasized in Hemingway's war stories: "I remembered one of Hemingway's stories. It was about a battle in World War I. . . . I wondered why he did not care to talk about the thoughts those men must have had. Certainly those suffering and sacred human beings must have wondered if their cause was worthy. The men in war novels and stories and reportage seem to come off the typewriter as men resigned to bullets and brawn. Hemingway's soldiers especially" (*Die*, 96–97). For O'Brien, soldiers' thoughts, memories, daydreams, and decisions are important: thoughts about the strategic and moral chaos of the Vietnam War, memories of their lives before the war, daydreams of escaping war, responses to the unspeakable horrors and mind-numbing boredom of war, recognition of their own insignificance and mortality, and tricks of the mind to control their fate and fears within the chaotic arena of the battlefield. All of these elements become essential topics in O'Brien's war stories as they help define the individual and the war and as they contribute to significant truths about a soldier's emotions and thoughts.

Obviously as O'Brien explores his own moral dilemma involving a separate peace, discusses his attempts to maintain his individuality within the military structure, or questions the nature of courage, he is probing the soldier's mind. But what connects these introspective sections in *If I Die* with other external scenes portraying battlefield occurrences involves the soldier's pursuit of order and control in his life and environment—another common motif in modern war literature and an overarching theme throughout O'Brien's writing. As I have already noted, one of O'Brien's arguments for not fleeing the war is that he values order in his life, and either draft resistance or army desertion would bring chaos into his somewhat organized and comfortable existence. On the other hand, O'Brien implies that one strong argument for fleeing the military is that such an act is an ultimate display of control as the individual flees the impersonality and overwhelming power of the military machine. Moving beyond these moral and authority issues in his book, O'Brien explores soldiers' routine efforts of establishing order, control, and psychological comfort in their often mixed up, chance-filled existence—one that has frequently been compared in war literature and movies *(The Deer Hunter)* to a game of Russian roulette. As O'Brien notes in an interview, "The ability to manufacture order out of seeming chaos is important to our psychological well-being—humans are causal animals. We have an impulse to order events, seek out causes and consequences" (McCaffery, Interview, 143). Perhaps the perfect depiction of this random, helpless existence of the combat soldier appears in O'Brien's chapter labeled "Step Lightly." Here the author presents an extensive catalogue of different hidden mines and booby traps and their devastating physical and psychological impact on anxious foot soldiers: "The moment-to-moment, step-by-step decision-making preys on your mind. The effect sometimes is paralysis" *(Die, 126)*.

Within such an unpredictable environment where logical cause-and-effect relationships and known consequences infrequently happen, soldiers' obsessions with reintroducing some degree of control into their lives are natural. These combatants discover that they are mere cogs in the military machine or at the mercy of the land and weapons of death. " 'It's more than the fear of death that chews on your mind. . . . It's an absurd combination of certainty and uncertainty: the certainty that you're walking in mine fields, walking past the things day after day; the uncertainty of your every movement, of which way to shift your weight, of where to sit down' " (*Die*, 127). Linked to this particular indecision are the horrors of seeing the results of a misstep, the debilitating fear generated by an active imagination, or the need to make instantaneous life-and-death decisions. Such conditions make probing the psyche of the combat soldier essential for war authors. To accomplish this task, O'Brien examines soldiers' devices for coping with these insecurities, fears, horrors, and decisions and their attempts to establish a modicum of order, if only temporary, in their existence. The resulting psychological mechanisms for coping and choosing fall under the label "tricks of the mind." Their goal of creating momentary order, control, and comfort—experienced by O'Brien and his friend Erik on a night of guard duty in basic training—is rarely achieved on the battlefield, "A sense of privacy and peace. We talked about whatever came to mind . . . and it was a good time. We felt . . . what? Free. In control. Pardoned" (*Die*, 55).

As noted by soldier-authors from previous wars, mental tricks to establish a feeling of control on the battlefield may involve an almost involuntary giving of oneself over to the war. Such an absence of thought leading to desensitization, or combat numbness, is described in Wilfred Owen's poem "Apologia Pro Poemate Meo": "Merry it was to laugh there- / Where death becomes absurd and life absurder. / For power was on us as we slashed bodies bare / Not to feel sickness or remorse of murder" (ll. 5–8). Moreover, soldiers may focus on simple routines, such as elaborate rituals of eating described in Remarque's *All Quiet on the Western Front*. Such mind games appear in *If I Die* in the form of macabre humor exchanged among soldiers over deaths of fellow soldiers; mindless submission to the rhythms, routines, and instinctive acts of the war; or preoccupation with the statistics of war—the body counts. Such coping methods are soldiers' attempts to keep from thinking about the realities of their existence, the hidden truths, and their innate fears. These tricks of distraction momentarily locate psychological order and comfort within the turbulence of the battlefield, and undertaking these activities temporarily relieves soldiers from guilt, horror, anxiety, and feelings of helplessness. For brief moments, they feel they have the upper hand.

Sometimes, such outwardly directed tricks of the mind are inadequate measures to establish inner sway. At these moments some participants become daydreamers, escaping into their memories or imagination. This ruse, in O'Brien's view, holds the most promise and peril for the soldier. Imagination and memory out of control can lead to fear, paranoia, and helplessness: "We would squeeze our eyes shut. What we could not see, we imagined. Then—only then—we would see the enemy. We would see Charlie in our heads: oiled up, ghostly, blending with the countryside, part of the land" (*Die,* 36–37). Used wisely, however, imagination and memory can produce the opposite effect. Instead of creating fear, mental imagery can aid soldiers by conjuring up possibilities for life during and after the war. This heuristic use of imagination is one that O'Brien employs as he plans his desertion from the army and considers the possibilities of this choice. It also allows him to think about courage in the abstract and concrete as he recalls his heroes from films and books, especially Frederic Henry in Hemingway's *Farewell to Arms*, and imagines heroic actions on the battlefield. Furthermore, envisioning what might be brings a temporary wonder, playfulness, and security into soldiers' lives: " 'I see a circus. No shit, there's a circus out there. Charlie's all dressed up in clown suits. Oh, yeah, a real circus.'. . . For a time we just sat there. We watched the dark grow on itself, and we let our imaginations do the rest' " (*Die,* 38–39). These various roles for a soldier's memory and imagination in combat will become the center-piece of *Going After Cacciato* as Paul Berlin, the central character, learns the power and limits of his mental faculties as a means to control fear, order events, and—most important—make decisions.

Writing

Unlike writers who in their autobiographies explicitly discuss the craft of writing (*graphein*), O'Brien devotes little space in this book to comments about the nature of autobiography or memoir. He does, however, begin to address directly and indirectly the art and purposes of his story-telling, a prominent subject in his later works: "I would write about the army. Expose the brutality and injustice and stupidity and arrogance of wars and the men who fight in them" (*Die,* 96). Equally important, distinctive features of style and structure of O'Brien's later books appear in this war autobiography as the author prepares for the more demanding writing tasks ahead. Specifically, O'Brien establishes his preoccupation with the carefully crafted sentence, one that is short, rhythmic, and devoid of many adjectives and adverbs. Interestingly, this description of sentence style also applies to his goals for the form of a story: "You should keep them as close to the bone as possible, without embroidery, without much but the facts" (McNerney, Interview, 8–9). It is the resulting dispassionate, unembellished form and content that critics praise. In *If I Die,* O'Brien also hones his "scene drawing," a staple of fiction, as he dramatizes events and develops story truths.[17] Further, he introduces patterns of chapter organization, integrated themes, iteration, and enumeration that shape his novels. For example, his technique of enumeration, briefly used in *If I Die* ("Step Lightly") with an extensive cataloging of mines and booby traps, becomes an important narrative device in *The Things They Carried.* O'Brien infuses a simple list of items with narrative power as the accumulation of detail leads to an emotional weight and a thematic and symbolic significance.

Perhaps foremost among these elements of incipient form in this war autobiography is O'Brien's emphasis on the structure of his chapters, or, in the case of *If I Die,* the 23 vignettes. Each can stand alone as an independent story, an illustration of a simple truth, or a character sketch, and each has a definite beginning, middle, and end. Such a structure would seem obvious given the fact that O'Brien had already published some of these stories as separate pieces in magazines and newspapers. In an interview, he notes two advantages of this form:

> I try to make chapters into independent stories. . . . I can publish chapters as stories in magazines. This has the advantage of making money, and also of testing things out, getting responses from magazine editors and readers. The other reason, which is more important, has to do with why chapters are chapters. I've always wondered why so many chapters end arbitrarily. It's much nicer to have your chapters conclude with a nice mini-resolution. There should be a sigh from the reader at the end of a chapter, the sigh signifying he's recognized a natural end and that the chapter has an internal integrity to it. (McCaffery, Interview, 137)

Such an emphasis on the "mini-resolution" within each chapter (for example, the setting, details of everyday life, action, and resolution of the sketch entitled "Lagoon") is also obvious in *The Things They Carried,* but it characterizes many of the chapters in *Going After Cacciato.*

Even so, with this stress on parts, the whole of *If I Die* and the novels does not suffer. As is true of *The Things They Carried,* O'Brien's war autobiography is more than a loose collection of stories connected by a title and an overarching setting and theme. O'Brien has used the label "integrated novel" (McNerney, Interview, 8) to describe the structure of *The Things They Carried* and to distinguish it from the more conventional novel form, but the term is also an appropriate label for *If I Die.* An obvious connecting link in *If I Die* is the narrative voice of Tim O'Brien, although his changing perspectives (I, we, and it), tones, and shifting times (immediate to retrospective) frequently occur. Yet O'Brien strives to do more than simply stitch together these vignettes with a single narrative voice. He integrates them, although not as successfully nor as consciously as he does in *The Things They Carried*. Across the chapters, connections occur through recurring images; thus, references to marching appear in several separate chapters to symbolize the routines and monotony of war, as well as the machinelike response of the soldiers to their plight: "The days were always hot, even the cool days, and we concentrated on the heat and the fatigue and the simple motions of the march. It went that way for hours. One leg, the next leg. Legs counted the days" (*Die,* 12). In addition, repeated references to mines suggest the haphazard existence of the soldiers. Settings also recur; thus, a one-paragraph passage on "old rituals, old fears" of night in the first chapter is expanded into a subsequent chapter ("Nights") detailing more about the imagination of a combat soldier at night while waiting in ambush. Later (chapter XV, "Centurion"), night becomes a setting and an occasion for a discussion of the night rituals of soldiers on the battlefield across time and wars, a subject connecting with a later extended digression ("Another War") on soldiers' distinctive routines at night in a safe rear area. O'Brien links all of these night scenes by exploring the soul of the soldier within the physical and symbolic setting of darkness, which has a conspicuous presence in all of his novels.

The most distinctive feature of this integrated structure in *If I Die* is O'Brien's technique of iteration. Not only are themes repeated throughout the book, but as is true with his collection of works, these motifs are viewed across chapters from different angles. Each new outlook adds to the accumulation of different realities, simple truths, moral ambiguities, difficult decisions, and philosophical issues related to a single theme. For example, courage becomes a central focus in the confessional portions of this autobiography, particularly O'Brien's bravery or cowardice in going to war. Throughout various scenes, O'Brien also explores gallantry and timidity within broader contexts: film and fictional heroes, individuals who attempt to flee the battlefield with self-inflicted wounds, the diluted courage of American soldiers in Viet Nam compared to their counterparts in World War II, common courage based on wise endurance in combat, and ideal courage of command as demonstrated by Captain Johansen. O'Brien also attacks the obstinate, misguided "courage of preserving" illustrated by Major Callicles. This officer steadfastly holds onto his notions of right and wrong conduct (He pursued

prostitution, pot, and sideburns "like an FBI agent; he prosecuted viola-
tors with inquisitorial zeal": *Die,* 189.) while the larger moral issues of
the war, such as the My Lai Massacre, are dismissed or disingenuously
explained as evidence of a lack of discipline among American soldiers.

As has been true in this entire war autobiography, O'Brien is not
preaching to his readers through these different perspectives of courage.
Instead, he is exploring the angles, complicating the decisions, and forcing readers to consider these substantive issues and decide for themselves what they would do. As O'Brien notes, "Fiction in general, and
war stories in particular, serve a moral function, but not to give you
lessons, not to tell you how to act. Rather, they present you with philosophical problems, then ask you to try to adjudicate them in some way
or another"(McNerney, Interview, 10). For O'Brien, this process and
purpose of storytelling, first introduced in his war autobiography, will
shape all of his later writings.

Northern Lights

Responding to a question about Paul Milton Perry, the central character
in *Northern Lights* (1975), Tim O'Brien judges his first novel harshly:
"That's a terrible book. I'm embarrassed by it; it's hard to talk about it.
It's the first novel I ever tried to write, and unfortunately it was published. It was done logically" (Naparsteck, Interview, 2). Written during
O'Brien's off-hours in 1973–1974 while he worked as a general assignment reporter on the national desk at the *Washington Post,* this novel is
one that, as O'Brien has noted on several occasions, he would like to
revise by cutting about 80 pages, some of the interior monologues, and
also the unnecessary repetition. Despite the author's unflattering assessment, the book provides fertile ground for a whole range of interesting
studies of symbolism, mythology, literary and religious allusions, literary
parody, irony, parallel scenes, and archetypal motifs. Scholars would
probably not subscribe to the "terrible" label but would agree that it is a
flawed first novel, the work of a young novelist searching for his own
sense of place, style, vision, and narrative voice. As a result, the story
lacks the focus and subtleties of theme, character, and structure distinguishing the later works. What readers and critics can agree upon is
that *Northern Lights* is unique among O'Brien's six books. First, unlike
his other books, portions of it did not appear in other publications prior
to the release of the novel. Also, the novel has received little critical
attention. In fact, it is the least known and examined work in the

O'Brien collection and currently remains out of print. As O'Brien becomes one of America's most prominent contemporary writers, however, a few scholars return to this novel to trace the evolution of O'Brien's theme and craft, and O'Brien in 1995 still talks about reworking it because the book contains a worthwhile story (Herzog, Interview).

At the time of publication, the book received generally tepid reviews that cited its "undramatic" ending, literary pretentiousness, excessive length, and "contrived" interactions. Positive comments focused on the "sensitive portrait" of provincial life in Minnesota, O'Brien's "sharp ear for dialogue," and the "good adventure story" comprising about 150 pages of the book. Perhaps the most interesting analysis is Roger Sale's. He notes that in places O'Brien shows himself "to be a real writer," but the book's major defect is its unmistakable origins in Hemingway's *The Sun Also Rises:* "Is it possible to read *The Sun Also Rises* too often? . . . Tim O'Brien has read it too often, let it sink into him too deeply."[18] Sale goes on to cite similarities in dialogue within the two books, the Hemingwayesque descriptions in O'Brien's book, and parallels among characters (with Addie of *Northern Lights* assuming the role of Lady Brett Ashley in *The Sun Also Rises,* and O'Brien's two central male characters sharing traits with Hemingway's Jake Barnes, Bill Gorton, and Robert Cohn). Without question such observations are accurate, but they do not surprise O'Brien: "I was trying to parody Hemingway. I wrote the book not knowing it was going to be published. I was just a beginner, and I was sort of having fun with it, so I tried to spoof *The Sun Also Rises*, *A Farewell to Arms,* and I thought I did a pretty neat job of doing the spoofs, but unfortunately good literature should be more that just gamesmanship, and I think there is too much gamesmanship in that book" (Naparsteck, Interview, 3). This debt to Hemingway also appears through O'Brien's use of nature as a crucible, rituals of outdoor life, themes (courage, manhood, and heroism), style (sparse sentences and simple adjectives), dialogue, characters (code and true heroes), and characters' edgy interactions. But within the novel Faulknerian influences, as O'Brien has admitted, also mold his evolving sensibility as a writer, particularly his interest in the influence of place, family, and culture on personality.

Some readers of O'Brien's books examining the Vietnam War might also be tempted to consider this first novel as an indirect commentary on the war and its aftermath: a wounded veteran suffering from Post-Traumatic Stress Disorder returns to an unappreciative and largely ill-informed America. Other readers may find the book to be an elaborate allegory about the relationship between the American frontier spirit and the evolution of the American soldier, perhaps, as one reviewer has noted, something akin to Norman Mailer's novel *Why Are We in Vietnam?*[19] But O'Brien dismisses attempts to inflate the significance of the Vietnam War in this novel: "The action of the book occurs after the war, and I wanted some kind of dramatic demonstration of Harvey's macho tendencies. So I had him go to war—you know, 'There's this brave son-of-a-bitch'—and he gets wounded as a result" (McCaffery, Interview, 141). Rather than political and social commentary, this novel presents, according to O'Brien, a simple story about people, "the genesis of personality, the genesis of one's moral outlook" (McCaffery, Interview, 140). O'Brien also examines characters' connections with the living, the dead, the land, and the self. Along the way, O'Brien returns to issues of memory, imagination, courage, control, and commitment introduced in *If I Die in a Combat Zone,* and he examines themes of love and mortality, which he will develop in later novels. Also prominent in this book is O'Brien's treatment of the complex associations of fathers and sons, another theme present in his remaining works.

The limited third-person narrative unfolds through the eyes and mind of Paul Perry. The setting is Sawmill, Minnesota, in 1970, a dying timber town located in the Arrowhead portion of northeast Minnesota, with its Indian, French, German, and Finnish heritages. The physical isolation of the community suggests the psychological separation of the central characters from external global forces, but threats of nuclear war and the fallout from the Vietnam War intrude upon some of the characters' lives. The central figures are 30-year-old Paul Milton Perry, a divinity-school dropout and county farm extension agent; his wife, Grace, described throughout as a mother figure; Paul's brother, Harvey, who has just returned from Viet Nam with a wounded eye; and Addie, the Brett Ashley character who fluctuates from "she could be very gay" to neurotic, to a collector of men, to an emasculator.[20] The Perry brothers live under the dark cloud of the bullying values and gloomy prophecies of their dead father (Pehr Lindstrom Pehri), a preacher for 57 years at Damascus Lutheran Church. They also live under the influence of the harsh "northern attitude" of their grandfather, a preacher who committed suicide. Both ministers, shaped by Finnish mythology contained in the *Kalevala* (Finnish epic poem of 1835), the Old Testament, and an "asexual northern attitude that excluded and eventually scorned things female" (*Lights,* 69), preached of the elements, hell, fear, heroism, the apocalypse, stoic endurance, and mortality. Notably absent in their teachings were references to love, heaven, and salvation.

Although divided into two major parts, the novel actually follows a traditional tripartite pattern of a coming-of-age or, in this case, maturation story: preparation, confrontation, and consideration (a pattern frequently used in war memoirs and war novels).[21] Within these three stages, O'Brien focuses on the Perry brothers' quests to arrive at a sense of self, an acceptance of their relationship with their father, and an understanding of courage and heroism. The central motif is the literal and figurative seeing that does and does not occur in the novel. Consequently, O'Brien replaces the symbolic night scenes and starlight scopes of *If I Die* with an interest in the flawed eyes of his central characters, Harvey's wounded eye and Paul's weak eyesight: "If you saw into the forest, then you saw. If you did not, then you did not. 'There's vision on the one hand and there's blindness on the other,' was the Kalevalian paraphrase used by his father to organize the Pentateuch sermons of 1962" (*Lights,* 191). Finally, perhaps as a result of O'Brien's "logical" approach to writing this story and his characteristic use of repetition, the novel's underlying structure involves pairings—similar and contrasting characters, settings, images, symbols, and events.

Preparation: Character Poses

The flawed first part of this novel, which runs 159 pages, is O'Brien's attempt to establish the personalities of his major characters, including Pehr Lindstrom Pehri (the dead father), and a limited dance of desire occurring among four individuals. In this section the Hemingway parody is the strongest with characters, dialogue, sexual repartee, and situations reminiscent of *The Sun Also Rises,* along with the playful, edgy, and sometimes neurotic exchanges between Frederic Henry and Catherine Barkley in *A Farewell to Arms.* In terms of the overall plot, this first section presents readers with the two principal characters who will undergo the physical and spiritual test in the book's second part, and it explains why both men so desperately need such a journey to self-discovery and independence from their dead father's continued smothering influence.

Furthermore, in a novel that pursues O'Brien's preoccupation (from *If I Die*) with what constitutes courage and heroism, the author presents in the early pages the quasi-Hemingway code (ideal) hero of this novel, Harvey Perry: high school football player, consummate outdoorsman,

pride of his father, and a "hard charger." Harvey, nicknamed "the Bull"
by the townspeople and his brother, is a wounded hero (first lieutenant
with two rows of medals) from the Vietnam War, who, despite losing his
eye, "didn't seem bitter and even sometimes appeared to treat it [war]
all as a great adventure that, if opportunity came, he wouldn't mind
repeating" (*Lights,* 33). As a boy, Harvey (the favored son delivered at
home by the father during a snowstorm) followed his father "into the
woods" (an important symbolic phrase repeated in this novel) to learn
the skills of a woodsman.

Years after his father's death, he remains the obedient son, burdened
with an authoritarian, frontier, pessimistic view of life preached by his
father. While in high school, Harvey, in response to his father's prophecies of a nuclear apocalypse, heeded the dying preacher's request and
built a bomb shelter in the backyard of their home during the Cuban
missile crisis in October 1962.[22] Years later, he continues to cling to the
belief that his father was not crazy. Furthermore, as the novel begins, he
is also the character who initially seems in control of his life—comfortable with his relationship to his dead father and secure in his manhood.
As O'Brien soon reveals, however, the symbolism of Harvey's "dead eye"
alerts readers to the blemishes in this hometown hero. Harvey is not the
ideal model in the Captain Johansen mold of temperance, justice, and
wise courage; instead, he is merely posing as a hero. He bullies his
brother about the latter's lack of courage, becomes obsessed about participating in a proper parade to honor his own heroism in the war, lacks
insight into his own personality and his father's, and simply cannot take
charge of his own life upon his return from the war. As O'Brien notes, "I
did intend Harvey's partial blindness as a symbol of a deeper personality-
blindness" (McCaffery, Interview, 141).

In contrast, Paul Milton Perry initially serves as the physical and psychological foil to his daring and physically fit brother. Paul's first name,
alluding to Apostle Paul's epiphany and temporary blindness on the
road to Damascus, and the middle name, a reference to the blind poet,
suggest his own personality blindness and a lack of order in his life. The
bespectacled Paul, who also smokes, is variously described as "chubby,"
"fat," and "out of shape." Finding himself in a midlife crisis at age 30,
Paul wallows in self-pity, " 'Pooooor me,' he moaned" (*Lights,* 8). He
indulges his jealousy of his brother, laments his dead-end job, and falls
into the role of an onlooker as he sleepwalks through his job, his marriage, and his life. Asked to join the local fire brigade during a fire, Paul
responds that he will " 'watch it from the window' ": " 'You [Paul] don't

join anything around here. You ought to show a little more citizenship' "
(*Lights,* 50). Such a lack of commitment carries over into his comfortable
but passionless marriage to Grace ("Marrying her after graduation had
been as easy and natural as falling asleep in a warm bath": *Lights,* 13.) in
which his spiritual impotence has turned into a sexual impotence,
relieved only by his wife's masturbating him. "Peeping Paul," as Addie
taunts him, also is incapable of acting on his sexual attraction to Addie
and her suggestive invitations to adventure. Rather, he prefers to talk
with her or fantasize while watching her from a distance. Hence, imagination for Paul is not a heuristic tool but a means of escaping life.
"Wishy-washy" Paul is directionless. He is torn between action—want-
ing to establish order, control, and meaning in his life (to find out where
things started)—and helpless inaction in the face of his fears, memories,
and a debilitating fatalism about his lack of influence over his destiny
and personality: "partly a combination of human beings and events,
partly a genetic fix, an alchemy of circumstance" (*Lights,* 9). Paul, like
Tim O'Brien in *If I Die,* faces a flee-or-fight decision, in this case
whether to commit himself to an active, meaningful life.

As Paul sorts through his options and memories, he is also guilt ridden
about his love-hate relationship with his dead father. Unlike Harvey, Paul
was not the good son. Despite his father's disappointment, the young
Paul did not go into the woods with his father and Harvey, eschewing
these outdoor adventures and never acquiring the temperament or skills
of a hunter. A recurring memory for Paul is of his terror at being ordered
by his father into nearby Pliney's Pond to learn to swim. Later, as an
adult on a brief outing with Harvey in the woods, Paul still feels "awkward and out of place" (*Lights,* 75) and has to be saved from drowning by
Harvey. In fact, symbolic of his unheroic nature, Paul later suffers the
taunts of Harvey and Addie for his inability to kill a rat. In contrast to his
macho brother, Paul grew up in their male household performing the
domestic duties after his mother had died giving birth to Harvey. And
unlike his obedient brother, Paul defiantly refused to attend church and
hear his father preach. Believing deep down that his father was crazy, he
also declined to help Harvey build the backyard bomb shelter. It is no
wonder that this emotional, physical, and psychological baggage induces
Paul to look for a revelation, an epiphany on his journey through life as
he attempts to seek "the bottom of things" (*Lights,* 84).

In this male-dominated Hemingwayesque world of outdoor life, the
two female characters, Addie and Grace, appear to have relatively minor
roles. The mysterious Addie (Is she part Indian?), as suggested earlier, is

also on a meandering journey toward self-discovery that in reality becomes an escape from life. But her principal role in the novel is that of a sexual catalyst as she plays the Perrys against each other in an unconventional love triangle that intensifies Paul's jealousy of Harvey and reveals Harvey's inability to understand his brother. Through her posing, she taunts, teases, and emasculates both men, eventually temporarily attaching herself to Harvey, but appearing still interested in Paul, " 'I love you anyway' " (*Lights,* 153). Most important, as she breaks down the Perrys' poses, she exposes their emotional and psychological weaknesses.

In contrast to the dark-skinned, slender, outgoing, alluring, and nasty Addie, the "heavy-breasted" Grace, Paul's wife, is the symbolic earth mother, whom Roger Sale compares to Hadley Hemingway (Sale, 31). Grace, as Addie notes, offers Paul "home" (a Hemingwayesque symbol of security) and "supper" in contrast to Addie's offer of the "badlands and Indian adventure" (*Lights,* 117). Grace is described as having "that vast womanly, wifely, motherly sympathy and understanding that both attracted and repelled him [Paul], often at the same time. 'Like somebody's goddamn mother,' his father had said" (*Lights,* 12). Grace also displays a "southern calm" in contrast to the "northern attitude" of Paul's father and grandfather. Not only is she the soothing, protective mother-wife for Paul, she is also the moral center of this novel. Comfortable in her role as wife-mother to Paul and eager to become a real mother, she is the only one of the four characters who is not posing, not searching for her true self. As Paul admits, she is "like a gyroscope. A warm self-righting center, soothing with those whispers" (*Lights,* 12). As a result, in a novel emphasizing "seeing," Grace is the only character without defective spiritual vision. She understands situations and accurately judges people. Thus, she immediately perceives how "awful" Harvey's belated homecoming parade turns out to be and recognizes that Harvey " 'isn't . . . such a great hero as he pretends' " (*Lights,* 127). Because Grace is the moral and emotional touchstone of this novel, the evolving relationship between Paul and his wife progresses from indifference to love and marks his progress on his journey to self-discovery, courage, commitment, and love.

Confrontation: Journey into the Woods

As is true of most initiation literature, this confrontation section, which comprises almost three quarters of part 2 of the novel, contains both a literal and a symbolic journey—a physical and spiritual testing of character. Yet unlike most conventional initiation literature, the outcomes of these journeys are unexpected. Within this piece of solid nature writing, O'Brien describes a multiday cross-country ski trip planned by Harvey. This trip takes the Perry brothers from the New Year's winter carnival and ski races at Grand Marais (the equivalent of the bull fights at Pamplona in *The Sun Also Rises*) to their home some distance away. In describing this outdoor adventure, O'Brien draws upon the Hemingwayesque symbolism of a trip into the out-of-doors where individuals test their skills and endurance, attempt to reestablish order and comfort in their disordered lives, and embrace the Romantics' view of nature as a spiritual guide and healer.

The ski trip takes the Perrys into the woods for a second time since Harvey's return from the war. On this occasion, the brothers are seeking more than adventure: For both, the trip is an opportunity to become "better brothers" and for Paul one more chance to achieve insight about himself—a revelation. "It was that long far-back tension, a kind of tugging, a feeling of vast bewilderment and eventual melancholy at not seeing so clearly. . . . Some sort of great and magnificent epiphany was what was needed" (*Lights,* 191). In addition, the ski trip allows the Perrys to do some brotherly bonding and to assume their customary roles: Harvey as leader shows off his "woodsman's tricks" (learned from his father) to an admiring Paul, who views him as someone who "knew what he was doing. Calm, building that fire, unafraid, a full-fledged undaunted hero, absolutely no question" (*Lights,* 172). Paul, presaging the position and attitude of soldier Paul Berlin with his Third Squad in *Going After Cacciato,* happily becomes the unthinking follower as they ski, "It was easy, following the orange rucksack, following the simple channel of the gully. It was easy. There was nothing to think about" (*Lights,* 178).

Within a short span of time, however, misfortunes occur. Symbolically, using their father's old map of the territory, they become lost. Close on the heels of this event are Harvey's illness, a blizzard, and Paul's loss of his glasses. These misfortunes precipitate a confrontation, as Paul must literally confront the wilderness he has desperately avoided and figuratively confront himself, his fears, the memories of his dead father, and his relationship with Harvey. A role reversal quickly occurs as Paul Perry, forced by circumstances, becomes leader and reluctant hero. As Harvey becomes sicker with pneumonia and wishes to give up the journey and die, Paul forces him to continue the journey and, at one point, administers CPR to save Harvey's life. Because of Paul's resolve and actions, both brothers are eventually rescued.

But as will be true with the rest of O'Brien's fiction, the details of the adventure are insignificant in comparison to the opportunities for O'Brien to explore relationships, characters, and moral issues. Without question, as numerous reviewers note, in this section of nature writing and psychological exploration, O'Brien moves away from the influence of other writers and assumes his own narrative voice. Consequently, he examines issues raised in *If I Die*. Thus, in *Northern Lights*, O'Brien progresses from exploring the issues of courage and a soldier's heart and mind in his war autobiography to examining the soul of an average person. This individual must deal with physical and mental stress, control his fears, act courageously, and order his life—experiences not at all unlike those a combat soldier encounters. Through his analysis of these experiences, O'Brien proves once again his adage that anyone can have a war experience; he or she does not have to participate in armed conflict to have the same feelings and face somewhat similar decisions.

As the lost brothers travel deeper into the woods, O'Brien journeys deeper into the brothers' essential nature. He describes Harvey's thoughts, fears, and memories during this episode, but clearly the focus is on Paul's mind and his apparent evolution into a brave leader. First, O'Brien describes how Paul gradually learns survival skills, begins to trust his physical and mental powers, becomes comfortable in this unfamiliar environment, and develops tricks of the mind to control his fears and establish order. For example, borrowing Harvey's trick taught to him by the father, Paul counts his glides while skiing, the equivalent of the combat soldier's preoccupation with the act of marching. Such a focus on routine details becomes for Paul a way of establishing order and connection, building his pride in his stamina, and ignoring the desperateness of the situation.

Next, O'Brien turns to the real drama of this adventure—Paul's efforts to use memory and imagination to arrive at the sought-after revelation. Linking himself with foot soldiers in *If I Die* and anticipating Paul Berlin's looking backward and forward in *Going After Cacciato,* Paul Perry uses his memory and imagination heuristically to consider the complex love-hate relationship with his father and to explore various possibilities for his own life. He attempts to recall what happened in order to get to the bottom of things and determine why these events occurred. He also imagines what could have happened. In contrast to his defective physical vision, heightened by the loss of his glasses, his mind's eye becomes quite sharp.

As Paul remembers what did and did not transpire in his relationship with his father, several traits dominate these memories, including the absence of communication and of outward signs of love between father and son. Dismissing Paul's "woman's work" and feeling disappointed at Paul's lack of interest in the woods, the father apparently showered his attention and affection on Harvey. Thus Paul vividly recalls his feelings of being an outsider in a "womanless household." Paul also remembers his own lack of sympathy for his father, his thoughts that his father was crazy, and his hope that his father would change. And he recalls living with the "wind of his father" (*Lights,* 191), which included the father's harsh views on life, endurance, and heroism. Most of all, he recollects his father's apocalyptic vision involving the elder Perry's fixation with death through nuclear destruction at the hands of the Russians and his obsession with having a bomb shelter built in the back yard. Paul's memories also include incidents when Paul attempted to assert his independence from his father and to display courage. For example, he refused to attend church to hear his father preach and later to participate in building the bomb shelter.

Equally important, mixed with feelings of guilt, resentment, confusion, and rejection are a few positive memories and the seeds of love, something that Paul desperately sought from his father and continues to seek even now. He recalls images of his father during the preacher's quiet time on Sunday mornings before church, "cooking his own breakfast and letting Paul sleep late, then waking him, the only gentle time, and a very fine time" (*Lights,* 198). Paul also remembers the pride he felt during the Cuban missile crisis when it appeared that his father's crazy prophecy might come true, "nobody was joking about the old man being crazy. Perry could have burst he was so proud" (*Lights,* 213).

Entangled with these memories are Paul's fantasies, many also related to his father, that become more tricks of the mind to forget the chaotic present and explore the possibilities for his own life. During moments of relaxation, physical exertion, fear, or courage on the ski trip, Paul imagines how he could change his life, become fitter, be a better husband, move from Sawmill, and start a new career. Like Paul Berlin in *Cacciato,* he also anticipates the heroic stories he will be able to tell about this great adventure to his wife, his son, and the townspeople. In his most frequent daydreams, however, he imagines what his relationship with his father might have been, "what he might have done differently, what he might have said to ease the old man's death or what he might have done to help with the digging, the pouring of cement" (*Lights,* 186). He also imagines conversations with his father about Paul's mother, about Grace, and about the disagreements with his father.

Above all, he imagines open communication between father and son, along with mutual love and acceptance: He would be courageous by killing an animal, and he would "at last huddle with the old man and eat with him and hold him and warm him beside a waxing fire, hold the old man and tell him, tell him . . . Hold him and warm him and not speak, knowing without language the way the old man knew every-thing without language and spoke without language" (*Lights,* 267).

Just as Paul Berlin will learn about reality and daydreams in *Going After Cacciato,* Paul Perry finds reality intruding upon his daydreams of heroic possibilities. In a key scene preparing readers for the inconclusive ending, O'Brien shows the limits of Paul Perry's imagination. After leav-ing Harvey in a small timberman's shanty, Paul searches for food. Imag-ining himself to be the enthusiastic and skilled hunter that his father wanted him to be, Perry begins to believe that he can indeed kill an ani-mal for the food that he and his brother so desperately need. He pictures himself a killer, stealthily stalking a deer: "Then he got up and waded deeper into the forest, again focusing his thoughts on the act of hunting, casting himself as a hunter and thinking only that he would find an ani-mal and then kill it with the blue-bladed knife and then eat it" (*Lights,* 268). Typical of the logical and mechanical way in which O'Brien con-structs this novel, he once again uses repetition to counterpoint this visualized scene with the real episode from part one at the town dump, when Paul is incapable of killing a rat. Reality interrupts fantasy as Paul quickly loses his courage and nerve to kill a deer and retreats instead to the shanty. In an ironic twist mirroring Stephen Crane's *Red Badge of Courage,* Paul, feeling "stupid, silly, and embarrassed," stumbles on a woodchuck (which Harvey later tells him is "a fucking big rat") buried deep in the snow and unable to move. Paul unthinkingly clubs it to death—not the heroic act that Paul envisioned. Despite his desire to conform to his father's expectations of maleness, Paul cannot change. Moreover, although he began the journey expecting to arrive at a revela-tion, to see the light, the end of the adventure is inconclusive for Paul—survival, rescue, but no enlightenment or completion of the spiritual journey. Paul ends the physical journey without self-understanding and without loving himself or his father.

Consideration: Choices

At one point near the end of the Perrys' ordeal in the woods, Harvey answers his own question as to " 'Why aren't we dead, brother?' " His response is quite simple, " 'We're heroes! We're heroes, that's why!' " (*Lights,* 274) True, as a result of Paul's stamina and desire to survive, the brothers are rescued. In addition, although Paul has not arrived at an epiphany, he, like Harvey upon his return from the war, considers himself a brave man and expects a hero's welcome. Yet is Paul Perry a hero? As O'Brien always does in his books, he complicates the situation and focuses on philosophical and moral ambiguities. Accordingly, this novel is not a typical initiation story with resolution and insight coming quickly on the heals of a protagonist's physical and spiritual test. Instead, two locals whom Paul meets after the rescue bluntly label the episode in the woods as " 'stupid' " (*Lights,* 306), and similar to Harvey's return from Vietnam, there are no parades for the rescued pair.

In the months following his return to Sawmill, a depressed and directionless Paul begins drinking, puts on weight, and buys a new pair of glasses that gives him headaches: "In the winter, in the blizzard, there had been no sudden revelation, no epiphany or sudden shining of light to awaken and comfort and make happy, and things were the same, the old man was still down there alive in his grave, frozen and not dead, and in the house the cold was always there, except for patience and Grace and the pond, which were the same" (*Lights,* 314). Like O'Brien's other central characters, Paul ultimately faces the hard choice about how to live his life—to flee or fight. In this classic existential dilemma, the scenario involves, on one hand, Paul's fleeing from self-discovery, choice (possibilities), and responsibility (the "sleepwalking default" of *If I Die*) and in the process escaping from integrating his past, present, and future. On the other hand, Paul can choose to fight—or act. This latter choice requires that he confront his past and in so doing choose a direction in his life, accept responsibility for who he is and what he can do, and embrace life itself. In choosing to act, Paul will establish order (the bottom of things and sequence of events) and seize control of his life.

Critics who discuss this novel (Bates, Kaplan, and Nelson) see these choices as intertwined with O'Brien's pervasive interests in courage and conscience. Bates believes Paul's life choices are connected to three types of courage: a rigid "masculine courage" (characterized by confrontation and endurance and represented by Pehr Lindstrom Pehri); a flexible "feminine courage" (typified by assimilation and love and represented by Grace); or a union of the two.[23] Nelson, basing her analysis on Erich Fromm's definitions of authoritarian and humanistic consciousness, sees Paul's choices related to submitting to a "punishing" voice of external authorities, such as his father's, or following an affirming voice of responsibility to self and the potential of human goodness.[24]

Unlike his brother, Harvey has already made his life choice to flee long before the adventure in the woods. Therefore, despite momentary insights into himself and his father, he is incapable of letting go of his illusions and his father's ideas of what it means to be a man. In short, Harvey remains the obedient son living with messages of death and urgency, and he remains the war veteran, the hero still waiting for a "decent parade" and searching aimlessly for adventure and direction through fantasies about trips to Nassau, Mexico, Africa, and even back into the woods. In some ways, Harvey has become his father: " 'The old man, all the outdoor crap. It's really a lot of crap, isn't it? But it's not the old man, anymore. It's me. Now it's in me and I can't get it out. Doing crazy things' " (*Lights,* 337).

In contrast, Paul chooses "patience and Grace and the pond" and a new incantation, "Not so bad, after all" (*Lights,* 349) instead of "Poooor me." But the choice to fight, to commit to life, occurs neither easily nor quickly. The process begins when Paul confronts his past, his universe of memories. First, he decides to shave off his beard, the last remnant of the ordeal in the woods. This act is quickly followed by his momentous decision to sell the family home, despite Harvey's waffling on the decision and his taunts that Paul is a "coward" for undertaking this plan. Both actions are important steps for Paul in snatching control of his life and integrating his past, present, and future to achieve a measure of harmony in his life. His shaving marks Paul's rejection of his need to be a hero in his brother's mold, and selling the house establishes his separate peace with his father and with this man's influence on Paul's life up to this point. Through this action, Paul does not completely reject his father, just the "crazy stuff and the histories." Both acts allow Paul to accept the past and move beyond it.

To confront the present, his universe of fears, Paul acts in two ways. First, he resumes short walks into the nearby woods. This time with Grace as his guide (a type of female-male relationship appearing in later novels), Paul experiences far different results from what occurred on the trips into the woods with Harvey. Grace offers a new perspective of the forest, not the primitive, threatening, competitive masculine view held by Harvey and the father. Instead, she presents a feminine view, one that suggests an inviting, sophisticated, sensuous haven: "She showed him the underbelly of the forest, the quiet and safe spots . . . soft tangles of weed and fern and moss and simple things. She showed him a delicate fern which she called maidenhair, plucking it from the soil" (*Lights,* 335).

Later, after a few of these excursions, Paul takes a momentous trip alone at night, without his glasses, to Pliney's Pond and swims to its center, the symbolic center of this novel and the figurative bottom of things for Paul—the awful smell, primitive organisms, ash, sewage, decay, and terror. As he submerges himself in the pond, the black bile of fear, which has been a constant force in Paul's life, flows from him. A symbolic rebirth occurs, complete with the dawn of revelation and hope provided by the Northern Lights: "Coming out, emerging, he saw the great lights. . . . and everything was very quiet and peaceful and things were not really so bad or so urgent as the old man had preached. And there was still Grace" (*Lights,* 344–45). This moment of insight occurs with the union of the past (his father's "northern attitude") and present (Grace's "southern calm").

Finally, to accept the possibilities for his future and to integrate them with his past and present, Paul chooses a new start; he returns from Pliney's Pond to his father's house to make love to Grace and create a son. The existential journey is complete, from start to finish to start. With this new beginning, Paul has chosen life and its responsibilities, the present and the future. In the process of making this decision, Paul has given meaning to his life and affirmed the power of self and of love. He has rejected the absolutes and stern masculine values of his father.

At the end of the journey, he has also displayed courage and become a hero. His courage is not the charge-up-the-hill type of his father or of Harvey; nor is it the "grace and poise" courage of Captain Johansen. It is the common courage that O'Brien describes in *If I Die*—a wise endurance, a willingness to put aside one's fears, regrets, and the past and to continue with life as an optimistic participant rather than as a pessimistic onlooker: "It is more likely that men act cowardly and, at other times, act with courage, each with varying consistency. The men who do well on the average, perhaps with one moment of glory, these men are brave" (*Die,* 146–47). In this optimistic ending to the novel, Paul Perry becomes one of Tim O'Brien's heroes, an individual who has chosen the right path, one of commitment and conscience. Typical of O'Brien's subsequent novels, the nature and outcome of Paul's future journey on that path remain mysteries filled with possibilities. In his later works, O'Brien will return to these issues of fathers and sons, fleeing or fighting, courage, control, love, and choices—but from new angles.

Chapter Three

A Soldier's Heart and Mind: *Going After Cacciato* and *The Things They Carried*

As Tim O'Brien in 1997 continues to admonish critics and reviewers not to typecast him as "just" a Vietnam War writer, this task is made more difficult by the ongoing acclaim given to two of his novels examining the Vietnam War: *Going After Cacciato* (1978) and *The Things They Carried* (1990). Separated by 12 years and another novel (*Nuclear Age*, 1985), these works form the core of O'Brien's writing in terms of content, style, numerous awards, and extensive critical attention they have received. Together they establish O'Brien as one of the most important soldier-authors (if not the premier) of the Vietnam generation; furthermore, they establish his reputation as one of America's most notable postmodernist writers—not only for his themes but also for the structure of his books and his exploration from multiple perspectives of the problematic nature of truth and reality.

For readers of O'Brien's previous works, these two novels also illustrate just how much this author has developed his literary skills. In these Vietnam narratives, O'Brien returns to the same battlefields and some of the same incidents of *If I Die in a Combat Zone*. But following the advice of his fictional Major Li Van Hgoc, he views the Vietnam War from many different angles, including points of his imagination rather than memory alone. He turns to imagination's creative playfulness and transforming power to extend his memories and travel along different invented paths. In addition, these two works connect with the other books through O'Brien's dominant purpose of studying the mystery, ambiguity, and complexity of the human heart and mind. Also present in these novels are persistent considerations of links between imagination and memory, the search for order and control, relationships between fathers and sons, and the problematic politics of life. And as is true of *If I Die,* he views these themes within the crucible of war, revealing its special influences on human personality, as well as universal philosophical, moral, and spiritual issues inherent in battlefield experiences: "My passion as a human being and as a writer intersect in Vietnam, not in the physical stuff but in the issues of Vietnam—of courage, rectitude, enlightenment, holiness, trying to do the right thing in the world."[1] In fact, O'Brien's assessment of *Going After Cacciato*—"It's a war novel on the surface, but it's about lots of other things too" (Schroeder, Interview, 144)—is particularly appropriate in describing the most significant subject matter for both of these works.

Finally, in these two novels, O'Brien takes the conventional war novel in new directions. In *Going After Cacciato,* he manipulates form and content as he introduces an elaborate interplay of past, present, and future time while mixing fact and fantasy. In *The Things They Carried,* he creates an integrated novel out of a collection of short stories, commentaries, confessions, character sketches, and notes. Together, the jumbled forms of these two books mirror the soldier's chaotic psychological landscape and the political, moral, and military disorder related to America's Vietnam experience. Moreover, in both works O'Brien explores his narrative craft along with the content and purposes of war stories. Rooted in O'Brien's own Vietnam experience, both works raise an interesting question, especially involving *The Things They Carried,* of what this soldier-author remembers and what he indeed invents. Another question involves O'Brien's purposes and methods for writing about the Vietnam War. Despite parallels with people, events, and places from O'Brien's war experiences, he claims that these narratives do not represent his efforts as a veteran to confront these experiences: "I'd never written for therapy or consciously for catharsis, or any of that stuff. It was just that the stories were so wonderful and the literary possibility seemed so rich" (Caldwell 1990, Interview, 75).

Going After Cacciato

With the publication in 1978 of *Going After Cacciato,* dedicated to Erik Hansen (O'Brien's soul mate from basic training who helped edit this book), this soldier-author burst onto the national literary scene with his second novel. He was helped by an unexpected National Book Award in Fiction, for which he was selected over the heavily favored John Irving *(The World According to Garp)* and John Cheever *(Stories)*. At the time, reviewers were surprised that a 32-year-old author won this major award with a book that had sold 12,000 hardback copies compared to Irving's sales of almost 20 times that number of his immensely popular work. Perhaps, however, O'Brien's success was not so unexpected as reviewers and critics had at first thought. Several short stories published from 1975 on, which O'Brien incorporated with minor or major changes into the novel, had already won short-story prizes.[2]

Furthermore, reviews of the book in 1978 are very enthusiastic. One reviewer describes the novel as "the best novel written about the war"; another praises O'Brien's ability to transcend the battlefield ("To call *Going After Cacciato* a novel about a war is like calling *Moby Dick* a novel about whales.");[3] a third applauds the author's "artistry and imaginative power," and another lauds the "philosophical" subject matter. A few dissenting voices focus on problems with the fantasy journey: One reviewer labels this material "an unworkable idea that nearly sinks the book," and another notes that this section has "too many of its symbolic braces showing." One other early criticism points out O'Brien's seemingly excessive literary debt to Joseph Heller's treatment in *Catch-22* of a separate peace. The reviewer notes parallels between the relationships of Orr and Yossarian in *Catch-22* and Cacciato and Paul Berlin in O'Brien's novel, as both sets of characters seek to escape war.[4]

Perhaps most notable of the early comments is Richard Freedman's positive assessment of the novel's "gritty realism" and "dreamlike state": "Clearly we are dealing with what the new South American novelists would call 'magical realism' " (Freedman, 21). This label has become unalterably linked to this novel as well as to O'Brien's later works, and it is a description from which, as noted earlier, O'Brien has spent considerable time distancing himself: "I see myself as a realist in the strictest sense. That is to say, our daydreams are real; our fantasies are real. They aren't construed as otherwise in any of my books" (Herzog, Interview). From the very promising initial critical reception, time has proven this book to be a worthy recipient of the 1978 National Book Award. It continues to entertain and enlighten critics and readers alike as it assumes its current position, described by Philip Beidler, at the core of the canon of Vietnam War literature and postmodernist literature: "a postmodernist classic of magical realism."[5]

In commenting on the place of this novel among his own works, O'Brien mentions that this book represents his first true effort at writing literature. According to the author, he and the book would not have succeeded if he had not already paved the way with his war autobiography *If I Die:* "I'm glad I got it out of my system. Otherwise I would have ended up writing . . . autobiography cast as fiction" (Schroeder, Interview, 148). Because O'Brien delayed writing this first war novel and had already written another novel, he did not fall into the trap that snagged so many inexperienced soldier-authors writing a first war novel: retelling their actual experiences with superficial changes rather than using their imagination to transform their experiences. Thus, for O'Brien this novel does not become a restating of his war experiences but is "the flip side of *If I Die*" (McCaffery, Interview, 133). Consequently, Paul Berlin, the novel's central character, begins a journey in his imagination at the point where soldier Tim O'Brien in *If I Die* stopped—deciding on two occasions not to flee the military. In *Cacciato* author O'Brien considers the "what if" of the flee-or-fight quandary; he employs the actions and daydreams of his alter ego Paul Berlin and other characters to analyze the process and consequences of running from war: What do people experience fleeing the war? Would they be happy? Would they be able to live with the consequences? Would their decisions end happily? At the same time, as O'Brien observes, key differences exist between soldier O'Brien and the fictional Berlin: The latter is "more of a dreamer than I was, I think. He spends much more of his time in dream. He takes the war and the possibility of running from war more seriously than I did. . . . He's more frightened. . . . He's more sensitive" (Schroeder, Interview, 142).

In addition to a few connections with O'Brien's life, this novel has several thematic and structural ties to the author's other works. At the heart of this novel is this recurring dilemma that many soldiers face and many authors write about—whether to defect or to stay in war and then live with the consequences. Such a choice links this novel to O'Brien's other works where central characters face wrenching flee-or-fight decisions. In this book, author O'Brien, primarily through a limited third-person narrative, explores the heart and mind of Specialist Four Paul Berlin who faces this moral dilemma, struggles to control his fear, and hopes to arrive at some understanding of himself and his situation.

The fear biles of Paul Perry in *Northern Lights* are a prominent feature of Paul Berlin's character, and Paul Perry's symbolic path ("Road to Damascus") into the woods of northern Minnesota becomes an imaginary road to Paris in this second novel, a city that, interestingly, Paul Perry would like to visit (*Lights*, 190). But Berlin's journey to Paris, unlike Perry's trip into the woods, leads to an epiphany. Also connecting Paul Berlin to Paul Perry and O'Brien's other central characters is Berlin's preoccupation with courage as represented by the shining Silver Star in *Going After Cacciato*, which connects with Captain Johansen's Silver Star described in *If I Die*. Finally, even the Hemingway influence that so dominates *Northern Lights* surfaces in this novel as O'Brien creates his Vietnam version of *A Farewell to Arms* by examining war, love, and a separate peace.

Furthermore, typical of O'Brien's angles-of-reality approach to structuring all of his works, the author examines his principal characters, the war, and major themes from various perspectives, each providing a different degree of insight. Central to this many-faceted approach is the novel's interwoven tripartite structure, which allows O'Brien to present three perspectives of Berlin's Vietnam experience artfully mixed with each other. Out of the book's 46 chapters, 10 of these, labeled "Observation Post," serve as the fulcrum of the narrative: the present time, at almost the midpoint of Berlin's 12-month tour of duty, when he uses his six hours of night guard duty to consider his war experiences and to daydream. The sights and sounds of the coast of Quang Ngai Province become the backdrop for Berlin's immediate thoughts, which lead to memories and an elaborate daydream found in the other chapters.

Sixteen of the remaining chapters (fact chapters), which are spread throughout the book, contain Paul Berlin's jumbled memories of important events during his tour—principally the deaths of eight soldiers. Several of these chapters, mirroring the self-contained chapters of *If I Die* and anticipating similar units in *The Things They Carried,* are standalone chapters—stories linked to each other by common themes and subjects. Finally, the remaining 20 chapters (Paris chapters) are devoted to Berlin's imaginary trip to Paris, which evolves from Third Squad's real efforts to capture the deserting Private Cacciato. This elaborate fantasy journey enables Berlin to evaluate himself and his Vietnam experience from a new perspective—one resulting in what Thomas Myers calls a "textual alchemy": Viet Nam is transformed by Berlin's imagination into the landscape one might find in a trip from Viet Nam to Paris (Myers, 174). This daydream also permits Berlin to create an imaginary story, one that he intends to conclude with a happy ending. Most important, this story within a story becomes Berlin's way of exploring possibilities related to the issues of courage, fear, self-knowledge and, of course, a separate peace, all of which are prominent concerns in Berlin's real Vietnam experience.[6]

Connecting the content of these seemingly randomly mixed chapters of past, present, and future time, is an in-depth study of Berlin's heart and mind, as well as O'Brien's focus on various quests for control: author O'Brien's command of his own novel, American soldiers' control of a chaotic war, soldier Berlin's domination of his fears and his memory, and storyteller Berlin's direction of his tale of an 8,600-mile journey to Paris. As O'Brien notes, "We are causal animals. That is to say, we try to impose on the world, to the best of our abilities, a sense of causation [a normal sequence of events]. . . . And life presents us with scrambled sequences, and as human beings we try to unscramble them, decode them" (Herzog, Interview).

Despite the novel's chaotic milieu and disordered structure, the book succeeds as a superb piece of writing because O'Brien never loses command of his material. The novel's intentional surface disorder and complexity mask an exquisitely crafted novel that has a simple structural, temporal, and thematic design—a soldier considering the present (observation-post chapters), remembering events (fact chapters), and imagining a future journey (road-to-Paris chapters) during six hours of night guard duty.

O'Brien artfully controls this structure by linking the chapters *within* each grouping through other organizational strategies, themes, images, words, time, and narrative intrusions. For example, one of the basic organizing features within the fact chapters is Paul Berlin's remembering, in random order, the deaths of eight soldiers in his squad. As Berlin struggles to recall the correct order of these deaths, O'Brien reminds readers of this recurring thematic and structural link. Thus, the first lines of the novel (a fact chapter), containing a list of eight names, will reappear with minor variations in three other fact chapters (see pages 185, 255, and 288): "It was a bad time. Billy Boy Watkins was dead, and so was Frenchie Tucker. Billy Boy had died of fright, scared to death on the field of battle, and Frenchie Tucker had been shot through the nose. Bernie Lynn and Lieutenant Sidney Martin had died in tunnels. Pederson was dead and Rudy Chassler was dead. Buff was dead. Ready Mix was dead" (*Cacciato,* 1). This litany of the dead influences, through scattered references, the content of all 16 fact chapters and shapes specifically the content of seven of these chapters in which Berlin remembers the deaths in some detail.[7] As another thematic linking of chapters within a grouping (Paris chapters), O'Brien describes the consequences for seven people who choose to flee the war. Their decisions become models for Paul Berlin.

In addition, O'Brien controls the structure and content of his novel by deftly interlocking all three groupings of chapters with repeated themes, settings, images, events, and words. For example, issues of courage surface in the three sections; the tunnels mentioned in fact chapters become an imaginary hole in the road during the invented trip to Paris; the image of the round-faced Cacciato appearing in the first fact chapter is transformed into an image of the moon, which begins the following observation-post chapter; an actual search-and-destroy mission in a Vietnamese village evolves into a search-and-destroy mission on a train trip during the journey to Paris; and the key word "Go," which ends a climactic scene in the first fact chapter, reappears on three other occasions in the Paris and observation-post chapters.

Perhaps the most prominent link across the three sections involves quests for control. O'Brien's rigid control, through integrated structure and content, counterpoints the disorder of the Vietnam War and contrasts with Paul Berlin's moments of losing command of the facts of his tour, his own imaginary tale, and his fear. Furthermore, within the formal and thematic implications of the soldiers' and authors' quests to order their experiences and war stories, O'Brien also occasionally turns this narrative into metafiction, a commentary on its own fictive nature, as he examines issues related to an author's mastery of the creative process. Finally, O'Brien involves readers in the same pursuit as they struggle to master the disordered events in this book, find the center, and separate the book's facts from fantasy. A careful analysis of the book's three sections may aid readers in this pursuit.

Memories and Facts

In stark contrast to O'Brien's control of his novel is his subject matter (borrowed from *If I Die*) present in the 16 chapters of facts and memories: the confusion and disorder characterizing the Vietnam War and the chaotic lives of the members of Third Squad in general and Paul Berlin in particular. Tom Myers describes this chaotic condition as forcing the American soldiers in *Going After Cacciato* to decide "how to act properly within a configuration that affords the entrapped soldier little historical understanding or moral justification as he experiences the most jarring imagery of waste and death" (Myers, 171). Within this context, Berlin remembers without order the people, fears, deaths, rituals, and horrors of war he has experienced during his tour of duty. Several of these subjects involve events, emotions, and individuals first introduced in *If I Die*. For Berlin and the other soldiers, the chaos and confusion lead them to view war as a form of Russian roulette, a metaphor used in several books and films dealing with the Vietnam War. Thus, a character in James Webb's Vietnam novel *Fields of Fire* notes that " 'If you want to know, I get the feeling this [Vietnam War] is kind of like Russian roulette. Just as senseless. And the players aren't excused until the gun goes off in their face.' "[8]

Also running throughout Paul Berlin's disordered memories is a related theme of a soldier's insignificance. Marching without will and direction, Berlin and the other members of Third Squad feel powerless in a war environment where they gamble with their lives and become mere extensions of a military machine. Among soldiers of all wars, such feelings of confusion, insignificance, and powerlessness are common. Compared to other wars, however, the snarled conditions of guerrilla warfare in Viet Nam were particularly acute. American soldiers "outmanned, outgunned, and outtechnologized" the enemy (*Cacciato,* 84) but showed little progress for their efforts. In this novel, such conditions intensify the sense of confusion, vulnerability, and insignificance shared by the ill-prepared soldiers in Berlin's squad. For example, as described in an important fact chapter, "The Things They Didn't Know," Berlin and the other members of Third Squad do not know the Vietnamese language, people, culture, geography, land, or friends from enemies. Unfortunately, this mystery and otherness of the Vietnamese do not heighten the self-centered American soldiers' curiosity about these people, their customs and emotions. On the contrary, this ignorance creates among the soldiers greater distance, distrust, fear, and occasional guilt.

Also contributing to the confusion is these soldiers' inability to understand the politics of this war. Among Third Squad, discussions of the political issues are rare: "There was no serious discussion. No beliefs. They fought the war, but no one took sides" (*Cacciato,* 240). Finally, Third Squad has difficulty distinguishing between good and evil in this chaotic environment. They also do not understand the military strategy in this war of attrition fought with an often unseen enemy: "They did not know even the simple things: a sense of victory, or satisfaction, or necessary sacrifice. . . . No sense of order or momentum. No front, no rear, no trenches laid out in neat parallels. No Patton rushing for the Rhine, no beachheads to storm and win and hold for the duration. They did not have targets. They did not have a cause" (*Cacciato,* 240).

For O'Brien and for Paul Berlin, this confusion and disorder are, perhaps, best symbolized by Third Squad's frequent experiences with the extensive tunnel system inhabited by the Vietcong and North Vietnamese Army (NVA) in Quang Ngai Province. These hidden complexes are part of the land that, as Major Li Van Hgoc emphasizes, often becomes the real enemy for American soldiers: " 'The soldier is but the representative of the land. The land is your true enemy' " (*Cacciato,* 77).

The tunnels are places of potential death for the intruding Americans, as Frenchie Tucker and Bernie Lynn discover. They force choices based on competing values. Accordingly, when a tunnel is discovered, the commanding officer of Berlin's platoon, who partially controls the fate of his soldiers, must choose a course of action. Standard Operating Procedure (SOP), embraced by many officers, calls for the military mission to be completed; thus, each tunnel complex must be searched before it is destroyed. This procedure involves having one soldier, a volunteer or someone selected, enter the tunnel head first. The Russian-roulette outcome might be an unoccupied tunnel or, in the case of both Frenchie and Bernie, a bullet in the head or throat. In contrast, informal Standard Operating Procedure, favored by most soldiers because it removes chance and preserves their lives, calls for destroying the tunnel without first searching the tunnel.

The different procedures represent competing values. Lieutenant Sidney Martin, Third Squad's first commanding officer, is a highly trained and conscientious young officer devoted to mission—the father figure as taskmaster who observes SOP when confronting tunnels. His attitudes toward his men and mission parallel those of the gung-ho Colonel Daud described in *If I Die*. As a result, Martin's gambling with his men's lives to accomplish the mission creates further uncertainty and evokes the same hatred from his men as Colonel Daud receives from his. Martin's decisions eventually result in his own murder, ironically a fragging (approved by the members of Third Squad) while he is searching a tunnel. The platoon's second commanding officer, the much older Lieutenant Corson, diminishes some of the uncertainty in his soldiers' lives by observing the informal SOPs when encountering tunnels, thus eliciting the admiration of his men: "Lt. Corson took no chances, he wasted no lives. The war, for which he was much too old, scared him" (*Cacciato,* 40).

As O'Brien probes the minds of soldiers confronting these situations, he examines ways in which Paul Berlin and Third Squad struggle to counteract these moments of uncertainty and disorder. One technique they use is to eliminate a commanding officer who increases the disorder. More often, these soldiers simply occupy their minds by focusing on the surface details of their existence and the routines of war—the informal SOPs—that govern everyday rituals, conversations, jokes, the order of march, and activities engaged in away from the battlefield. Such preoccupation with superficial details and routines becomes a coping mechanism to establish order, comfort, and causation within the chaotic battlefield. And engaging in these familiar and comfortable tricks of the mind temporarily relieves soldiers from moments of guilt, anxiety, powerlessness, self-reflection, grief, and fear characterizing their chance-filled existence.

This approach to surviving—unthinking actions—also cuts down on the choices the soldiers must make. For Third Squad, if decisions about searching the tunnels represent the disorder in their lives, then a symbol of their efforts to establish order and control is playing a basketball game. In the fact chapter entitled "Pickup Games," members of Third Squad and the rest of the platoon, during a lull in the fighting, start a pickup basketball game lasting on and off for weeks. In contrast to the uncertainties of the Vietnam War, this game provides a sense of order—a clear objective, rules to govern play, a visible opponent, and a clear way to determine the outcome. "Bad places and good places. Winning—you knew the score, knew exactly. The odds could be figured. Winning was the purpose, nothing else. A basket to shoot at, a target, and sometimes you scored and sometimes you didn't, but you had a true thing to aim at, you always knew, and you could count on the numbers" (*Cacciato*, 98). Such tricks of the mind and ritualized activity for coping with the insanity of the battlefield dominate these disordered fact chapters as Paul Berlin struggles to corral his fears and maintain some order in his life and memories: "Keeping track wasn't easy. The order of things—chronologies—that was the hard part" (*Cacciato*, 44).

Berlin is an average 20-year-old grunt, "a straightforward, honest, decent sort of guy" from Iowa. His mother is an alcoholic who hides liquor in large cologne bottles, and his father, with whom Berlin has a positive relationship, builds homes. As a child, Berlin had one constant in his otherwise uneventful life—fear, "Yes, the issue was courage. It always had been, even as a kid. Things scared him. He couldn't help it" (*Cacciato*, 72–73). Another constant in his childhood was his propensity to escape into a world of daydreams and pretending. Years later, much like Paul Perry, Berlin's fears, reveries, and indecisiveness remain parts of his personality. Hence, this soldier arrives in Viet Nam ill prepared for the war's physical and psychological realities. He is an innocent among the lost whose constant fear is attributed to "overabundant fear biles." In addition, he lacks any commitment to the war or understanding of it; in fact, he has never thought about whether it is right or wrong. Instead, he went to war because of the law, a desire to avoid censure, and a trust in country—automatic responses echoing O'Brien's earlier quoted reaction to the draft in his war memoir, "But I submitted . . . by a sort of sleepwalking default" (*Die*, 31). Once Paul Berlin is in Viet Nam, this pattern of reflex overriding reflection continues.

Not everyone within the novel views Berlin as powerless and out of control. At one point readers receive opposing perspectives of Berlin's character and condition. The first is from an outsider, Lieutenant Sidney Martin, who observes Berlin marching up a hill: "He admired the oxen persistence with which the last soldier [Berlin] in the column of thirty-nine marched, thinking that the boy represented so much good—fortitude, discipline, loyalty, self-control, courage, toughness. The greatest gift of God . . . is freedom of will" (*Cacciato*, 150). The second assessment of Berlin is an insider's view from the limited third-person narrator: "But Paul Berlin had no sense of the lieutenant's sentiment. His eyes were down and he climbed the road dumbly. . . . He was dull of mind, blunt of spirit, numb of history, and struck with wonder that he could not stop climbing the red road towards the mountains" (*Cacciato*, 150). Marching machinelike at the rear of Third Squad, his customary position, Berlin is helplessly dragged along by the day-to-day events: "Powerless and powerful, like a boulder in an avalanche . . . [he] marched toward the mountains without stop or the ability to stop" (*Cacciato*, 150). Hence, the unthinking Berlin endures his tour of duty without considering the significance of the war or the deaths that occur around him.

Similarly, although concerned about what the Vietnamese think of him ("He wanted to be liked": *Cacciato*, 233.), Berlin displays a disturbing indifference to the poverty, suffering, and deaths of South Vietnamese civilians. He views this foreign land and its people through the filter of images gathered from American media and popular culture. He is a tourist. In short, this soldier does not connect emotionally to the hardships and horrors of the Vietnamese: "He was not stricken by it; he was not outraged or made to grieve. He felt no great horror. He felt some guilt but that passed quickly, because he had seen it all before seeing it" (*Cacciato*, 226). Instead, the self-centered Berlin's recurring activity in these fact chapters is his quest to control his fear and his environment through rituals and daydreams, an activity linking him to soldiers in all wars.

From his first day in country, Berlin has two goals—to survive and maybe to win a Silver Star for his father, the equivalent of Henry Fleming's Red Badge of Courage in Stephen Crane's novel about the American Civil War. The first goal is a possibility; the last is merely a daydream based on an unrealistic desire to be courageous. But to survive, he must master his fears: "True, the war scared him silly, but this was something he hoped to bring under control (*Cacciato*, 36). He must also develop a sense of order, rhythm, and meaning in his life. In three significant ways in these chapters, O'Brien directly portrays this soldier's struggle to command his life and indirectly addresses Berlin's efforts to "act wisely in spite of fear" and to consider "whether to flee or fight or seek an accommodation" (*Cacciato*, 72). To dramatize Berlin's efforts, O'Brien draws upon a common pattern in war stories in which outward actions symbolize inner conditions. For example, precise physical signs, such as a soldier's defecating in his pants during moments of extreme fear, signal emotional states. Thus, Berlin's control of his excretory functions, like Paul Perry's control of his bowels, becomes a significant barometer of this soldier's success in controlling fear. Soon after arriving in Viet Nam and before experiencing fear on the battlefield, Berlin, calm and in control, defecates in the enlisted men's latrine at the in-processing center: "And for a long time he sat there. At home, comfortable, even at peace" (*Cacciato*, 39). But during a particularly harrowing experience with a booby trap, Berlin urinates in his pants, and later in the novel's climactic scene, when fantasy and reality merge, Berlin loses control of his gun, loses control of his fear, and loses control of his body: He again urinates in his pants.

Next, O'Brien introduces a trick of the mind from *Northern Lights* to indicate Berlin's efforts to keep his mind occupied on surface details, to control his fear, or to establish order in his life. Just as Paul Perry counts his steps during moments of anxiety during his ski trip, so on several occasions Paul Berlin counts, but for different reasons. The first occasion occurs during a moment of extreme fear as Berlin attempts to calm himself immediately after a smoke grenade exploded in front of him: "The numbers kept running through his head, and he counted them, but he could not move. Dumb, he thought as he counted, a struck dumb little yo-yo who can't move" (*Cacciato*, 18–19). Next, he counts in order to pass the time: "Counting, that was one trick. Count the remaining days" (*Cacciato*, 43). Finally, he counts to keep from thinking—an attention to surface details to keep from confronting his inner and outer war: "There were tricks to keep from thinking. Counting. He counted his steps along the dirt path, concentrating on the numbers, pretending that the steps were dollar bills" (*Cacciato*, 187).

Finally, in these chapters of fact, Berlin attempts to control his fears and order his existence through his lifelong penchant for pretending and daydreaming: "Pretending was his best trick to forget the war" (*Cac-*

ciato, 9). Such an activity and its purpose—psychological survival—connect Berlin to soldiers from other wars. Therefore, the epigraph for this novel ("Soldiers are dreamers"), a line taken from soldier-author Siegfried Sassoon's observation about the habits of World War I soldiers, accurately describes Berlin's approach to surviving this war. Daydreams allow this soldier a temporary escape from the war and partial solace as he follows his father's advice "to look for the good things" (*Cacciato,* 58) during his tour of duty. For Berlin, who is scared by the world around him, the good things are in his mind. At times his reveries, like the mechanical counting, merely pass the time as he invokes memories of home, parents, and childhood or explores possibilities for his life after departing Viet Nam. Frequently, Berlin attempts to calm his fear by imagining an end to the war, a time when he can stop being afraid, or a comforting, invented conversation with his father around a campfire. Most significant, however, is Berlin's time spent daydreaming about Cacciato, the soldier who actually deserted from Third Squad in late October. As Berlin begins to imagine what may have happened to Cacciato, he establishes the foundation for the elaborate six-hour fantasy (presented in the 20 chapters devoted to the "Road to Paris") that he will create during his night of guard duty.

Imagination: The Road to Paris

As readers move back and forth among chapters of fact, observation post, or the trip to Paris, they find the narrative anchor to be Paul Berlin's thoughts while he stands night guard duty perched high in a teetering tower in Quang Ngai on the Batangan Peninsula surrounded by the South China Sea. Berlin's platoon is enjoying a brief period of easy duty and a temporary break from the war. The time frame (the present time of the novel) is from midnight until approximately 6 A.M. This night, somewhere around 20–25 November 1968, marks an approximate midpoint in Berlin's tour of duty (he arrived in Viet Nam on 3 June 1968) and an appropriate point for a self-reflective journey into this soldier's mental and spiritual makeup: "The real issue was the power of the will to defeat fear. A matter of figuring a way to do it. Somehow working his way into that secret chamber of the human heart, where in tangles, lay the circuitry for all that was possible, the full range of what a man might be" (*Cacciato,* 73). Over the next six hours, Berlin not only looks backward, randomly recalling the facts of the previous six months, but he also devises his most elaborate trick of the mind to escape the war, control his fear and destiny, consider possibilities, and create an ordered world. Through his imagination this confused soldier leisurely views the war from a new vantage point—peering into the darkness through the starlight scope of his mind. In addition to passing the time, he attempts through daydreaming to transform the turmoil of his war experiences into logical, ordered, and understandable events. Unlike the memories of his tour of duty, which he is eventually able to order chronologically but which still remain "separate and haphazard and random . . . no sense of events unfolding from prior events" (*Cacciato,* 185), this daydream about the journey to Paris will have order, transitions, and cause-effect relationships.

To accomplish this feat of escape, control, and consideration, Berlin becomes an author creating his own elaborate fictional war story based on raw materials stored in his mind from the occasional daydreaming about Cacciato he has done during the previous months. Berlin is also the central character in his own story. This extended daydream begins with the last known fact that concludes the first chapter: In late October while pursuing the AWOL Cacciato, who wants to see Paris, Third Squad had cornered the soldier on a grassy hill and attempted to capture him. Soldier Berlin shouted the command "Go" to Third Squad as he fired a flare to begin this real ambush of Cacciato. As Cacciato escaped, Berlin's "Go" also became a shout of encouragement. Now, almost a month later, author Berlin contemplates how far Cacciato might have led the pursuing Third Squad on a continuing journey to Paris. In a little over six hours, the quasi-author imagines a six-month, 8,600-mile odyssey as Cacciato conducts Third Squad through a host of countries in Asia and Europe.

Although John Updike labels them "picaresque interludes," together the 20 chapters devoted to this story-within-a-story are the core of this novel and distinguish this Vietnam War narrative from other such books.[9] They contain snatches of adventure, romance, allegory, black humor, psychology, philosophy, and the so-called magical realism that so many critics identify. O'Brien would respond that these chapters are not magical or surrealistic; they are real in the sense that they contain an accurate portrait of how the mind of this one soldier functions. For author O'Brien, daydreams are real. According to O'Brien, these chapters also re-create the process and product of "what I do with a typewriter. . . . my own process of imagining that book [*Cacciato*]—not dreaming it and not just controlling it, but a trancelike, half-awake, half-alert imagining" (Naparsteck, Interview, 11).

Linking the episodes in Berlin's extended daydream is the narrative voice of Paul Berlin, an experienced soldier but an amateur storyteller and traveler. Typical of a novice author writing his first book, Berlin fashions a story combining the realism of his war experiences with the innocence, romance, and superficiality of an American tourist who has learned about the rest of the world through the media, including Hollywood movies, and American popular culture: "A true tourist feeling. . . . He [Berlin] watched the islands slide by like pictures in a travel magazine" (*Cacciato,* 227). Often the postcard settings ("It was the India that Paul Berlin had always believed in": *Cacciato,* 131.), Americanized characters (Jolly Chand living in Delhi but educated for two years at Johns Hopkins), cartoonlike events (the helter-skelter escape from jail in Tehran), and chaste romance of this imaginary adventure seem to parody the Bob Hope-Bing Crosby "road" films—Berlin's own "On the Road to Paris" (a phrase appearing in several of the chapter titles)—or to imitate the 1952 romantic film *April in Paris* (the month when Third Squad arrives in Paris).

Yet despite one critic's claim that this tourist's fantasy represents Berlin's "complete denial of lived experience, a total immersion in a representational world which prevents unmediated confrontation with the horrors of Vietnam," this imagined journey is not pure escape from the war.[10] Although occasionally transforming the horrors and serious issues of war into a Hollywood romance, Berlin uses this extended daydream to interpret the all-too-real experiences of his tour of duty (the deaths and horrors) and to explore possibilities for his own life. Even in this illusory mission, Berlin the character is still a soldier and still part of a war. Therefore, the ordered narrative of a fancied trip to Paris emerges as Berlin-the-author's oblique treatment of Berlin-the-soldier's experiences in the actual war, the facts presented in the fact chapters. Thus, transformed events and dilemmas from Berlin's real war surface in his fictive world: mission (a search-and-destroy mission on a train to Chittagong); horrors (a beheading in Tehran of an AWOL soldier); and issues of responsibility, courage, and cowardice ("Tell me that it [the mission after Cacciato] is an alibi to cover cowardice": *Cacciato,* 206.). Moreover, this war story forces Berlin the soldier to confront his fears from the real war and to decide whether to flee or fight. Finally, this exercise in pretending also teaches author Berlin the limitations of imagination.

Surprisingly, despite the free play of his imagination, Berlin the novice author does not turn his central character into a brave and self-assured soldier who wins the elusive Silver Star. Perhaps as further evidence of author Berlin's practical purpose for his daydream as an interpretive vehicle rather than just an escape from the war, the real and fictional soldiers are often similar, dragged along by events. Like Berlin the real soldier, who at times acts like a detached tourist making his way through the Vietnam War, this imaginary Berlin, with postcards and camera in hand, marches at the end of the squad, daydreams, and is frequently afraid. Thus, even in this daydream, character Berlin is unable to act upon his desires. For example, the relationship with Sarkin Aung Wan, the Vietnamese girl, remains platonic as Berlin can only pretend to make love with her. Also, even in this imaginary tale, he is unable to control his fears, thus becoming incontinent during moments of fear: "[F]alling, he felt the fear fill his stomach. He had to pee. . . . He couldn't control himself" (*Cacciato,* 75). Furthermore, Berlin the character also searches for order and rhythm, not in a basketball game but in the cities to which Third Squad travels. In Mandalay and later in Paris, Berlin is happy: "There was order in the streets. There was harmony . . . there was color, there was concord and human commerce and the ordinary pleasantries" (*Cacciato,* 104).

Yet Berlin of the fictive world occasionally differs from his double in the real world. Unlike Berlin's mission in the real war, which seems purposeless, this imaginary mission has order, sequence, and purpose—to bring back the missing Cacciato. As a result, he occasionally casts off his role as a follower and actively searches for Cacciato. In Tehran, he drives the escape car; in Mandalay, he becomes angry, disrupting the monks' evening prayers as he struggles to capture Cacciato ("such a hero. . . . Such a brave Spec Four": *Cacciato,* 110); and when the train finally arrives in Paris, he is the "first to step down" (*Cacciato,* 260). Most important, Berlin the character can neither ignore the difficult issue that Berlin the soldier has steadfastly avoided, whether to flee or fight, nor avoid confronting his fears. Throughout the 20 daydream chapters, these issues of a separate peace and Berlin's fears become the central thematic focus. Also, similar to the structuring device of the soldiers' deaths in the fact chapters, these issues organize the fantasy chapters. Thus, within the road-to-Paris chapters, Berlin the character repeatedly encounters others who have the fled the war, are fleeing the war, or encourage Berlin's flight. In between Cacciato's desertion and Sarkin Aung Wan's imaginary arguments in Paris for Berlin's leaving the war, he confronts five other characters choosing a separate peace of one form or another or living with the consequences of such a choice. Each becomes a guide for his flee-or-fight decision.

Cacciato's unexpected desertion—a brilliant plan, an unthinking act, or a consequence of his refusal to support the fragging of Lieutenant Martin (the answer is never clear)—provides character Berlin with the first of several examples of a defecting individual. According to O'Brien, the genesis for Cacciato's befuddling character traits is a real person, Kline, the inept soldier O'Brien encountered in his own basic training and later described in *If I Die* (Schroeder, Interview, 150). Furthermore, the name, which author O'Brien found intriguing while he was in Viet Nam, is that of a real officer with whom O'Brien worked (McNerney, Interview, 5). Cacciato, variously described in the fact chapters as " 'missing Mongolian idiocy by the breadth of a hair' " (*Cacciato,* 7) and a brave soldier because of his winning the Bronze Star for shooting an enemy soldier, becomes the first guide in author Berlin's extended fantasy: "Cacciato. He's our guide" (*Cacciato,* 55). Similar to Orr, a pilot in *Catch-22* who leaves the war, Cacciato intentionally or unintentionally illustrates the possibility for a separate peace for all of Third Squad— and for Berlin in particular. Yet unlike *Catch-22*'s Yossarian, who does not learn until late in the novel that Orr was providing him with a model for escaping the war, author Berlin has known, even before beginning his imaginary story, that if character Berlin chooses, his actions, like Cacciato's, can result in peace and an end to his war.

But Cacciato is not the only character in Berlin's fantasy to depart from his unit. Early in the fictive mission to bring back Cacciato, Harold Murphy, one of the seven members of Third Squad, raises the recurring question of whether the unit's pursuit of Cacciato is a legitimate military mission or merely "plain desertion." He elects not to continue the journey because he feels the mission is nothing more than desertion and fears the consequences, an anxiety that Berlin subconsciously shares. Soon after Murphy's flight, Third Squad encounters another soldier who has spurned the war, North Vietnamese Major Li Van Hgoc, who is imprisoned in a tunnel. He confesses to Third Squad that as a draftee, he too never felt committed to the conflict and, consequently, deserted from the army, or as he describes it, " 'I decided to resist. I . . . well, I ran' " (*Cacciato,* 86). Eventually captured and tried for desertion, he has been sentenced to live in a no-exit tunnel complex in South Viet Nam. For 10 years a prisoner of the land, he has gathered intelligence data and observed the war through his periscope. Later in the journey Third Squad encounters another deserter, an Iranian soldier who is beheaded in Tehran for going "merely AWOL" from his military unit. Soon after, when Third Squad believes it will be captured by the authorities at

Piraeus, Stink Harris abandons the war and his unit by jumping into the sea. Finally, in Paris, another act of running—this one motivated more by exhaustion rather than conscience—occurs when the squad's figurehead leader, the "sick old man" Lieutenant Corson, disappears with Sarkin Aung Wan just before the assault on Cacciato's apartment.

Although character Berlin never directly comments in his imaginary tale on these departures—except for Cacciato's—he cannot help but consider these actions and their consequences as he nears a decision on whether to run from the war or stay. During the trip to Paris, moreover, attendant issues of mission, responsibility, refugees from the war, and cowardice become conspicuous connecting threads in author Berlin's extended daydream. Most important, it is left to the one civilian fleeing the war to force Berlin finally to choose a path of action.

Sarkin Aung Wan, who like many things and many people in this daydream is Paul Berlin's creation, is a refugee from Saigon (the Cholon area), fleeing the war and accompanying Third Squad on its mission. For the naive and romantic tourist-author, she is an idealized refugee, one who does not even have a true Vietnamese name. Nevertheless, unlike the brief unflattering caricature of an American coed-protester, whom Third Squad and readers quickly judge as an irrelevant antiwar voice, Wan is a strong character. In O'Brien's words, she may even be an "example of a hero" (McNerney, Interview, 21). Even so, Berlin constructs Wan as a representative of an American male's romantic vision of idealized Asian women, figures whom critic Kali Tal labels "shadow characters who embody men's needs and desires." In Berlin's case such a character serves as a "mother and lover."[11] Like Cacciato, her male counterpart in this imaginary journey, Wan also serves as a guide for Third Squad, in particular leading them out of the complex tunnel system into which they fell: "Sarkin Aung Wan led them on with the sureness that comes of knowledge" (*Cacciato,* 89). Equally important, like the mother-lover Grace in *Northern Lights,* she intuitively understands Berlin's fears and indecisiveness, but unlike Grace, she becomes a much more forceful spiritual guide for this soldier as he considers the possibilities of acting on his desire for an end to the war and securing a life of order, peace, and happiness.

Accordingly, one of the climactic scenes in this extended daydream is a version of the real Paris Peace Talks, convened in May 1968 to negotiate a peace settlement in Viet Nam. In these imaginary peace negotiations, Berlin the author presents Berlin the character with carefully delineated choices forcefully argued by Sarkin Aung Wan. She presses him to overcome his fears, his pretending, and his indecisiveness. She urges him to act bravely on his dreams by giving up the search for Cacciato, remaining in Paris, and declaring a separate peace from the war: " 'I urge you to act. Having dreamed a marvelous dream, I urge you to step boldly into it, to join your dream and live it. Do not be deceived by false obligation. . . . Do not let fear stop you. Do not be frightened by ridicule or censure or embarrassment' " (*Cacciato,* 284). At this moment, daydream and reality merge as character Berlin ultimately faces the decision that soldier Berlin has intentionally avoided during the five and one-half months of his tour. He must choose between two significant actions. This moment, toward which O'Brien has steadfastly been leading his central character and readers, is the most significant of the recurring political decisions in the novel, those that involve adjudicating competing moral and political values. These are values and arguments that, as O'Brien notes, have an autobiographical ring to them, since they emerge from his own choices and widespread reading in political philosophy at Harvard (Herzog, Interview). With a "resonant and firm" voice, Berlin the character chooses.

Despite the soundness of Wan's arguments and the attractiveness of life away from the war, Berlin decides to remain with Third Squad. He cites arguments strikingly similar to Tim O'Brien's explanation in *If I Die* for not deserting the army: "Family, the home town, friends, history, tradition, fear, confusion, exile" (*Die,* 73). Berlin's reasoning also anticipates the fictional Tim O'Brien's similar response to his draft notice in "On the Rainy River" in *The Things They Carried*. Berlin justifies his decision by referring to obligations and tacit promises " 'to my family, my friends, my town, my country, my fellow soldiers' " (*Cacciato,* 285). Furthermore, as was true of O'Brien's rationalization in *If I Die,* he admits that he fears society's censure: " 'I am afraid of running away. I am afraid of exile. . . . I fear the loss of my own reputation. . . . I fear being thought of as a coward' " (*Cacciato,* 286). Even in his imagination, Paul Berlin cannot escape his fear of social consequences. To his credit, character Berlin acknowledges his timorousness, but reasons that he hopes to attain an "honorable and lasting" inner peace by continuing the search for Cacciato. Neither the bonds of community—with the soldiers in Third Squad and the people at home—nor the fears of estrangement are to be ignored. Berlin's explanation for his decision echoes the civilian O'Brien's comments in *If I Die* that he accepts his induction notice because he seeks comfortable order in his life rather than inevitable chaos resulting from fleeing the war. Therefore, Berlin, deciding with his head rather than with his heart, acts out of social and human realities: society's reaction to deserters, his own frailties (cowardice?), his sense of obligation, and a sense of his true self (personality and background).

More so than soldier O'Brien's parallel decisions in *If I Die,* this decision has evoked numerous conflicting assessments, even if it is only one more imaginary act in the odyssey played out in the novice author's imagination. Comments come from critics who see Berlin's decision to stay in the war as credible and from those who believe the choice represents a failure of this soldier-author's imagination. For example, Arthur Saltzman condemns Berlin's refusal to leave the war as a "disqualification of imagination as a means of salvation" from chaos;[12] Robert Slabey comments that "Paul's choice of chauvinism over pacifism is undercut by his quotation of patriotic cliches";[13] Kali Tal views Berlin's decision to remain in the war as a failure of the imagination because it "conforms . . . to the traditional myths of male romance" and Berlin is unable to acknowledge his female side (Tal, 78). However, Milton Bates notes that Berlin's decision to remain with Third Squad is a "kind of courage" combining "masculine endurance with feminine commitment" (Bates, 278), and Maria Bonn also justifies the decision, noting that Berlin "has discovered the values he wishes to live for."[14]

Further confusing the issue are O'Brien's own views, detailed in his war autobiography, on wise courage and courage of endurance and responsibility. Accordingly, one might argue that Berlin's thinking action—and it is a purposeful action rather than a "sleepwalking default"—seems to fit O'Brien's definition of courage as a "wise endurance" described in *If I Die.* Berlin's decision to remain with Third Squad reflects an ordinary bravery, one based upon wise endurance in spite of fear and found among average, decent people: "You promise, almost moving your lips, to do better the next time; that by itself is a kind of courage" (*Die,* 147). Hence, Berlin, in his exchange with Sarkin Aung Wan, appears to display a spiritual valor combining understanding, fortitude, and commitment. In addition, even in this daydream, character Berlin acknowledges the reality of his situation and his feelings: "You could run, but you couldn't outrun the consequences of running, even in imagination" (*Cacciato,* 201).

For this novice author, his fantastic war story can never become too removed from the realities of his experience and his personality. Because of his background, relationships and obligations to people at home and in Third Squad, and the stigma attached to deserters, soldier-author-character Berlin realizes that leaving the war will bring him an uneasy peace—embarrassment as well as physical and spiritual exile: " 'The realities always catch you' " (*Cacciato,* 275). O'Brien's comments in an interview about this novel and his own flee-or-fight choices reinforce Berlin's reality argument and underline the purpose of the daydream— to explore the possibilities before choosing a course of action: "My conclusion was basically that Paul Berlin's fantasized run for Paris would have been an unhappy experience—it wasn't compatible with his background, personality, his beliefs. . . . I found I couldn't write my way into a happy ending, just as in my life I couldn't live my way into it" (McCaffery, Interview, 133). Perhaps the most important point about this controversy over the courage or cowardice of Berlin's decision is that the ambiguity associated with his choice is intentionally fostered by O'Brien. "The issue isn't to judge a character. . . . It is rather to watch a character . . . deal with the complications of life" (Herzog, Interview). In commenting on a related subject, O'Brien observes that one reason he does not like the ending to *Catch-22* when compared to his own ending is that Yossarian's decision to defect is an easy solution, "a simple thing to tack onto the book" (Herzog, Interview). In contrast, Berlin's decision to stay remains complicated and controversial.

Observation Post

The third group of chapters (10), each entitled "Observation Post," establish the present time of the book. They contain O'Brien's ongoing exploration of the heart and mind of Paul Berlin through this soldier-author's meditations (in the third person) and confessions during this night of remembering and creating. These chapters also serve as the fulcrum for the book: the point at which the "what-really-happened" chapters extend into the "what-might-have-happened" chapters. The observation-post sections also allow Berlin, the quasi-author, and O'Brien, the real author, to pause momentarily in their jumping back and forth in time and place and between fact and fantasy.

More important, in these chapters, as he has in the other two sections, O'Brien continues to focus on soldier Berlin's struggle with fear: "The issue, of course, was courage. How to behave. Whether to flee or fight or seek an accommodation. The issue was not fearlessness. The issue was how to act wisely in spite of fear" (*Cacciato,* 72). Finally, through metafictional passages within these 10 chapters, O'Brien complicates Paul's consideration of the issue of control. Through the reflections of Berlin, a surrogate, O'Brien examines this author's quest to control his materials and imagination in creating a war story, a subject that will have a more prominent place in *The Things They Carried*. Therefore, although Berlin is constructing only an elaborate daydream about the journey to Paris, he struggles with the rudiments of artistic creation: musing on such issues as the power and limits of imagination, the strategies of narrative, the relationship between the author's experiences and the world he or she creates, and the purposes of a war story. O'Brien, portraying the artist as a young soldier, reveals Berlin's thought process as this soldier turned author visualizes events never consciously anticipated or moves back and forth between facts of his Vietnam tour and their fictional transformations. Finally, O'Brien, through Berlin, explores how stories may lead to consideration of possibilities and self-knowledge.

At night sitting in the observation tower adjacent to the South China Sea, Berlin the author periodically reflects on his problems in shaping the basic elements of the tale—the facts of a soldier's stint in Viet Nam—into a war story. He, like real soldier-authors, has difficulty giving form to these war experiences because they lack order, development, and a unified plot. Accordingly, author Berlin notes his problem in creating a coherent story: "Order was the hard part. The facts even when beaded on a chain still did not have real order. Events did not flow. The facts were separate and haphazard and random, even as they happened, episodic, broken, no smooth transitions, no sense of events unfolding from prior events" (*Cacciato*, 185).

Yet, like any skilled author, Berlin trusts his imagination to transform this material into a coherent story about Cacciato's trip to Paris: "A truly awesome notion. Not a dream, an idea. An idea to develop, to tinker with and build and sustain, to draw out as an artist draws out his visions" (*Cacciato*, 24). He believes that during this one night of guard duty, such an act of invention will give him the sense of order, control, power, and meaning that has been missing for him during the previous months. His most elaborate trick of the mind will be an opportunity to separate past, present, and future; to explore the possibilities; to find answers about fear and flight; to view the war from a new angle; and to survive the psychological turmoil of uncertainty and helplessness.

In the daydream chapters, Berlin the author begins with the last known facts, Cacciato's actual desertion and his escape from the ambush sprung by Third Squad on a grassy hill. Anticipating a logical conclusion and a happy ending, he proceeds carefully with his story of what might have happened after this event. Inspired by his fear biles, he is "excited by the possibilities" and feels in control of the situation and the story. After a symbolic relaxed bowel movement in the sea, he returns to the tower—ready to create his imaginary journey: "That was the important part—he was in control. He was calm. Clear thinking helped. Concentrating, figuring out the details" (*Cacciato*, 58). This apprentice author, then, builds and sustains his idea; orders the facts; describes appropriate sights, sounds, and feelings; establishes cause-and-effect relationships among events; provides proper motivations and background for characters; and even anticipates skeptical critics' remarks. Along the way, his imagination swiftly cuts through obstacles in the narrative (trivial details such as money, passports, and plausibility) and moves to important issues: courage, fear, flight, accommodation, and happiness.

Nevertheless, despite Berlin's initial success in controlling his creation, the narrative does not proceed smoothly. This author, as revealed in the observation-post chapters, unexpectedly learns lessons about pitfalls novelists face, including limits to their powers of imagination. Soon he finds himself unable to concentrate solely on the story. Chapters of fact and the observation post momentarily interrupt the tale and eventually merge with it as short passages of present thoughts and memories briefly interrupt nine of the road-to-Paris sections (see chapters 6, 13, 21, 27, 29, 33, 36, 40, and 46). Other moments occur in the creative process when Berlin loses control of the narrative as his imagination lapses and events lead to unexpected outcomes. The anticipated story, a smooth arc from war to peace, assumes a direction and tone independent of the author's plan: "How it started as one thing, a happy thing, and how it was becoming something else. No harm intended. But it was out of control. Events taking their own track" (*Cacciato*, 121). Consequently, during the climactic Paris peace talks, Berlin the author's anticipated happy ending is impossible as Berlin the character feels obligated to remain in the war: "It was a failure of the imagination" (*Cacciato*, 280).

Order in the final episodes of the Cacciato story is achieved; however, it is not imposed by this novice author. Instead, the order emerges internally from the logic of the narrative and externally from the realities of Berlin-the-soldier's character and his impending decisions. Art and life merge as Berlin's imagination fails to break the constraints of the empirical world. As a result, this author, like many artists, must acknowledge his limitations. Just as the character Paul Berlin acknowledges his obligations to others when deciding not to flee the war, so author Berlin accepts the realities of the responsibilities in the fictive world he has created: " 'Even in imagination we must be true to our obligations, for, even in imagination, obligation cannot be outrun. Imagination, like reality, has its limits' " (*Cacciato*, 286).

In the book's final chapter, "Going After Cacciato," disorder reigns. Fiction merges with facts as Berlin's past, present, and future narrative strands collide and as the three Berlins (soldier, character, and author) lose control. After character Berlin rejects the long-anticipated separate peace, author Berlin cannot imagine an ending for the Cacciato tale; he can only remember a real event: Berlin-the-soldier's fear during the real confrontation with Cacciato at dawn on a hill in Viet Nam, the last known fact. As a result, O'Brien must intrude and assume control. Weaving together the three narrative strands in this last chapter, the real author arranges the disordered form and content and completes this exploration of Berlin's heart and mind. Consequently, the daydream briefly continues.

After character Berlin takes control of his destiny by rejecting Sarkin Aung Wan's offered peace, happiness, and the relative harmony of Paris, he joins Third Squad in a dawn ambush outside Cacciato's Paris apartment. Crouching outside the door, he responds to an order to charge into the room. Immediately he is afraid, but he also thinks about the elusive Silver Star. "Go"—he enters the apartment, and then "he felt the fear" (*Cacciato*, 295). O'Brien and Berlin, the two soldier-authors, have been inexorably moving toward this scene, for with the word "Go," the three Berlins merge, as do the chapters of fact, observation post, and daydream. Berlin's ongoing fear of consequences if he deserts merges with his ever-present physical fear on the battlefield. In this last chapter of fantasy, the "Go" uttered in Paris returns O'Brien, Berlin, and the readers to the "Go" ending the first fact chapter and uttered on the seventh day of the real journey after Cacciato: " 'Go,' whispered Paul Berlin. It did not seem enough. 'Go,' he said, and then he shouted, 'Go!' " (*Cacciato*, 23)

In intervening pages, Berlin's imagination and memory have avoided or suppressed one of the most important facts of the book, the real event occurring after the "Go" of chapter 1: soldier Berlin's embarrassing moment of uncontrollable physical fear during the actual hillside ambush of Cacciato. Perhaps Berlin's fantasy tale about Cacciato has been more than an exploration of possibilities involving a separate peace; it may have been an escape, a simple alibi to cover this moment of real cowardice. Whatever the case, unavoidably the character's panic in the imagined Paris ambush suddenly turns into a soldier's remembered terror in the actual ambush of Cacciato: a moment when Berlin lost control of his fear, lost control of his weapon (fired wildly), and lost control of his body (urinated in his pants). The real Cacciato escaped. With this final truth, Berlin and O'Brien arrive at the end of the story and the beginning, for this event marks the point where reality ends (" 'And who knows? He [Cacciato] might make it. He might do all right' ": *Cacciato*, 301.) and fantasy begins in the form of the six-hour daydream.

The significance of Berlin's six-hour journey of memory, observation, and imagination through a physical and metaphysical darkness is that this soldier turned author, who before this night existed in the war without understanding, ponders from various angles the consequences of fleeing. He also directly confronts his dread of exile and indirectly faces his cowardice. No longer an unthinking soldier helplessly dragged along by Third Squad, the war, and his anxieties, he attempts to explore and release the potential of what he might be: "Somehow working his way into that secret chamber of the human heart, where, in tangles, lay the circuitry for all that was possible, the full range of what a man might be" (*Cacciato*, 73). Using imagination heuristically, Berlin investigates possibilities before choosing a real course of action. Finally, he engages in the activity that Lieutenant Sidney Martin believes is a soldier's most significant task: "The overriding mission was the inner mission, the mission of every man to learn the important things about himself" (*Cacciato*, 148). Admittedly, in this mission Berlin does not achieve complete understanding. Yet through his memory, he faces the facts of his tour, and through his imagination, he briefly establishes order in and control over his life. Furthermore, as Berlin the soldier-author notes in the final observation-post chapter, he realizes the limits of his imagination: "The war was still a war, and he was still a soldier. He hadn't run. The issue was courage, and courage was will power, and this was his failing" (*Cacciato*, 288).

Does Berlin fail? True, his final assessment reveals his weakness. Conversely, it highlights his newly found strength of character and the extent of his change from an unthinking soldier to one who completes Lieutenant Martin's spiritual mission and momentarily controls his destiny. As already noted, for some readers, the truly courageous act might have been for Berlin, in both the real war and in the imaginary journey, to follow the dictates of his heart and declare a separate peace. But despite doubting the war and having to live with his physical embarrassment on the battlefield, Berlin refuses to flee. His courage to remain, affirmed in imagination as well as in reality, is an ordinary insignificant bravery, one based upon a wise endurance in spite of fear and found among average, decent people. Once again, O'Brien purposely muddies the moral issues.

At the thematic level, however, *Going After Cacciato* appears to be a straightforward novel. Just as Cacciato leads Berlin through a literal and figurative pilgrimage to partial understanding, O'Brien takes readers on a journey exploring a soldier's heart and mind as Paul Berlin confronts his apprehensions and chooses between competing values. These trepidations and choices are part of a larger theme involving a soldier's, a character's, a quasi-author's, and even an author's pursuit of control to overcome fear and arrive at some degree of understanding in the midst of confusion and chaos. The setting for this quest, the disorder of the Vietnam War, complicates the novelist's task and turns this narrative into a complex work. O'Brien faces the problem of capturing the special character of the Vietnam experience (episodic, confused, and illogical) within a fictional framework providing unity, coherence, perspective, and meaning. His solution to these artistic problems is to create a structure that counterpoints and mirrors the content. Order opposes disorder. The disordered facts of the soldier's existence oppose the orderly progression of the tale about Cacciato, which ends in confusion.

On another level, the novel's underlying unity and meaning counterbalance the surface disorder and multiple perspectives present in O'Brien's telling of Berlin's story. Unlike his quasi-author, O'Brien controls his material. Among the chapters, he carefully establishes structural, metaphorical, and thematic connections through a controlled juxtaposing or mixing of the three narrative strands, and he ties the multiple perspectives to one person. Indeed, O'Brien's imagination and craftsmanship succeed in creating an intricate, thoughtful novel. He achieves a formal completeness in this work missing in Berlin's tale, and he sustains a thematic depth and unity absent from *If I Die* and *Northern Lights*. Moreover, O'Brien reveals the value of imagination, his own and Berlin's, as a means of holding events in one's consciousness so they can be confronted, studied, and perhaps understood. Having followed Major Van Hgoc's advice to view things from many angles, O'Brien transcends the boundaries of time and place to consider once more central issues of traditional war stories—courage, fear, and manhood. As a result, *Going After Cacciato,* through its form and content, establishes the war story as salvation in the midst of chaos: a source of order and story truth in a study of the ambiguous human spirit. This sophisticated war story also

extends the form and content of this genre and anticipates similar
themes and narrative structure in O'Brien's next Vietnam War story, *The
Things They Carried*.

The Things They Carried

After publishing in 1985 his comic home-front novel about the Vietnam
era, *The Nuclear Age*, O'Brien spent the next five years returning in his
memory and imagination to the battlefields of *If I Die* and *Going After
Cacciato*. He also returned to a short story, "Speaking of Courage," that
he had written for inclusion in *Cacciato* but removed because it dealt
with a postwar veteran. The result is O'Brien's third Vietnam War narrative, *The Things They Carried* (1990), which, like *Cacciato,* has received
enthusiastic critical response and numerous literary honors. It is one of
five books nominated in 1991 for the National Book Critics' Circle
Award honoring the best novel of 1990. In France, where the novel was
published under the title À *Propos de Courage,* O'Brien won in 1992 the
prestigious *Prix du Meilleur Livre Étranger* award for fiction, competing
with such luminaries as Ingmar Bergman and Philip Roth. The novel
was also a finalist for a Pulitzer Prize.

At the time of publication, reviewers noted this novel's "lean, vigor-
ous style of [O'Brien's] earlier books"; its "raw force of confession"; its
"lyrical," "visceral," and "autobiographical" qualities; its place as "essential fiction about Vietnam"; and in comparison to *Cacciato* its "more pol-
ished and manipulative" style. Related to this last assessment, one recurring criticism about the book at the time centered on "too many fact or
fiction games," a reference to readers' and critics' questions about how
much of the material is straight autobiography from soldier-author Tim
O'Brien and how much is invented. But perhaps the final judgment
about the book should come from the author himself, who in a 1989
prepublication interview commented that this novel is "my best book.
There's no doubt in my mind about it" (Naparsteck, Interview, 8).

One reason for O'Brien's fondness for this book is its form: "In this
new book, I forced myself to try to invent a form. I had never invented
form before" (Coffey, Interview, 60). In this novel, written in the mode
of a war autobiography, author O'Brien invents a soldier-author narrator, also named Tim O'Brien, to tell stories of his life and Vietnam War
experiences, to relate war stories told to him by other soldiers, and to
comment on the art of storytelling. If this structure and content seem to
imitate the contents of his other two war narratives, they, in fact, do.

Furthermore, reminiscent of the publisher's and critics' difficulties in classifying *If I Die* (fiction or nonfiction; a collection of stories or an integrated book), readers and critics face similar problems in assessing *The Things They Carried*. Although many of the chapters can stand alone—as is true with *If I Die*—O'Brien has invented an integrated novel with 22 sections ranging from two-page vignettes to lengthy stories (several of which appeared elsewhere prior to or after publication of the book.)[15] In these sections, readers find passages of story, autobiography, memoir, confession, anecdote, character sketches, and lyric prose poems—all united by the narrative voice of 43-year-old soldier-author Tim O'Brien and linked by questions of fact (details from the memory of the real author O'Brien?) and fiction. O'Brien describes this new framework as one in which "I blended my own personality with the stories, and I'm writing about the stories, and yet everything is made up, including the commentary" (Naparsteck, Interview, 8). If readers and critics agree that O'Brien has invented a new form, they need only to look to *If I Die* and *Going After Cacciato* for its origins. The integrated tripartite subjects of O'Brien's war autobiography (I, we, and the art of writing a story) and the tripartite time-oriented structure of *Cacciato* (past—memory; present—commentary; and future—daydream) certainly merge and appear in this novel.

Whether new or not, the book's form has intrigued and puzzled readers, as well as compelled them to ask many questions. Is the narrator "Tim O'Brien" the same person as the author Tim O'Brien? If not, why is the narrator named Tim O'Brien? Did the real O'Brien, like the narrator, travel to the Rainy River to decide his fate in regard to the draft? Does the real O'Brien have a daughter? Are some of these stories factual, based on the war experiences of soldier O'Brien or on war stories he heard in Viet Nam? Are the content and the form of the book more examples of O'Brien's proclivity for "disingenuous game playing?" O'Brien's response to these questions is predictable: The fact or fiction debate should not be an issue. As he reiterates in lectures and interviews concerning his books and life, the key question for readers should be whether the content "rings true," that is, presents emotional truths. Working with and against conventional notions of truth and lies as well as conventions of author-narrator and author-reader relationships, O'Brien in *The Things They Carried* once again lies to tell the truth.

To accomplish this goal, he plays with the book's form and content to affect readers and illustrate points about the craft of storytelling. But despite O'Brien's efforts to deflect autobiographical questions emerging from this novel, the inquiries continue, and in some ways O'Brien invites them because he wants readers to be uncertain about the book. All of the literary tricks are part of the mystery and ambiguity that O'Brien purposely cultivates about his life and writing. The truth, according to O'Brien, is that in this novel, he invents and embroiders material based on his own experiences to make himself and his readers feel emotions of hatred, peace, love, loss, horror, confusion, anguish, and wonder—to get a "quick truth goose" from the stories (*Things,* 39). The ambiguity and complexity of the book's form and content also mirror for readers the experience of war, a subject of his previous war narratives: "In war you lose your sense of the definite, hence your sense of truth itself, and therefore it's safe to say that in a true war story nothing is ever absolutely true" (*Things,* 88).

Furthermore, in this integrated novel, author O'Brien follows the advice of his narrator, Tim O'Brien, who notes that the way to have an audience understand a story is "tell it one more time, patiently, adding and subtracting, making up a few things to get at the real truth" (*Things,* 91). This novel, like his two earlier war books, is a multifaceted war story examining O'Brien's recurring themes of courage, fear, the interplay of memory and imagination, the nature of war stories, a separate peace, and the ever-present soldier's heart and mind. Therefore, the war portrayed in this novel is the same war of the previous narratives with many of the same issues, some of the same characters, and several of the same events and related questions. All, however, are viewed from different angles and with modifications to get at the elusive truths of war. As if to draw attention to this intertextuality of his war stories across books and to his notion of retelling a true war story, O'Brien in *Things* mentions Stink Harris waking up "screaming with a leech on his tongue" (91), a story that takes readers back to the first page of *Cacciato* where "Stink Harris woke up screaming one night with a leech on his tongue" (1).

More significant repetitions from these earlier works also occur. For instance, the elusive Silver Star, which represents the multiple forms of admirable courage possessed by Captain Johansen in *If I Die* and receives such prominent symbolic attention in *Going After Cacciato,* symbolizes false courage and failure in this novel. Moreover, Calloway observes that the "Speaking of Courage" story in *Things,* with its focus on Norman Bowker's almost winning a Silver Star, becomes a related but different angle on events in *Going After Cacciato* (chapter 14, "Upon Almost Winning the Silver Star"), where Paul Berlin chooses not to enter the tunnel to retrieve Bernie Lynn (Calloway 1995, 251). Other intertextual repetitions include the graphic description of soldiers shooting a water buffalo in *If I Die* (135–36), which becomes a gruesome scene of Stink Harris's mindless massacre of Sarkin Aung Wan's buffalo in *Cacciato* (47–48), and finally evolves within *The Things They Carried* (85–86) into the chilling scene of Rat Kiley's systematic killing of a baby buffalo as this soldier succumbs to overwhelming grief at the loss of a friend. Even more significant, O'Brien transforms the brief references in *If I Die* to the death of his African-American friend Chip (each wrote letters to the other's sister) into a recurring event in *Things* involving the bizarre death of Curt Lemon. Specifically, narrator Tim O'Brien, much like the narrator in Joseph Heller's *Catch-22* who incrementally relates information about Snowden's death, keeps adding details each time he recalls Chip's character and death.

Finally, a version of O'Brien's flee-or-fight decisions in *If I Die* and of Berlin's similar dilemma in his imaginary journey to Paris surfaces in this novel. The narrator describes an agonizing decision not to evade the draft during the summer of 1968 after his graduation from college. This latter thematic connection among the three books establishes an intriguing biographical link among the real O'Brien and his fictional alter egos Paul Berlin and Tim O'Brien. Typical of author O'Brien, he repeatedly tells this fight-or-flight story, as well as other incidents, from various perspectives to create new insights and emotional impacts. As O'Brien notes, "The element of perception has to do with uncertainty. . . . The whole stew of variables determines what we perceive and what we call real" (Herzog, Interview).

Another recurring theme from O'Brien's repertoire appearing in *The Things They Carried* is the search for order and control conducted by characters, storytellers, the narrator, critics, and readers. As in O'Brien's previous works, soldiers and the narrator seek command of their fears, existence, and choices; tellers of war stories within the book search for control of their material through a closure or moral to their stories; critics and reviewers impose an artificial order on the book as they attempt to discuss it; and readers attempt to arrange, connect, and understand the recurring events within the book's episodic structure.

Furthermore, as is true with both *If I Die* and especially *Going After Cacciato,* the surface disorder of this book is part of the meaning; the medium is the message. The confusion and ambiguity of the form and content, as noted earlier, mirror the disorder of the Vietnam War. More important, the narrator's inability or indifference to presenting the

events in a chronological or sequential fashion merely reflects the work-
ings of his mind. Just as Paul Berlin is unable to recall in order the factual events of his tour, so narrator Tim O'Brien jumps back and forth in
time, place, and action as he tells and retells stories. Events lead to stories, to confession, to commentary, and to stories within stories, all without an apparent pattern.

Yet, just as in *Going After Cacciato,* author O'Brien firmly guides this
novel. Surface disorder masks the tight interlocking structure of the
book. As in *If I Die,* O'Brien carefully links the individual sections
through recurring themes, and as in *Going After Cacciato,* O'Brien weaves
together the three major groupings of content—details of the narrator's
life and war experiences, war stories, and passages and separate chapters
of commentary—with recurring images, characters, and events. Thus,
similar to his beginning *Cacciato* with a list of eight soldiers who die during Berlin's tour, O'Brien dedicates *Things* to six of his fictional characters in the novel who become subjects of the stories and storytellers. In
addition, as in *Cacciato,* where O'Brien connects the fact chapters
through intertwined deaths of eight soldiers, deaths—not always war
related—link sections of *Things* and unite the book's thematic and narrative strands in the final chapter, "Lives of the Dead." For instance, the
death of Kiowa, one of Tim O'Brien's friends, becomes a prominent
subject in four stories; the death of Curt Lemon appears six times during
the course of the book, each time with additional details; and the death
of a North Vietnamese soldier is the central event in three stories. These
interconnected tales do more than simply repeat information; they contain both new and conflicting details on the same events as O'Brien
manipulates these accounts by altering the angles of reality.

In two other ways, O'Brien directs this novel by linking this collection of 22 sections: through an underlying theme developed in the first
section (a prologue to the book) and through the first-person narrator.
In the story titled "The Things They Carried," O'Brien mixes storytelling with his technique of enumeration to introduce objects, memories, fears, dreams, hopes, and—most important—stories that the narrator and other soldiers carry with them (the physical and emotional
baggage of life) on their tour of duty in both the Vietnam War and the
war of life. As O'Brien notes, *"Things* is framed around the burdens we
carry, not just in war, not just physical, but spiritual as well" (Herzog,
Interview). Consequently, a central activity in the book involves the narrator and characters telling stories about these burdens identified in this
first section.

O'Brien also unifies this novel of stories, as he does with the nonfictional *If I Die,* through the limited center of consciousness and observation of a first-person narrator, who carries with him guilt and disturbing memories from distant and recent events in his life: "The bad stuff never stops happening: it lives in its own dimension, replaying itself over and over" (*Things,* 36). As O'Brien has noted on several occasions, *Things* is intended to be read as a memoir, a writer's memoir. Therefore, everything in the book (stories, interpolated stories, confession, commentary, fragments, and sketches) is filtered through the eyes, memory, and imagination of Tim O'Brien, a fictional 43-year-old narrator recalling people, events, and stories from his life and Vietnam War experience. This fictional O'Brien also creates new stories and comments on his career as an author.

Since *The Things They Carried* exhibits some of the same content, structure, narrative strategies, and themes of O'Brien's previous books, the work receives similar criticism: charges of perceived racism (absence of the fully developed Vietnamese perspective) and sexism (objectifying, excluding, or silencing women). It should also be noted that such criticism is certainly not targeted at O'Brien alone but has been directed generally at many modern war authors, particularly male American authors writing about the Vietnam War.[16] As in *If I Die* and *Going After Cacciato,* O'Brien devotes minimal space in *The Things They Carried* to developing Vietnamese characters, examining war experiences from the Vietnamese perspective, or exploring the larger political issues involved in this war. Granted, in this novel and in his two previous war narratives, the land of Viet Nam plays a prominent role, becoming a character—threatening, ever changing, mysterious: " 'The whole country. Vietnam. The place talks. It talks. Understand? Nam—it truly talks' " (*Things,* 82). Only a few native inhabitants of this land, however, appear in *The Things They Carried:* a poppa san who leads American troops through a dangerous minefield, two Buddhist monks living near an abandoned pagoda, a dancing Vietnamese girl traumatized by the burning of her hamlet and the killing of her family, a corpse of an old Vietnamese man, and a Vietnamese farmer described in the narrator's story about his return to Viet Nam 20 years after his tour of duty. Yet, as is particularly true in *If I Die,* the roles of these individuals in the book are insignificant, either as victims of the war or background figures in the war stories.

Perhaps narrator Tim O'Brien's most noticeable attempt to humanize and understand these mysterious others occurs in his description of a young Vietcong draftee killed in an ambush. This death-recognition story, told in "The Man I Killed" and repeated with variations in two other sections, seems a prose version of Thomas Hardy's famous World War I poem "The Man He Killed." It connects with a tradition in war literature of a protagonist engaging in a sympathetic identification with the enemy, but an experience always presented from the protagonist's point of view. In O'Brien's story, narrator Tim O'Brien imagines his enemy—a Vietnamese citizen-soldier—being the same age as the narrator (born in 1946), beginning college in the same year (1964), and responding to the war in a similar fashion: "The young man would not have wanted to be a soldier and in his heart would have feared performing badly in battle" (*Things,* 141). Although linking the two soldiers, such a self-centered perspective of this other soldier suggests an effort at projecting the narrator's own traits onto this unknown Vietnamese rather than imagining a separate person. As noted earlier, author O'Brien responds to criticism about his excluding the Vietnamese voice in *Things* and other books by arguing that he is neither capable of presenting a Vietnamese perspective he is unfamiliar with nor required to speak for people who can speak for themselves.

If, for the most part, O'Brien excludes the Vietnamese from meaningful roles in this novel, he does include more women in this book when compared with their presence in the earlier war narratives. Specifically, females figure prominently in several of the stories: Kathleen, narrator Tim O'Brien's nine-year-old daughter; Linda, the narrator's nine-year-old girlfriend from his childhood in Worthington, Minnesota; Martha, Lieutenant Jimmy Cross's girlfriend; and Mary Anne Bell, a 17-year-old who has a "heart-of-darkness" experience at a fire base in Vietnam. In addition, the narrator briefly refers to Curt Lemon's sister, a woman in an audience listening to one of the narrator's war stories, a dancing Vietnamese girl, and Norman Bowker's girlfriend and his mother.

But such inclusions do not diminish some feminist criticism of this book. Significantly, all of these female characters, along with the war itself, are presented through the words of male storytellers, and only Kathleen and Linda are given a voice of their own in the stories.[17] For these and other reasons, a few critics view O'Brien's portrayal of the female characters in *Things* as antifeminist, in particular because they lack an "agency and sensibility of their own" and instead are "projections of a narrator trying to resolve the trauma of war" (Smith 1994, 19). Specifically, Lorrie Smith in examining *The Things They Carried* notes the verbal and emotional hostility directed toward women in the story "How To Tell A True War Story" and their exclusion from the war throughout O'Brien's book because of their supposed inability to understand the male war experience.[18] She comments that the story "Sweetheart of the Song Tra Bong," which becomes O'Brien's attempt at deconstructing gender differences within the context of war by describing a woman's violent battlefield experiences, simply "portrays the woman as *more* masculine than the men, hence monstrous and unnatural" (Smith 1994, 32).

O'Brien's response to such criticism is a cryptic "I think I often am much more a feminist than the so-called feminists criticizing me" (McNerney, Interview, 17). In a 1994 interview he characterizes some of the objectionable language and comments directed toward women in his stories as a realistic "recording" of details rather than an "endorsing" of such language and views. Furthermore, O'Brien disagrees that "Sweetheart" is an antifeminist story; in fact, he sees it as just the opposite, an "utterly feminist" story promoting gender equality. He argues that the story promotes the notion that American women, who are currently excluded from serving in ground combat, would have the same experiences and feelings on the battlefield as their male counterparts, given the chance: "They would be going to the same dark side of the human hemisphere, the dark side of the moon, the dark side of their own psyches" (McNerney, Interview, 21).[19]

Within this context of critical debate and this novel's place within O'Brien's efforts at interconnecting his books, we will examine the specific form and content of *The Things They Carried*. Because of the diverse content and structure within the 22 sections, finding a workable approach to synthesizing the whole book may appear problematic. But as noted previously, the numerous thematic and character links among the chapters, as well as the first-person point of view, create an integrated novel based on an interdependence Philip Beidler characterizes as "each story needing another or others for completion" (Beidler, 33).

Also linking the different stories is a loose tripartite structure somewhat paralleling the form of O'Brien's other two war narratives. For example, drawing upon the relationships of past, present, and future time so artfully manipulated and intertwined in *Going After Cacciato,* the author establishes roughly equivalent time relationships in this novel. Similar to the present time in the observation-post chapters of *Cacciato,* the narrator's commentary, constituting separate chapters or appearing within other chapters, represents the present time in *Things*. Yet unlike the fixed present time in the observation-post chapters, which is restricted to a six-hour period, the sections and passages in *Things* devoted to present-time commentary range over an imprecise period during the fictional narrator's 43rd year of life. During this time, Tim O'Brien assesses his life up to this point; he considers his current state of mind ("I feel guilty sometimes. Forty-three years old and I'm still writing war stories": *Things,* 38.). He comments on the stories he is about to tell ("This is one story I've never told before": *Things,* 43.) and analyzes the purposes and nature of stories ("By telling stories, you objectify your own experience. You separate it from yourself. You pin down certain truths": *Things,* 179.).

Corresponding to the relationship between past (Paul Berlin's memories of his civilian life and Vietnam tour) and present time in *Cacciato,* the past in *The Things They Carried* is represented by the memories of this 43-year-old narrator recalling people, events, and stories from his childhood ("Linda was nine then, as I was, but we were in love": *Things,* 258.); from his Vietnam experiences ("As he passed me on the trail I threw a grenade that exploded at his feet and killed him": *Things,* 147.); and from his more immediate past ("A few months after completing 'In The Field,' I returned with my daughter to Vietnam, where we visited the site of Kiowa's death": *Things,* 207.). Future time (imagination) in this novel, similar to Paul Berlin's daydream about his trip to Paris, is contained within the stories themselves:

> And sometimes remembering will lead to a story, which makes it forever. That's what stories are for. Stories are for joining the past to the future. Stories are for those late hours in the night when you can't remember how you got from where you were to where you are. Stories are for eternity, when memory is erased, when there is nothing to remember except the story. (*Things,* 40)

Unlike *Going After Cacciato,* in which chapter breaks mark clear delineations among time shifts, *Things* lacks such signals. Contrasting the time shifts within these two novels, Don Ringnalda observes that *"Carried* no longer holds up city limits signs as it moves from past to present, from memory to imagination, from reality to fantasy. Plot, and the continuity and coherence it assumes, is possible only in 'spots of time and space' " (Ringnalda, 110).

The other obvious all-encompassing unity among the stories and fragments emerges from the modified autobiographical content of this novel, although O'Brien uses the label "memoir." With its 22 interlaced sections, *The Things They Carried* may simply be a more literary, more sophisticated, fictional version of *If I Die*, with its 23 intertwined sections. As he does in his earlier work, O'Brien accordingly eschews a chronological approach to structuring *Things* and intersperses confession, commentary, vignettes, short stories, fragments, and character sketches throughout the book. Similar to the structure of *If I Die*, a pattern exists to this arrangement of subject matter in *Things*, one that approximates the tripartite form of a modified war autobiography and memoir described in the earlier discussion of O'Brien's nonfiction book. As noted earlier, such a form of autobiography/memoir contains a traditional focus on the inner life of the narrator (autos), an examination of the interaction between the narrator and significant events and people in his or her life (bios), and commentary on the techniques, content, and purposes of such a written document (graphein). O'Brien's fictional autobiography more closely follows this tripartite pattern than does *If I Die*. Consequently, Tim O'Brien, the fictional subject of this autobiography, engages in introspection more readily than does the real O'Brien of *If I Die*. He explores his own heart and mind at various times in his life and in different situations: as a 43-year-old author, a father of a nine-year-old daughter, a 21-year-old college graduate about to be drafted, a combat soldier in Viet Nam, and a veteran. This fictional autobiography also ranges more widely over time and events in the subject's life as well as in the lives of others, and the narrator ponders long and hard the art of writing—in this case stories, including autobiographical ones.

Analyzing the content and connections within and among these three major groupings in *Things* thus seems another appropriate point of view for examining this book. Nevertheless, Ringnalda's earlier warning about the absence of clear signals for merging time in *Things* is also relevant to these intertwined categories of subject matter. O'Brien does not provide prominent road signs for his readers as he glides effortlessly among sections and passages of introspection (narrator Tim O'Brien), observation and storytelling (the war and us), and commentary (the war story).

Narrator Tim O'Brien

A frequent point of confusion for readers of *The Things They Carried* is the fact that the names of the fictional author-narrator of this autobiography and the real author are identical; author O'Brien, however, notes that despite the same name and many of the same characteristics, "it [the narrator] isn't really me" (Naparsteck, Interview, 9). Nevertheless, comparisons between the two O'Briens are inevitable, as are questions about how much of the material in this book is invented and how much is recalled by author O'Brien from his own life. Why did he use the same name? O'Brien responds to this question by describing a significant moment in his life and his writing career: "A month into the writing of the book [*Things*] . . . I found my name appearing." After about an hour of writing he began to feel the words and stories in his stomach and heart as a result of writing and reading his name in the manuscript. Such a magical intersecting of his writing life and real life became an important influence on this book and resulted in O'Brien's decision to continue using his name (Caldwell 1990, Interview, 74).

O'Brien has, however, used more than his own name in developing this fictional narrator's background and personality. Readers familiar with O'Brien's life will find several parallels between the lives of author and narrator, along with a few key differences. As revealed in the course of this fictional autobiography, the 43-year-old subject, who in 1989 – 1990 is the same age as O'Brien, lives in Massachusetts with a wife and daughter. He is a Vietnam veteran who has written about the war, specifically a novel called *Going After Cacciato* and an award-winning short story titled "Speaking of Courage." The fictional Tim grew up in Worthington, Minnesota; played shortstop in little league; graduated Phi Beta Kappa and summa cum laude from Macalaster College in 1968, where he was a McCarthy supporter in the presidential campaign; and soon after receiving a draft notice, reluctantly entered the army. He served his Vietnam tour in an area of operations just south of Chu Lai in Quang Ngai Province. During this time he was wounded twice. An "easy adjustment from war to peace" marked this Tim's return from the war and his enrollment in a graduate program at Harvard. So far the facts about this fictional character are strikingly similar to those in author O'Brien's life—except that he does not have a daughter and he was wounded only once. Furthermore, the views of the two O'Briens toward war and the citizens of Worthington are remarkably alike. At age 21, the fictional Tim believed the "American war in Vietnam seemed to me wrong. Certain blood was being shed for uncertain reasons" (*Things,* 44). Also at this age, he condemned the ignorance of the adults in Worthington toward the war: "I held them personally and individually responsible—the polyestered Kiwanis boys. . . . They didn't know Bao Dai from the man in the moon. They didn't know history" (*Things,*

48 – 49). Both of these quotes contain words author O'Brien has used in several interviews to comment on the same issues.

The question emerges whether author O'Brien's efforts at confusing the reader by including so many of these real facts from his life are more literary tricks? Or is the technique part of the overall message of the book about truth, literary lies, angles of perspective, storytelling, and the relationship between memory and imagination? The answer seems to be the latter; the method is the message illustrating the elusiveness of truth. As he does throughout this interconnected novel, frequently telling the same story from different perspectives and with different information, O'Brien seems to be exploring his own life from different angles that combine facts and invented details. The results are a heightened dramatic intensity to incidents, increased emotional responses from readers, and perhaps from O'Brien's point of view additional opportunities to explore possibilities for himself and his characters.

As the fictional Tim O'Brien presents the confessional thread of this autobiography, revealing his heart and mind, readers begin to understand that author O'Brien and narrator Tim O'Brien are also preoccupied with analogous issues—courage, embarrassment, cowardice, fear, death, revenge, guilt, and healing. Again, they face many of the same doubts, fears, emotions, and character changes that soldiers in all wars have confronted. Many of these moral, philosophical, and emotional topics first appeared in the nonfictional *If I Die* and reappear in the later works. In *The Things They Carried*, however, they are viewed from new angles and with much more story depth and emotional impact. For narrator Tim, and possibly author O'Brien, these confessions become an exorcising of guilt, a way to "relieve at least some of the pressure on my dreams" (*Things*, 43). The narrator's moments of introspection also become emotional releases, opportunities to cut through the numbness that the war has created in him so he can feel again.

Perhaps the most dramatic confessional passages are those dealing with the narrator's guilt. Author-soldier O'Brien's guilt over his participation in the Vietnam War ("I was a coward"), described in *If I Die*, becomes narrator Tim's culpability over a similar decision to go to war. But this Tim's transgression also widens to include self-blame for the deaths of friends and foes and a sense of personal fault for the way the war has changed him. Although passages of autobiographical introspection appear throughout this novel, a few key stories focus exclusively on the narrator's examination of his memories, feelings, and this guilt—the things that 20 years after returning from Viet Nam "would never go away."

Some of this feeling of wrongdoing emerges from Tim's uneasiness about combat numbness to death and destruction, a condition to which many soldiers involuntarily succumb to stave off emotional collapse from viewing brutality on a daily basis. In Tim's case such dullness has remained with him years after the war: "There were times in my life when I couldn't feel much, not sadness or pity or passion, and somehow I blamed this place [Viet Nam] for what I had become" (*Things,* 210). Some of the narrator's confessions of sin involve another occurrence common among thoughtful individuals who confront the horrors of war—the frightening realization that during the war they have become very different people. As described in the story "Ghost Soldiers," Tim, who has undergone his own heart-of-darkness experience in war, is shocked that feelings of revenge and meanness inhabit the core of his character: "For all my education, all my fine liberal values, I now felt a deep coldness inside me, something dark and beyond reason. It's a hard thing to admit, even to myself, but I was capable of evil" (*Things,* 227).

Among these various forms of guilt to which Tim confesses, one of the most poignant and familiar emerges from the narrator's dilemma of whether to flee or fight, a recurring theme in O'Brien's works. As described in the short story "On the Rainy River," Tim O'Brien, like the real O'Brien, confronts this issue after his graduation from college. With a "draft notice tucked away in [his] wallet" (*Things,* 47)—a similar line also appears in *If I Die* (25)—the narrator spends six days at a fishing lodge on the Rainy River, which literally divides northern Minnesota from Canada and symbolically divides fighting from fleeing. The opportunity for a separate peace surfaces as Tim ponders escaping across the border into Canada. The competing arguments for and against flight raised in *If I Die* and *Going After Cacciato* reappear in this story, although they contain a dramatic intensity and depth of feeling missing in the earlier works: the argument of conscience—the war "seemed to me wrong" (*Things,* 44); the argument of personal safety—"or at the very center, was the raw fact of terror. I did not want to die" (*Things,* 47); the argument of society's censure—"I feared the war, yes, but I also feared exile" (*Things,* 48); and the argument of comfort and order—"all I wanted was to live the life I was born to—a mainstream life" (*Things,* 53).

On the last day of his stay, Tim is taken fishing on the Rainy River by the lodge's 81-year-old proprietor, Elroy Berdahl, who as a quasi-father figure and confidant plays a role in this story similar to Lieutenant Corson's in *Going After Cacciato* and Claude Rasmussen's in *In the Lake of the Woods*. Berdahl forces O'Brien to act when the old man takes the boat into Canadian territory and stops a short distance from land: "but I think he meant to bring me up against the realities, to guide me across the river and to take me to the edge and to stand a kind of vigil as I chose a life for myself" (*Things*, 58). Like civilian O'Brien in *If I Die*, draftee O'Brien about to depart for Vietnam in the same book, and Paul Berlin the fictional soldier, this narrator Tim O'Brien must adjudicate competing personal values and choose a course of action. As his tears mix with hallucinations about fleeing to Canada or returning home, Tim, like his counterparts in the previous stories, decides to go to war.

Readers have read his rationale before in the previous war narratives: "I couldn't risk the embarrassment. . . . Even in my imagination . . . I couldn't make myself be brave" (*Things*, 61–62). At this point the 43-year-old narrator condemns his earlier decision with words used previously in *If I Die* but with a conviction missing in that book: "I was a coward. I went to the war" (*Things*, 63). With this judgment, Tim O'Brien the civilian, soldier, and author seems to merge with the fictional Tim O'Brien, but perhaps not with Paul Berlin—whose situation and character create a somewhat different angle on this dilemma.

Another type of guilt, also borrowed from *If I Die*, surfaces in some of the introspective stories and commentaries as narrator Tim O'Brien broods over memories of battlefield deaths: "Here is the happening-truth. I was once a soldier. There were many bodies, real bodies with real faces, but I was young then and I was afraid to look. And now, twenty years later, I'm left with faceless responsibility and faceless grief" (*Things*, 203). To explore this guilt, author O'Brien transforms his uneventful "Ambush" chapter in *If I Die* and another chapter from the same book titled "Mori," describing the death of a North Vietnamese Army nurse, into three very dramatic and personal sections within *The Things They Carried* titled "The Man I Killed," "Ambush," and "Good Form." In these chapters, Tim O'Brien examines his responsibility—direct as well as indirect—for the death of a Vietcong soldier. Consistent with his pattern of mixing memory with imagination, fact with fiction, one detail with a conflicting detail, the narrator describes from different perspectives this soldier's death and Tim's subsequent remorse. In the first two stories, Tim recalls in detail a night ambush during which he killed the Vietnamese soldier. Years later still haunted by images of the body lying on the trail, the narrator confesses that "Even now I haven't finished sorting it out. Sometimes I forgive myself, other times I don't"

(*Things,* 149). But later in "Good Form," a commentary section, the 43-year-old narrator confesses something even more startling: He saw this enemy soldier die on a trail, but "I did not kill him. But I was present, you see, and my presence was guilt enough" (*Things,* 203).

Such confessions of accountability for his actions or mere presence (the facts are left purposely vague) related to various deaths also lead to Tim's survival guilt. For instance, the recurring brief passages describing from various angles the death of fellow soldier Curt Lemon (Chip from *If I Die*) suggest such a self-censure, a typical reaction among soldiers. Moreover, in the section titled "The Lives of the Dead," the deaths of other squad members, of the Vietnamese soldier Tim did or did not kill, and of Vietnamese civilians merge with the death of nine-year-old Linda, Timmy's girlfriend in fourth grade. These fatalities across time and place link with each other and pierce the narrator's emotional numbness created by the war. In particular, memories of Linda's death resurrect Tim's feelings of intense loss, along with a form of survivor's guilt and embarrassment over his inability to be brave in standing up to a class bully taunting the young girl dying of a brain tumor.

The death that seems to haunt Tim the most, however, is Kiowa's gruesome demise in a shit field just outside a Vietnamese village. Once again mystery surrounds the death of this Bible-carrying Native American, who is one of Tim's best friends. As the event is described in "Speaking of Courage," readers wonder whether squad member Norman Bowker is responsible for the casualty (a failure to act) or whether, as suggested in "Notes," "In the Field," and "Field Trip," Tim is guilty of unintentional complicity in Kiowa's death (a similar failure to save the soldier). This contradiction of happening-truths is never resolved; the story-truth is, on the other hand, quite plain. At age 34 Tim returns with his daughter to Viet Nam and the site of Kiowa's death ("Field Trip"): "This little field, I thought, had swallowed so much. My best friend. My pride. My belief in myself as a man of small dignity and courage" (*Things,* 210). In a scene somewhat reminiscent of Paul Perry's symbolic submersion in Pliney's Pond at the end of *Northern Lights,* Tim seeks forgiveness, closure, and healing for his war experiences by immersing himself in the river bordering the shit field and burying in the river bottom Kiowa's moccasins, which Tim has kept for 20 years: "Twenty years. A lot like yesterday, a lot like never. In a way, maybe, I'd gone under with Kiowa, and now after two decades I'd finally worked my way out" (*Things,* 212).

The War Experience

The bios sections, or fact chapters, of this novel (we, they, and it involved in the Vietnam War and the war of the living) contain descriptions of events, people, and relationships quite familiar to readers of O'Brien's other two Vietnam narratives. Also, as narrator Tim links himself with other squad members, he journeys into familiar territory—the souls of combat soldiers living in the crucible of war. In these sections of *The Things They Carried,* Tim moves from personal introspection and confession to more storytelling or relaying the stories of others, but the presence of a controlling narrative voice in these sections is much more noticeable than in similar sections in *If I Die.* Readers are constantly reminded that this is Tim's story. Combining techniques of iteration and enumeration with character sketches and war stories, Tim presents familiar images of machinelike and purposeless marching or of the ever-changing and haunting Viet Nam landscape at night. He describes soldiers, like those in *Going After Cacciato,* who find themselves in a world of uncertainty and confusion over mission, strategy, and the people they are fighting against and those they are fighting for.[20] It is also a world of land mines, tunnels, and an invisible enemy.

Within this psychological and physical landscape ruled by superstition, luck, and chance, these soldiers attempt to establish some control over their lives and their world. To succeed, they escape into games, such as checkers, that have clear winners; into their memories through filtered facts and images; and into their imagination through daydreams and war stories, which, according to battlefield protocol, have definite rules for presentation, form, and meaning. Such control gained through these mind games is fleeting, however. Memories can also unsettle and weigh down the mind and spirit; stories can end without closure or certainty; and daydreams replacing concentration during a combat mission can kill.

As Tim observes, disorder also emerges from contradictions inherent in these troops' battlefield existence: The horror of war is yoked with soldiers' story humor created to deal with war's obscenity and numb the emotions—"A pisser, you know? Still zipping himself up. Zapped while zipping" (*Things,* 17). Also, war's ugliness contrasts with its unexpected beauty—"But in truth war is also beauty. For all its horror, you can't help but gape at the awful majesty of combat. You stare out at tracer rounds unwinding through the dark like brilliant red ribbons" (*Things,*

87). In addition, a soldier's understandable revulsion toward death, destruction, and evil occurring in war links with an incomprehensible attraction to war's action, technology, power, and mystery. Such a "fascination of the abomination" (using Joseph Conrad's words) emerges in Mary Anne's addiction to her war experience as described in "Sweetheart of the Song Tra Bong." One final paradox occurs as shooting oneself to escape the mission and the nightmares (Rat Kiley in "Night Life") replaces shooting the enemy to accomplish mission.

This contradictory war experience also elicits competing emotions: love and hate; compassion and indifference; sacrifice and revenge. But the most prevalent and familiar of these is the opposition of courage and cowardice. Soldiers, readers, and the narrator sort through the ambiguities of this dichotomy as they have done in O'Brien's previous war narratives. In *Things,* does Rat Kiley's self-inflicted wound constitute bravery through his taking control of his situation and escaping battlefield absurdity? Does soldiers' endurance in war define a simple courage ("It was not courage, exactly. . . . They were too frightened to be cowards": *Things,* 21.)? Is Jorgenson, the medic in "Ghost Soldiers," courageous for apologizing to Tim for not treating his wound properly? Are soldiers' efforts to hide their fears and battlefield humiliations a false courage bordering on cowardice? Is the Silver Star for heroism that Norman Bowker almost wins also a symbol of false courage; is his suicide a cowardly act? Does a soldier's presence in an unpopular war represent the ultimate act of cowardice: "Men killed and died because they were embarrassed not to. It was what had brought them to the war in the first place, nothing positive, no dreams of glory or honor, just to avoid the blush of dishonor. They died so as not to die of embarrassment" (*Things,* 21). For narrator Tim O'Brien, readers, and author O'Brien, these questions are purposely left unanswered.

The War Story

"Can the foot soldier teach anything important about war, merely for having been there? I think not. He can tell war stories" (*Die,* 32). Using these words from his first book as a guide, author O'Brien devotes a significant portion of this fictional war autobiography to a consideration of the writing and telling of war stories. He indirectly analyzes his own stories while directly commenting on those of fictional author-narrator Tim O'Brien in *The Things They Carried.* Once more, author O'Brien is in familiar territory, but he is examining this subject from a new standpoint and in much greater depth than in his previous works. O'Brien plants the seeds of this metafictional quality of his writings in *If I Die in a Combat Zone,* and they germinate in *Going After Cacciato.* As noted earlier, in several of the novel's observation-post chapters, O'Brien, through his inexperienced author Paul Berlin, explores the difficulties of merging fact and fiction. Furthermore, in these chapters and those devoted to Berlin's Paris chapters, O'Brien raises issues of control, order, and responsibility as they relate to writing and storytelling. In *The Things They Carried,* such matters reach full bloom as author O'Brien, the fictional Tim O'Brien, and an assortment of other soldiers turned storytellers explore the form, content, pace, and purpose of war stories (oral and written), as well as related issues of audience, truth, lies, memory, and imagination. Three sections in particular—"How to Tell a True War Story," "Notes," and "Good Form"—contain the bulk of these musings about story and storytelling, but because this topic becomes one of the novel's principal themes, other passages on the process and content of storytelling appear throughout this integrated novel.

As author-narrator Tim analyzes war stories, his own and others', he considers the creative process, specifically the relationship between memory and imagination. As the daydreamer Paul Berlin discovers in *Going After Cacciato,* the raw materials for his imaginary Paris journey come from his memory—the facts, people, events, and moral quandaries from his Vietnam tour. Once he begins transforming memories into story, Berlin discovers that imagination often shapes these materials in totally unexpected ways and with surprising outcomes. In *The Things They Carried,* Tim's analysis of his own process of creating a story reveals similarities to Berlin's storytelling, as this experienced writer also draws from the details of his life and then allows imagination to take over: "The memory-traffic feeds into a rotary up in your head, where it goes in circles for a while, then pretty soon imagination flows in and the traffic merges and shoots off down a thousand different streets. As a writer, all you can do is pick a street and go for a ride, putting things down as they come at you" (*Things,* 38). Another soldier-storyteller in *Things,* Mitchell Sanders, turns a similar description of the process ("go for a ride") into advice for telling a story. He notes that good stories are ruined by too much involvement of teller through analysis, commentary, and clarification: "[T]rust your own story. Get the hell out of the way and let it tell itself" (*Things,* 116).

Such observations from Tim and Mitchell provide interesting contexts for examining the storytelling in this novel. Expanding the traffic metaphor to include repeated trips on the same rotary of stories leads to a description of exactly what occurs with Tim's and O'Brien's creative processes. Often they use the same raw materials, but each time they pick or find themselves on a different street to travel and view the material. As a result, the author may begin with the same basic information but always ends with a different story. For example, throughout his fictional autobiography narrator Tim O'Brien turns the raw materials of Curt Lemon's and Kiowa's deaths into different stories with different truths as he adds or subtracts information or as he examines the deaths from different narrative angles. On the other hand, Mitchell's advice about an author's direct involvement appears to be a rule that most of the storytellers, particularly Tim, ignore throughout *The Things They Carried*. They seem reluctant to let their stories tell themselves. Instead, commentary, explication of their stories, and assertions of authenticity ("It's all exactly true. It happened to me": *Things,* 77.) become commonplace for these storytellers and this fictional author.

In addition to scrutinizing the creative process, narrator Tim also probes the appropriate content of a war story; specifically, he considers what makes a story true. Indirectly, author O'Brien also explores this issue. Since readers' and critics' questions of fact and fiction related to O'Brien's own storytelling and life continually dog him, he seems to respond to such inquiries through his fictional narrator-author. For just as O'Brien has acknowledged such questions about facts and truth by labeling them irrelevant, so author Tim suggests that stories should be judged not by their literal truth but by other criteria. Foremost among these criteria is Tim's notion of story-truth opposed to happening-truth. The latter requires the author's recall of facts associated with events and people; story-truth requires the author to employ imagination to reveal emotional truths transcending the limits of memory and facts: "I want you to feel what I felt. I want you to know why story-truth is truer sometimes than happening-truth" (*Things,* 203).

Tim's words parallel a passage from Norman Maclean's autobiographical novella, *A River Runs Through It,* in which a father talks to his oldest son, the narrator, about stories: " 'You like to tell true stories, don't you? . . . After you have finished your true stories sometime, why don't you make up a story and the people to go with it? Only then will you understand what happened and why.' "[21] Such advice confirms Tim's notion that story-truth may come from what "seemed to happen" rather than what did happen, from a combination of memory and imagination, or from pure imagination. Or this truth may occur because the storyteller, like Rat Kiley, may exaggerate the facts in order to "heat up the truth" so listeners can "feel exactly what he felt" (*Things,* 102).

Whatever the case, true war stories, according to author Tim, do not contain an easily grasped moral, are not instructive, do not have certainty, and are not comforting. The true war story focuses on details, on an event, on a moment, on the obscenity and evil of war. Such a story does not generalize; instead, it particularizes and clarifies. Furthermore, a true war story may contain literal lies but feel true: "A true war story, if truly told, makes the stomach believe" (*Things,* 84). Tim's deconstruction of the war story becomes O'Brien's construction of a response to issues of truth in his own life and works. The real son-soldier-author O'Brien did not travel to the Rainy River in the summer of 1968. Nevertheless, this O'Brien did ponder the same arguments about fleeing the war and felt the same emotions about the decision to enter the army as the fictional Tim in "On The Rainy River." The story heats up the story-truth and allows readers to feel what O'Brien felt. This fictional story is true, just as true as narrator Tim's story that he killed a Vietcong soldier, although he later confesses that he was present but did not actually kill the soldier. Tim's death story contains story-truth; Tim's confession contains happening-truth. His imagined response to his daughter illustrates both: " 'Daddy, tell the truth,' Kathleen can say, 'did you ever kill anybody?' And I can say honestly, 'Of course not.' Or I can say honestly, 'Yes' " (*Things,* 204).

Finally, if war stories cannot teach but can make listeners and readers feel, they also fill other roles for the audience and the storyteller. Among fellow soldiers and veterans, war stories become basic ways of establishing a community of the battlefield through shared experiences, feelings, understandings, combat discourse, and catharsis. On a superficial level, the stories may be a way for the storytellers to display their skills in crafting and telling the story. Among civilians, the veterans' telling of war stories may become intentional or unintentional efforts at excluding the nonparticipants from the war experiences and reaffirming the notion that only combatants can understand war. But such storytelling may also be a desperate effort on a veteran's part to connect with family and friends or to explain the Vietnam War experience, something at which Norman Bowker fails because neither friends nor his father is available to listen. Consequently, Norman can only imagine telling his story of almost winning the Silver Star: "A good war story, he thought, but it was not a war for war stories, nor for talk of valor, and nobody in town wanted to know about the terrible stink" (*Things,* 169).

Narrator Tim notes other functions for these stories. Echoing the earlier quote from Maclean's short novel, Tim observes that stories allow authors to objectify their experiences, to step back and view events from new slants in order to "pin down certain truths . . . make up others" (*Things,* 179). Such stories also allow authors to invent a new life and history for themselves, consider possibilities, create a person out of a scrap of dialogue or a few details, or give concreteness to concepts and abstractions. These stories may even save lives and keep the dead alive. As O'Brien notes in an interview about *The Things They Carried,* "If there is a theme to the whole book it has to do with the fact that stories can save our lives. . . . the livingness that's there as you read and that lingers after" (Coffey, Interview, 61). What O'Brien means by such a comment connects with the notion of storytelling as a "magic trick" (*Things,* 272)—a way for the storyteller to remember the dead and hold on to the living by keeping their essence alive through dreams, daydreams, and story. This trick of the mind Tim uses in this book and in his life to hold on to dead friends from the war or to a childhood friend who died at age nine. It is a ploy that O'Brien's fictional character John Wade in *In the Lake of the Woods* will use to communicate with his dead father. Yet most important for author O'Brien and narrator Tim O'Brien, these stories keep the dead and the living alive in the minds of readers and listeners: "The thing about a story is that you dream it as you tell it, hoping that others might then dream along with you, and in this way memory and imagination and language combine to make spirits in the head" and create an illusion of "aliveness" (*Things,* 259–60). Such a goal for his stories connects O'Brien with all great storytellers.

Chapter Four

Wars at Home: *The Nuclear Age*

Seven years after publishing *Going After Cacciato,* O'Brien in his third
novel, *The Nuclear Age* (1985), returns readers to familiar territory
encountered in *Northern Lights:* an apocalyptic epigraph, a backyard
bomb shelter, and one man's obsessive fears of a nuclear holocaust and
his subsequent efforts to warn all who will listen about this reality of
modern life. Beginning with a lengthy epigraph taken from the apocalyptic *Second Book of Esdras* (*The Apocrypha*), O'Brien, through narrator
William Cowling, examines memories and visions, doomsday and the
Bomb, and personal and global instability. Furthermore, the novel continues O'Brien's consideration of the Vietnam War, but this time from a
new angle—an emotional, intellectual, and political "battlefield" situated within America's home front and involving the antiwar movement.
As a result, the novel occasionally resembles one more of O'Brien's
many war stories, this one chronicling the tour of duty of civilian
William Cowling, a soldier of peace, love, and family, confronting a hostile and chaotic world.

   Also present are features of form and content found in the author's
previous works: facts from O'Brien's own life transformed by the
author's imagination; fictional autobiography exploring the heart and
mind of a central character; a time sequence involving past (memory),
present (consideration), and future (imagination); a tripartite grouping
of chapters; and recurring themes, such as the possibility of a separate
peace, the search for order and control, courage versus cowardice, the
power of imagination to influence behavior, and global and personal
politics. Furthermore, in *The Nuclear Age,* O'Brien once again explores
the mysteries and ambiguities of human existence, particularly the fear
of the unknown. As Kaplan notes, the prominent nuclear bomb in this
novel becomes a "metaphor for all the unanswered questions human
beings have about their existence" (Kaplan 1995, 132). Finally, like all
of O'Brien's protagonists, the central character in this novel seeks control, stability, and understanding within a chaotic existence. But
O'Brien develops these familiar themes within a new literary landscape
for him. He struggles to create a sustained dark comedy similar to

Joseph Heller's *Catch-22* with its sprinkling of offbeat characters, bizarre humor, absurd situations, tension between sanity and insanity, and serious underlying messages about conflict, power, and mortality.

According to a brief background article about the publication history of *The Nuclear Age,* O'Brien found writing this book particularly difficult during the approximately seven years it took him to complete it. "There wasn't any writer's block exactly. . . . The agony was in just going over it. I must have rewritten it thirty times."[1] As the work passed through three publishing houses, he also struggled to make suitable production arrangements, eventually residing with Alfred A. Knopf.[2] Once published, the book, like *Northern Lights,* has received over the years minimal critical attention from literary scholars and generally negative reviews. Reviewers tend to disagree with O'Brien's own succinct evaluation of his efforts after seven years of writing: "I liked this book. I think it's better than *Cacciato*" (Weber, 269). A few of these critics are upset that O'Brien strays so dramatically in subject and style from the form and content of *Going After Cacciato* ("an awkward polemic sure to disappoint readers of *Going After Cacciato*)."[3] Others seem unaware of the book's thematic and stylistic connections to O'Brien's earlier works, especially *Northern Lights.* Nevertheless, most of the early negative criticism focuses on O'Brien's characters, with reviewers labeling them "tepid cartoons," criticizing O'Brien's inability to "create believable urban guerrillas" and in one case describing the central character (William Cowling) as "little more than an aberration—a kook, and a pretty boring kook at that."[4]

On the other hand, reviewers comment favorably on O'Brien's sympathetic portrait of the central character's childhood and, as usual, on O'Brien's carefully crafted prose, supporting structure, and psychological insights: The book is "notable for the lean clarity of O'Brien's prose and the finesse with which, as ever, he evokes states of mind."[5] For the most part, critics fail to note the depth to which O'Brien explores the essence of his central character as well as O'Brien's relevant messages about mortality, love, commitment, and accommodation. They also, according to O'Brien, fail to appreciate his intentional distortion of characters to create a cartoonlike effect: "The *Nuclear Age* in general was meant to be a big cartoon of the nuclear age, with everything heightened and exaggerated. . . . the way Trudeau does it in *Doonesbury*" (Kaplan, Interview, 100).

Most vexing, perhaps, to O'Brien is reviewers' common failure to acknowledge the overall comic intention of the novel. Bluntly commenting on such an oversight, O'Brien remarks that *Nuclear Age* is "a book I still like, in spite of all the negative reviews. I think it is funny, and people who don't think it is funny, Fuck-em. . . . Not to have the comedy mentioned in so many reviews, not even mentioned, makes me wonder about either my own sense of humor or that of others" (Herzog, Interview). Without question, some of the incidents, character relationships, and character descriptions are indeed humorous and exaggerated, and ironic plot twists add to the drollness. But much of the book treats important political and moral issues in a serious manner. Spread throughout the novel are sympathetic views of characters, poignant scenes, thought-provoking messages, a balanced treatment of the antiwar movement in the United States, and links to characters, themes, and narrative strategies in O'Brien's other works. Furthermore, the basic subject, as described by O'Brien, is weighty: William Cowling "believes the world is going to end. . . . Such an end is only a metaphor for something much larger in the book, which is the business that we are all going to die—the whole business, in other words, of mortality" (McNerney, Interview, 11). Consequently, critics and readers might be excused for failing to view this novel as a fully realized work of comic satire or an uproariously funny book.

Other problems arise. For example, as reviewer Grace Paley notes, the book falls between realism and surrealism, "an untranscending middle which muffles the important cry of 'Doom, doom.' "[6] In addition, abrupt plot shifts mar the third section of the book ("Critical Mass"), and tenuous connections between the chapters devoted to the antiwar movement and those exploring nuclear annihilation constitute other shortcomings. Overall, for readers and critics this novel is less satisfying than *Going After Cacciato* because the narrative is driven by incidents and details rather than by themes, ideas, and a complex narrative form. Consequently, in *The Nuclear Age,* O'Brien also is less successful than in his previous work in creatively meshing narrative form, underlying themes, and a consistent development of key characters' souls. Finally, unlike O'Brien's highly acclaimed *Going After Cacciato* and *The Things They Carried,* this book does not explore the craft and purpose of fiction. *The Nuclear Age* is a novel of stories but not a novel about the art of storytelling.

Perhaps O'Brien's forceful defense of *The Nuclear Age* reflects his strong emotional and intellectual connections with the principal subjects of this book—the Vietnam War and the nuclear age. Comparable to his other works, this novel and its central character (like O'Brien, born in October 1946) emanate from some of O'Brien's own experiences, obsessions, and perspectives on the world: "I grew up scared on the flatlands of southern Minnesota. An unlikely ground-zero."[7] In the late 1950s and early 1960s, dinner conversations at the O'Brien home occasionally involved the latest news on nuclear weapons and inevitably led to speculations about the potential for nuclear war, the chances of the Midwest being attacked, and possible consequences for Worthington of such a nuclear strike. Fueled by Cold War rhetoric, disaster drills, "duck-and-cover" jingles, and a bomb-shelter mentality sweeping America during this time, the young O'Brien found himself building a miniature fallout shelter under a Ping-Pong table in his basement—a pivotal incident in the novel.[8] The Cuban missile crisis in October 1962 also left an indelible mark on O'Brien's psyche as it too becomes a significant event in both *Northern Lights* and *The Nuclear Age*. O'Brien recalls that in October 1962 he had a key role in a high school play, *Curious Savage* by John Patrick, that describes the eccentric dreams of a group of young inmates in a mental institution. O'Brien remembers that as the dress rehearsals for the play occurred, the crisis in Cuba kept escalating. "That combination of the mental instability, which was in the play, with the instabilities in the world at the time—the fragilities in the world and the fragilities in these personalities we were depicting—will never go away. That combination will be in my memory forever. The two are locked forever" (Herzog, Interview). This description of O'Brien's emotional and intellectual state in 1962 summarizes the underlying global and personal brittleness first introduced in *Northern Lights* and featured in *The Nuclear Age*.

O'Brien's concern over this potential nuclear Armageddon did not end with his graduation from high school. In fact, after his return from Viet Nam, his fears intensified so much that he journeyed to Kansas to confront the source of his nightmares—Titan II missiles with nuclear warheads. In a 1979 article for *Feature* magazine, O'Brien describes these anxieties, the trip to Rock, Kansas, the indifferent responses of the town's residents who live next to the missile silos, the dangers of an intentional or unintentional nuclear war, and the ways people in the nuclear age cope with mortality—their own and civilization's. In the article O'Brien intentionally or unintentionally introduces the essence of his 1985 novel: "In September of this year, after more than a decade of nuclear nightmares, I went to Kansas to track down the source of all this fear. I went on an ICBM hunt. Stalking the mysterious Titan II missile. The objective of this trek was simple: to touch the nuclear age" ("Darkness," 42).

At times, O'Brien's confessions about his response to the nuclear threat anticipate the paranoia, obsessions, and prophecies of doom of William Cowling, the central character in *Nuclear Age*. In his magazine article, O'Brien writes that "as a kid, I had nuke fever. It was the work of imagination. I heard the scream of incoming ICBMs, I watched New York turn to cinders. I saw strontium-90 curdling my milk. I sat aghast as the TV hissed its one-note test of the Emergency Broadcast System. *Déja vu*. A voyeur at my own thermal funeral" ("Darkness," 42). These doomsday visions of the young O'Brien are similar to those of the young Cowling: "I'd been dreaming of war—whole continents on fire, oceans boiling, cities in ash—and now, with that dreadful silence, it seemed that the universe had died in its sleep."[9] In the 1990s, O'Brien, like many people, still lives with these fears, believing the threat of nuclear terrorism is increasing: "I will bet it [detonation of a nuclear weapon] will happen [in a large American city], maybe in say fifty years. Too many crazy people! Too many evil people in the world! The technology is too simple" (Herzog, Interview).

In addition to O'Brien's transforming fact into fiction and his life into art, readers of his previous works will find other familiar patterns in *The Nuclear Age*. As in all of his other works, O'Brien organizes this novel around the psyche of a central character—in this case William Cowling. Yet in this work, instead of using the limited third-person narrative form of *Cacciato* and *Northern Lights,* O'Brien employs a first-person narrative voice, a feature also found in *If I Die* and *The Things They Carried*. Consequently, memory chapters in this novel become a war-at-home autobiography with emphasis on the autos and bios but no interest in the *graphein*. Readers familiar with *Going After Cacciato* will also find structural parallels between the two novels in terms of chapter groupings and narrative shifts between past and present time. Like the interspersed observation-post chapters of *Cacciato,* which establish present time in the novel and serve as the narrative anchor, in *The Nuclear Age* O'Brien intersperses chapters titled "Quantum Jumps" that serve a similar role in this novel but have a time frame of a few months rather than Paul Berlin's six hours of guard duty.

Present time is 1995, roughly a three-month period from the middle of April to the middle of July, and the setting is the home of 49-year-old William Cowling. As the book opens, Cowling begins to dig an underground fallout shelter in his backyard located in the Sweetheart Mountains near Fort Derry, Montana, "the energy state." Throughout these five narrative-frame chapters, Cowling relates, in roughly chronological order, his progress in completing the shelter, his interactions with his wife and daughter, and his contemplations as he works. These chapters become the springboard, as occurs in *Cacciato,* for the novel's remaining eight autobiographical units, which contain Cowling's memories in chronological order of his youth, college years, and adult life up to 1995. Occasionally, present-time reflections interrupt these flashbacks, and all the past events appear against a historical backdrop of significant people, dates, and events related to the Cold War, the Vietnam War, and Cowling's personal war against nuclear annihilation. Like Paul Berlin on his one night of guard duty, Cowling spends approximately three months in his metaphorical subterranean observation post looking backward, inward, and forward by utilizing memory, consideration, and imagination. Unlike Berlin, who has difficulty recalling the order of remembered events, Cowling easily establishes order and connections among his recollections. For Cowling, cause-and-effect relationships are quite clear.

O'Brien provides an overarching structure to this content by separating the book's 13 chapters, including the quantum-jumps chapters, into three major sections: "Fission" (seven chapters), "Fusion" (four chapters), and "Critical Mass" (two chapters). The titles of these divisions, as well as of many individual chapters, through their scientific jargon and nuclear-age vocabulary ("Civil Defense," "First Strikes," "Escalations," "Underground Tests," "Fallout"), suggest both the planet's inexorable movement toward "the end of the world" and the stages in William Cowling's life.[10] In this story of William Cowling's coming of age in the nuclear era, the central character confronts atomic annihilation, the Vietnam War, and the disintegration of his nuclear family. Consequently, the three chapter groupings parallel the three-part stages of character development O'Brien uses in his earlier rite-of-passage novel *Northern Lights* (preparation, confrontation, and consideration). In addition, the stages closely approximate those identified by Paul Fussell as shaping the paradigmatic British World War I memoir.

Such a structure appears in many of the best pieces of modern war literature, including fictional and nonfictional narratives about the Vietnam War. In his seminal work *The Great War and Modern Memory,* Fussell describes the stages of a soldier's development as follows: "first, the sinister or absurd or even farcical preparation [for battle]; second, the unmanning experience of battle; and third, the retirement from the line to a contrasting (usually pastoral) scene, where there is time and quiet for consideration, meditation, and reconstruction. The middle stage is always characterized by disenchantment and loss of innocence" (Fussell, 130). The third stage, a more open-ended period of contemplation, begins on the battlefield but may continue long after the war has ended and the soldiers have returned home. It may even extend into a fourth stage, one that Fussell does not identify, that may be labeled an aftermath stage in which veterans reflect on their war experiences and struggle to adjust to civilian life.[11] Obviously, Fussell's three-way pattern of innocence (preparation), experience (loss of innocence), and consideration-aftermath has archetypal connections, and in various forms it shapes much of the content and structure of a bildungsroman, or rite-of-passage novel, focusing on the education, maturation, or mythic quest of a young central character. Since, in many respects, *The Nuclear Age* falls within this genre and connects with home-front war literature, *The Nuclear Age* seems an appropriate work to be analyzed within this structural and thematic paradigm. This novel presents the initiation and aftermath story of a "soldier" in the anti-Vietnam War movement and in the greater movement to educate people about the madness of the nuclear arms race.

Finally, in typical O'Brien fashion, the author thematically links his three major sections, as well as individual chapters devoted to past and present time, through underlying narrative techniques of iteration and angles: "[P]resently I was made aware of numerous unique perspectives. It was all in the angle" (*Nuclear,* 270). Accordingly, O'Brien presents new points of view on recurring themes from previous works and different angles on repeated themes within the novel. For example, one of the ongoing issues explored in this novel involves the tension between individual derangement and the madness of the age. From childhood into his adult life, Cowling is haunted by a question: "Am I crazy?" Is he neurotic as a child to be obsessed with fears of nuclear war and his own mortality? Is he demented as a 49-year-old father and husband to be digging a fallout shelter in his backyard? Is the world mad because people are apathetic about the Bomb and nuclear war?

O'Brien also introduces several familiar themes from his other works: the role of memory to establish connections within one's life and the role of imagination to escape chaos, explore possibilities, and influence behavior; Cowling's continuing quest to establish control and order in his chaotic life; relationships between fathers and children; and the politics of living with global political forces (the Vietnam War and nuclear war). Further, as is true with all of O'Brien's novels, this book examines personal choices and their significance in revealing the character of those making the decisions. Once again courage, cowardice, passivity, and commitment become competing elements in these selections. Three particularly significant quandaries involve literal and figurative flee-or-fight decisions: One requires a response to a draft notice; the second involves a commitment to the antiwar movement; the last decision relates to living in a precarious world. Together, Cowling's resulting choices, according to O'Brien in several interviews, establish this central character as "the only hero I've written" because he "manages to do for the most part what he thinks is right" (Naparsteck, Interview, 5).

Readers might question some of Cowling's motives for his so-called heroic actions, and on occasion O'Brien admits that under certain circumstances other O'Brien characters might be considered heroes. Nevertheless, Cowling seems to fulfill O'Brien's central definition of a hero as someone displaying a "correspondence between moral judgment and one's behavior in the world" (McNerney, Interview, 11), manifested in Cowling's real and symbolic acts of going underground. As a child, he hides under a basement Ping-Pong table to assuage his fears of nuclear war; as a young adult, he lives in an underground network of draft resistors and war protesters to escape the Vietnam War; and as a 49-year-old father and husband, he digs an underground sanctuary to keep his nuclear family intact and protect them from nuclear destruction.

Innocence

This first stage of Cowling's development lasts from age 12 through his college graduation, a point at which he must choose between entering the military or fleeing the draft. With its portrait of William's unusual personality and inherited or conditioned fears, the first major section ("Fission") contains many of the humorous and bizarre incidents in the book, particularly Cowling's relationships with two doctors (one a family physician and the other a child psychiatrist) and with the strange members of an antiwar group at his college. These sections are also a study of the conflicting roles of Cowling's imagination as the origin of both disorder (doom) and order (hope) in his life. At the same time, in this section O'Brien sensitively portrays the growing pains of a precocious young boy desperately attempting to be normal and to give his father "the son he deserved" (*Nuclear,* 42). Young Cowling lives in an average middle-class family that "pursued all the average small-town values" (*Nuclear,* 11). But the "extra-sensitive" and "even a little cowardly" Cowling is different from the other kids, as he struggles with frightening daydreams and his unappreciated conviction that "the world wasn't safe for human life" (*Nuclear,* 10). His request to his parents for a Geiger counter rather than a chemistry set only emphasizes his differences. He, like Paul Berlin as a youth, has an active imagination, one that conjures up visions of bombs, missiles, and annihilation, as well as possibilities for saving the world. At a young age, he understands the disturbing realities of the world and acknowledges the seriousness of living in it.

As a result, Cowling is different from the typical innocent central character in the traditional war initiation story who is filled with romantic notions of war, courage, and individual conduct. Quite the opposite, the youthful Cowling faces the truth as he recognizes the horrors and consequences of nuclear war, acknowledges his fears, and understands, like soldier-author Paul Berlin, the fragility of imagination: "A wonderful faculty, but sometimes it gets out of control, starts rolling downhill, no brakes, and all you can do is hang on for dear life" (*Nuclear,* 62). Even so, Cowling is out of control, unable to prevent this knowledge from leading to unhealthy obsessions and paranoia. He is also ignorant of the degree of people's apathy, including that of his sympathetic parents, toward the potential end of the world. Engaging in meaningless routines of Cold War drill and mind-numbing rituals of daily life, Americans are simply impervious to the realities ("nuclear war and sirens and red alerts"). Furthermore, Cowling is inexperienced at relaying his vision to others and unaware of the personal commitment and passion needed for addressing such momentous political issues (the evolution and responsibilities of politicization). On a personal level, he is unsure how to achieve order and control in his own life within the utterly chaotic nuclear age. Because of these truths, doubts, and instabilities, Cowling struggles with a horror of becoming crazy. He walks a fine line between sane and bizarre behavior as he acts according to his seemingly unheroic philosophy of life—"safety": "to seal myself off from potentially threatening situations. Locked doors were essential. Solid walls and a solid roof—shelter" (*Nuclear,* 56).

Cowling's first significant act of establishing some control and a sanctuary in his life occurs in 1958 when, for the first time, he flees underground to escape the terrors of the real world. This 12-year-old builds a fallout shelter in his basement using the family Ping-Pong table, cardboard boxes, newspapers, charcoal briquettes to absorb the radiation, and piles of lead pencils, which, his father gleefully notes, are really made of graphite. The act, which brings comfort to Cowling in the form of a peaceful night's sleep, evokes derisive laughter from his caring but confused parents and sparks their suspicions that their son is not normal.

This first instance of going underground and its attendant feelings of control and safety will become a recurring memory and a symbol of safety and inner peace for the 49-year-old narrator. Later, to assuage his parents' concerns about his behavior, the adolescent Cowling attempts to establish some outward normalcy in his life by carrying on lengthy phone conversations with Sarah Strouch, a popular high-school cheerleader. The chats, however, are imaginary; no one is on the other end of the line. Soon after, the Cuban missile crisis causes Cowling to experience constipation (the beginning of a Paul Berlinesque fixation with his bowels), headaches, and a breakdown—all resulting in a trip to a psychiatrist who seems to have worse problems of loneliness, insecurity, and doomsday visions than Cowling. In a humorous plot twist, the unstable doctor becomes the young man's patient.

In 1964, as American involvement in Viet Nam accelerates and nuclear threats remain, Cowling takes his visions and fears with him as he goes off to a college located 10 miles from the Little Bighorn battlefield (site of a much earlier episode of mass destruction) and 40 miles from the Strategic Air Command's (SAC) northern missile fields. His classmates seem no different from the townspeople of Fort Derry, if not worse: They "so daringly refined the meaning of mediocrity. A dense, immobile apathy. Ignorance on a colossal scale" (*Nuclear*, 77). For Cowling, safety and control in this setting emerge through his major in geology as a model of "how the world could be and should be. . . . Calm and stable" (*Nuclear*, 79). His imagination also provides temporary stability: "It's true, I lived in my head, but my head was a secure residence. There were no fracture lines" (*Nuclear*, 81).

Soon, his uncontrollable inventiveness creates inner disorder as images of missiles rising from their silos in Kansas and scenes from the Vietnam War fill his head. To regain control, Cowling makes the first of several key decisions in his life as he acts to educate his fellow students about political realities. As a symbol of his nascent politicization, he stands alone in the cafeteria every Monday holding a sign, "THE BOMBS ARE REAL," to protest nuclear craziness and the Vietnam War, a confused and dangerous war that Cowling views as conveying the world closer to doomsday. This protest begins Cowling's efforts to publicize his concerns, leave the safety of isolation, and demonstrate a commitment to his visions of good and bad possibilities. His silent protest also attracts allies—"The Committee." This group of four other campus outcasts, including cheerleader turned antiwar activist Sarah Strouch, support Cowling's efforts. These student radicals, especially Sarah, who becomes Cowling's lover, are eager to escalate the level of protest and subversive acts, but William, consistent with his philosophy of safety first and "never take chances," wants to continue with passive demonstrations.

Not unfamiliar with death and destruction because of having grown up in a funeral home, Sarah plays a very prominent role in this novel. She combines traits of the adventurous, troubled, and sexually provocative Addie from *Northern Lights* and the wise Sarkin Aung Wan from *Going After Cacciato*. In her passionate commitment to the intensity and allure of domestic guerrilla terrorism waged against America's involvement in Viet Nam, she anticipates Mary Anne Bell's aggressive attraction to combat in "Sweetheart of the Song Tra Bong": " 'This goddamn war. I hate it, I *do* hate it, but it's what I'm here for. I hate it but I love it' " (*Nuclear,* 196). For Cowling, Sarah becomes lover, guide, and catalyst. Although she matches Cowling in the intensity of her obsessions and moments of craziness, she does not believe in safety and isolation from the world. She is assertive, passionate, committed, and adventurous—all the attributes that the timid Cowling lacks. "She was out to change the world, I was out to survive it" (*Nuclear,* 186). Accordingly, their relationship is doomed from the beginning, a relationship for which William cannot imagine a happy ending. Initially, Cowling perseveres in both his relationship with Sarah and in the Committee's escalating protests against the war. Like his counterparts Paul Berlin and Paul Perry, also onlookers, he is dragged along by the momentum, "My own role was minimal" (*Nuclear,* 123).

Echoing Sarkin Aung Wan's urgings to Berlin to commit himself to a personal peace, Sarah presses William to commit himself to this public peace movement: "She told me to pay attention to my dreams. . . . 'You can't straddle fences forever. In or out. Let me know' " (*Nuclear,* 137). Like the timid Berlin, Cowling resists commitment and puts off the decision: "But no decisions. Vaguely, stupidly, I was hoping for a last-minute miracle. In Paris they were talking peace, and I wanted the miracle of decision deferred into perpetuity. I wanted resolution without resolve" (*Nuclear,* 138). This stage of William's innocence ends with his draft notice in the summer of 1968 after he has graduated from college. Like O'Brien in *If I Die* and Berlin, he can no longer postpone making decisions or acting on his fears and convictions—in or out!

Experience

With the "Fusion" section, O'Brien tests this central character, as he has
Paul Perry and Paul Berlin, through a series of difficult decisions Cowling must make as he confronts the self, people, and global politics.
Specifically, how does a nonviolent person promote his knowledge and
beliefs throughout a world that increasingly requires violent action to
gain attention for these beliefs? Hence, this section examines in detail
one of O'Brien's major themes in the book: "the whole question of how
and why we become politicized and depoliticized" (McCaffery, Interview,
141). Specifically, Sarah, driven by personal need for attention and commitment ("wanted to be wanted") and a public motivation to protest a
war that deeply offends her, becomes very politicized; at the same time,
Cowling, with values of passivity, love, peace, and personal safety, moves
in the opposite direction. Consequently, despite the exaggerated characterizations of the members of the Committee with their wacky personal
traits, motives, and activities, O'Brien superficially but sympathetically
portrays the antiwar movement's goals, disagreements, and methods
(violent and nonviolent protest). In a way, this section presents the flip
side of the battlefield scenes and moral issues found in O'Brien's Vietnam War narratives. The underground network of the antiwar movement is a different army with a different agenda carried out in a different setting, but it encounters some of the same concerns with training,
organization, strategy, commitment, control, courage, and power confronting a conventional army.

    Within this political context, Cowling begins his second stage of
development by encountering, from a new position, author O'Brien's
recurring moral and political dilemma of fighting or fleeing. Analogous
to his choice to flee under the Ping-Pong table in the "Fission" section,
Cowling must decide for a second time whether to run—this time figuratively underground. In this instance, like the real O'Brien before him
and the fictional Tim O'Brien in The Things They Carried after him,
Cowling must choose whether to enter the army or become a draft resis-
tor. Unlike in his other books, O'Brien downplays his central character's
decision. Thus, compared to Berlin's and the two O'Briens' torturous
decisions about commitment or flight, Cowling's decision is rather
straightforward, primarily because he has the wholehearted support of
his parents for resisting the draft and the logistical support of Sarah and
her links to an extensive underground antiwar network. As Cowling
ponders the options, familiar reasons for absconding surface ("Certain

blood for uncertain reasons": *Nuclear,* 16, and the desire not to die); and Sarah, like Sarkin, urges commitment to principles and action, " 'Sooner or later you have to walk' " (*Nuclear,* 163).

In contrast to the agonizing dilemmas in the other books, opposition arguments (entering the war) in this novel are nonexistent, or not articulated, and Cowling's imagination plays a limited role in exploring options. After failing to secure a medical deferment (the safe alternative), Cowling ultimately chooses to flee and go underground for the second time in his life. Yet his decision, despite O'Brien's claims of heroism for his central character, seems unheroic and without conviction; his decision to bolt is based on the personal-safety argument articulated in *If I Die.* Although downright selfish, this justification is consistent with Cowling's value of safety and his belief that nothing is worth dying for: "I was running because I couldn't envision any other way, because the dangers exceeded the reach of my imagination. Safety I said. Nothing else. Not honor, not conscience. All I wanted for myself was a place to ride out the bad times" (*Nuclear,* 170).

Cowling's choice forces him to experience the realities of life on the run and the responsibilities of political protest and terrorism. Operating from a safe house in Key West, Florida, Cowling soon learns that decisions have a price and lead to other difficult decisions. Thus, his choice to become a part of the underground network requires, as Sarah forcefully explains, a commitment to the guerrilla war against the Vietnam War: " 'Crawl out of your goddamn hidey-hole' " (*Nuclear,* 186). Sarah also asks for a personal commitment to their relationship. Like Paul Perry and even Paul Berlin, William must suddenly confront his passivity and lack of courage when dealing with these people and issues. Still, for a confirmed pacifist, his eventual decision to commit himself to Sarah and her war is similar to his earlier choice to avoid the draft, more of a sleepwalking default than resolve: "It was gravity. Something physical, that force that keeps pressing toward the end" (*Nuclear,* 160).

Like Paul Berlin marching at the end of Third Squad, William is again dragged along by Sarah and the Committee, this time to a terrorist training base in Havana, Cuba, for a lengthy basic-training session on domestic terrorism conducted by psychotic drill sergeants Ebeneezer Keezer (Vietnam veteran) and Nethro. Here the recruits train in weaponry, listen to stories about the evils of American involvement in Viet Nam, including a story familiar to O'Brien's readers about American soldiers' indiscriminate slaughter of water buffaloes. Once again, Cowling finds himself with disorder in his life and confusion about his options and want of courage: "Coward I thought. . . . I did not want to kill, or die, yet I did not want to do this thing we would now be doing. I had no zeal. For me, it was just a ride, and there were no convictions beyond sadness" (*Nuclear,* 193). The results of these feelings of disorder and helplessness for Cowling are paralyzing. In a Berlinesque moment of fear and panic on the firing range, Cowling loses control of both his weapon and his bowels: " 'This development,' said Ebeneezer Keezer, 'gives scared shitless a whole new meaning' " (*Nuclear,* 213).

Because Cowling fails terrorist training, he spends his three-year tour of duty in a "rear" job as a courier within the underground network. The experience in Cuba has forced him to evaluate his heart and solidify his conviction that "there is nothing worth dying for." As Sarah's war of bombs, break-ins, and protests at selective service offices escalates to the point that she becomes a radical celebrity with her story in *Newsweek,* Cowling retreats more and more into the security of anonymity and the state of noninvolvement. He ponders the definition of craziness—"a lapse of imagination"—and daydreams of romance and imaginary conversations with Bobbi, a quirky poet-flight attendant he met on a flight to Key West. In contrast to the real life of conflict and confrontation offered by Sarah, Bobbi represents an imaginary life of mystery, escape, and a happy ending. As Cowling daydreams about Bobbi, these brief retreats into imagination parallel Berlin's escape into the imaginative journey to Paris, but without similar connections to reality and without psychological, moral, and political significance. In Cowling's situation, imagination is not a heuristic tool.

Finally, typical of an initiation story, Cowling is tested for a second time, as he is forced to adjudicate competing values and to act—by neither gravity nor fear. Similar to Berlin's response at the imaginary Paris Peace Talks, William eventually acts out of conviction, knowledge, and faith in the restored active powers of an imagination enabling him to see the gap between what was and what might be: "I knew my limits. I also knew my heart" (*Nuclear,* 219). Finding his values of love for his family, nonviolence, and safety inconsistent with his life in the underground, Cowling twice acts courageously to restore control over his life.

First, with the help of another member of the Committee and guided by his principles, he destroys 14 cases of M-16 semiautomatic rifles stolen by Sarah's group and intended for use in escalating antiwar activities. Next, he returns home to Fort Derry, and his gradual reintegration into society culminates with his surrender to the authorities. Soon after (1977), he receives a pardon from President Carter, along with 10,000 other draft resistors, and enters a graduate program in geology (again studying the hard, real, and stable rocks). This stage of Cowling's involvement with global politics, in this case the Vietnam War and the "war" against the war, is over. Like many pieces of modern war literature structured around a three-part pattern of an individual's innocence, experience, and consideration, this second stage ends with Cowling, echoing the words of Hemingway's Frederic Henry ("that life was over"), declaring a separate peace ("For me, at least, the war was over": *Nuclear,* 299.), and affirming his sanity ("If you're sane, I realized, you take the world as you find it": *Nuclear,* 302.).

Consideration—Aftermath

In O'Brien's third section of this novel, "Critical Mass" (a point at which a nuclear chain reaction is sustainable), the sane and in-control Cowling enters a period of postwar, apolitical calm and consideration. He exhibits a renewed desire not to hide from the world but to live in it: "What I wanted above all was to join the world, which was to live and to go on living. . . . I didn't give a damn about missiles or scruples, all I wanted now was my life, the things of the world. . . . I was hard and sane and practical" (*Nuclear,* 302). With this section, the book frankly becomes more cartoonlike but not necessarily funnier. The exaggeration is more pronounced, the events more bizarre, and the inconsistencies greater.

As memories occur at a dizzying pace, the narrator recalls the next 14 years of his life. In short order, Cowling discovers a uranium deposit in the Sweetheart Mountains; he and the suddenly amoral Committee sell the mining rights to Texaco for 25 million dollars; Cowling, accompanied by Sarah, who wants to continue their relationship, searches for Bobbi— a decision leading to a strange love triangle. Cowling marries Bobbi, and they have a daughter. The Committee, without Cowling, steal a nuclear warhead and store it at Cowling's home in the mountains. Sarah dies from encephalitis; the Committee die in a government raid on a safe house in the tropics; and "flashes" of nuclear disaster again torment William. These snapshot memories lead the narrator to the present time of the book, April through July of 1995, and the five "Quantum Jumps" chapters interspersed throughout the three major sections. These five divisions form the core of the consideration-aftermath stage of his life and function as the observation-post chapters of this novel.

In these sections, like Paul Perry and Paul Berlin, Cowling confronts issues of love, commitment, courage, and optimism. In April 1995, at age 49, Cowling once more finds his life out of control, his imagination active, his sanity questionable, his fears for his family's safety growing, and his sense of the world's fragility increasing. Again, as O'Brien explores the unstable mind of his central character, William withdraws from life and literally and figuratively goes underground. This time Cowling's quest for safety, security, and sleep to allay his fears requires a fallout shelter in Cowling's backyard, not a Ping-Pong table in a basement. He spends three months digging this underground shelter in the hope of reestablishing control in his life: "After a life of insomnia and midnight peril, the hour has come for seizing control" (*Nuclear,* 4). Cowling's apocalyptic incantations dominate these chapters—"Bombs are real," "Doom," "Kansas is on fire"—but like Paul Perry's father's predictions of a nuclear holocaust, these warnings from the self-labeled "voice of reality" go unheeded in the deaf, "sanitized" world and within his own family. Is Cowling crazy for digging, or is the world crazy for ignoring the possibilities and not digging? Is this digging a sign of courage (facing the realities of life in the nuclear age) or cowardice (another selfish escape from the world)? Are Cowling's resurrected visions of the end of the world a continuation of childhood dreams, or, in 1995, do they now have more legitimacy and urgency?

Within this context, William, like Paul Perry and Paul Berlin, faces a difficult choice of how to live one's life, in this case in the nuclear age, and how to imagine a happy ending for this life. Such a decision requires action, courage, and guidance. For the last time, Cowling must also confront issues of love, control, family unity, flight, and madness. As he shovels out the hole, his mind jumps among memories, present thoughts, and visions of the end of the world symbolized by the Titan II missiles in their Kansas silos. Also, like Paul Perry and Paul Berlin, he hears voices urging various responses. Cowling listens to three guides as he decides whether to give up his underground retreat and live in the world or to dynamite the hole with his wife, daughter, and himself inside. The latter choice will save his family from experiencing the horrors of a nuclear war, and it will keep this nuclear family together forever—the ultimate act of commitment and love according to Cowling's confused thinking.

One guide is the bizarre and sometimes humorous voice of the hole, a talking shaft that is Cowling's subconscious. As Cowling's digging becomes more desperate and as the frequency of dialogues between Cowling and the hole increases, this voice becomes more vocal and assertive. It speaks in riddles, prophesies doom, plays word-association games, reaffirms Cowling's sanity, and urges William to "Do it" (blow up the hole). This advice seems to be a nuclear-age parody of the logic behind the famous quote from an American officer in Viet Nam rationalizing that American troops destroyed a Vietnamese village in order to save it from the Vietcong. In fact, one of Bobbi's poems to William during this time seems to affirm such a mode of thinking: "Remember this / as though in backflash: / A bomb / A village burning. / We destroyed this house / to save it" (*Nuclear,* 228). Accepting the hole's advice is to reject faith in possibilities, to acknowledge the failure of imagination to create a happy ending, and to embrace nothingness.

Two other voices are those of family members. The first of these is Bobbi, who speaks to William through her poems and whose desire to leave her husband and take their daughter with her (destroy the nuclear family) has been one of the catalysts for Cowling's excavation. Bobbi, who according to Cowling cannot process hard data, articulates through her poetry of "clean metaphors" and "clean language" an abstract vision of life that Cowling, the self-styled realist, quickly rejects. In Cowling's words, she, like the world, is "drugged on metaphor, the opiate of our age" (*Nuclear,* 143). The other guide is Melinda, Cowling's irreverent, brave, practical, and precocious 12-year-old daughter. Her role anticipates that of daughter Kathleen in *The Things They Carried.* Her voice prevents Cowling from escaping entirely into his thoughts, visions, and the hole as she questions her father about the digging and his sanity. Like Sarah years earlier, she also urges him to come out of his "hidey hole."

In the book's last chapter, a quantum-jumps chapter, Cowling sits in the hole with the firing device in his hand and his drugged family near him. He wavers between action—blowing the hole—or inaction. He feels "powerful and powerless" (*Nuclear,* 347), a condition also ascribed to Paul Berlin. Reality, in the form of his daughter's voice, intrudes as Cowling for the third time makes a key decision. He chooses life over death, love over nothingness, sanity over insanity, and a happy ending over a final ending. Just as Paul Perry in *Northern Lights* emerges from Pliney's Pond with a renewed commitment to life, so William Cowling emerges from his hidey hole with a similar resolve. Thus, as is true with *Northern Lights* ("Not so bad after all") and *Going After Cacciato* ("Maybe so"), this novel ends optimistically, with an affirmation of possibilities and the power of imagination to counteract madness.

O'Brien again explores the nature of courage, the use of imagination, and the redemptive power of love. Cowling's decision seems to combine the "feminine" courage of love and assimilation offered by Grace Perry and embraced by Paul Perry at the end of *Northern Lights* and the common courage of endurance and responsibility described in *If I Die in a Combat Zone* and displayed by Paul Berlin. Cowling's decision to live justifies O'Brien's labeling his character a hero. In choosing not to flee but to live in a chaotic world (the more difficult path), Cowling accepts his and everyone else's mortality. In the process, he acknowledges the paradox of living sanely in such a world—"To live is to lose everything, which is crazy, but I choose it anyway, which is sane. It's the force of passion. It's what we have" (*Nuclear,* 357). He also remains true to his values of peace, safety, love, and family unity. Above all, Cowling reaffirms the power of imagination to create hope and order in the midst of chaos and uncertainty: "I will take my place in the procession from church to grave, believing what cannot be believed, that all things are renewable, that the human spirit is undefeated and infinite, always. . . . I will endure. . . . I will live my life in the conviction that when it finally happens [nuclear war] . . . that E will somehow not equal mc^2" (*Nuclear,* 359). Such optimism might be equated with Lieutenant Corson's assessment of the odds on the real Cacciato's actually arriving in Paris: " 'Miserable odds, but—' " (*Cacciato,* 395).

Cowling, a veteran of the war of the living, has traveled on a path from innocence, through experience, to consideration-aftermath, but his journey, like those of Paul Perry and Paul Berlin, remains unfinished and full of possibilities—good and bad. This significant feature of all O'Brien's novels—the mystery of events and human existence—once again surfaces at the end of this book as readers ponder William Cowling's future. Such mystery and possibilities assume an added universal significance for readers as they consider the world's future—a happy ending or nuclear destruction?—and live with this uncertainty in their own lives.

Chapter Five

Mysteries of Life, Love, and Storytelling: *In the Lake of the Woods*

"There are certain mysteries that weave through life itself, human motive and human desire" (*Lake,* 30). "It is my view that good story-telling involves, in a substantive sense, a plunge into mystery of the grandest order" ("Magic," 179). Together these two quotes, the first from O'Brien's most recent novel and the second from his essay published in 1991, suggest the purpose, essence, and power of *In the Lake of the Woods* (1994): exploring mysteries of the human spirit—our own and others'—and forcing readers to live with uncertainty. Readers of O'Brien's previous works are accustomed to books containing mysterious characters and endings with possibilities. But in his 1994 novel, O'Brien takes his notion of mystery as a fundamental characteristic of great storytelling to a new level. Not only does he forge a mystery story, but he also gives readers an opportunity to solve the mystery from a series of scenarios provided by the book's narrator. Or readers can simply accept the inconclusive ending as a reality of life—a postmodernist notion that some important things can never be known. Thus, the fictional narrator-author of *In the Lake of the Woods* observes in one of his many footnotes in the book, "if you require solutions, you will have to look beyond these pages. Or read a different book" (*Lake,* 30).

Despite its unusual form and inconclusive ending, the book is at times comfortable for readers of O'Brien's other works. Present are familiar O'Brien themes—courage, cowardice, fear, control, memory, imagination, politics, fathers and sons, choices, tricks of the mind, and the crucible of war. Another important subject is the human heart, specifically an individual's all-consuming need for love and the impact of such an obsession on actions and character: cowardice, deception, manipulation, atonement, and guilt. As the culminating work in O'Brien's collection of integrated books, beginning with *If I Die in a Combat Zone,* this 1994 novel also marks one more opportunity for O'Brien to explore moral issues and the nature of storytelling from new or familiar angles.

Consequently, moral, thematic, historical, and narrative issues that author O'Brien has always cared about—and always will—appear in this novel. Furthermore, the work brings readers full circle, back to confessions, observations, and events in his war autobiography *(If I Die)* that relate to the My Lai massacre (March 1968) and soldier O'Brien's experiences in this area (Pinkville) one year later. The book also resurrects husband-wife and father-son relationships of *Northern Lights,* metafictional passages and memory-imagination relationships of *Going After Cacciato,* narrative tensions between happening-truth and story-truth in *The Things They Carried,* and the fragile heart and mind of William Cowling in *The Nuclear Age.* Also emerging from *In the Lake of the Woods,* through the portrait of the central character (John Wade) and the confessions of the unnamed narrator, is the recurring question of how much of author O'Brien's own life, heart, and mind appear in this piece of fiction, which O'Brien has labeled his "most personal" (Herzog, Interview).

Finally, the confluence of several recurring writing influences shapes this work. The opening chapter has a Hemingwayesque feel in establishing the setting, mood, and symbols for the entire novel. Also present are the narrative ambiguity and mystery of character and plot at the heart of Faulkner's stories (particularly *Absalom! Absalom!*), the multiple endings and metafictional techniques of Fowles's *The French Lieutenant's Woman,* and Shakespeare's themes of honor, guilt, and responsibility. Perhaps the most pervasive literary influence to be detected is that of Joseph Conrad. Specifically from *Heart of Darkness,* the intertwined relationship of narrator and character (Marlow and Kurtz) involved in psychological and moral heart-of-darkness journeys foreshadows a similar relationship between the unnamed narrator and John Wade in O'Brien's novel. In addition, O'Brien's themes of flight, cowardice, guilt, self-deception, and redemption, along with shifting points of view and manipulations of time sequences, are reminiscent of Conrad's novel *Lord Jim.*

Because *In the Lake of the Woods* extensively recapitulates O'Brien's literary influences, themes, craft, and life, examining this novel serves as an appropriate conclusion to this critical commentary on O'Brien's life and works. This final chapter of my book also leads readers deeper into the heart and mind of Tim O'Brien—son, soldier, and author. Moreover, O'Brien notes that this work caps almost 25 years of writing that has created a significant intertextuality for his six books, beginning with *If I Die in a Combat Zone:* "I had the feeling when I was finishing *In the Lake of the Woods* that there was a finality in my career in a funny way, like the idea about which you [Herzog] are organizing this book [for Twayne]. And even if I do write another novel, there's a sense of finality to this one" (Herzog, Interview).[1]

In the Lake of the Woods, O'Brien's fifth novel, is not his most critically acclaimed work, but it has received numerous accolades, including *Time* magazine's designation as "the best work of fiction published in 1994" and the 1995 James Fenimore Cooper Prize for the best novel based on a historical theme. This book is also O'Brien's most commercially success-ful. It was designated a "Book-of-the Month Club Selection"; hardback sales far surpassed those for *Going After Cacciato* and *The Things They Carried;* and Hallmark Entertainment adapted the novel for a made-for-TV movie appearing on the Fox network in March 1996 (starring Peter Strauss and Kathleen Quinlan). Whether the novel is O'Brien's best work to date is open to debate. Nevertheless, it is his most ambitious and experimental novel in terms of form, narrative strategies, and blend of fact and fiction. It is also O'Brien's most controversial work, shrouded in mysteries of O'Brien's own life, enigmas surrounding the central characters in the book, mystery created by a storyteller who does not know the ending for his story, and mystery of an author (O'Brien) who in several interviews immediately after the novel's publication indicated that he might not write another novel.

Although O'Brien finds writing any book a slow and agonizing process, we do know that this project was particularly difficult. He post-poned working on the story for several years after the publication of *Nuclear Age,* focusing instead on *The Things They Carried* because, in O'Brien's words, " 'I knew *The Things They Carried* would be well re-ceived. . . . And I knew I'd get nailed on this one. I was afraid of doing it, of writing a book without an ending—or seemingly without an end-ing. Those are real terrors for a writer who publishes once every four or five years. On top of that, to be writing about deceit, knowing I'd be using footnotes from my own life—I didn't want to face it.' "[2] Once he resumed working on *In the Lake of the Woods* in 1990, O'Brien, over the next four years, faced numerous personal crises: the breakup of his mar-riage; bouts of depression and guilt; his sister's serious illness; and the death in January 1994 of his long-time friend and publisher Seymour Lawrence. In addition, approximately eight months before publication of the novel, he embarked on a well-publicized and emotional return trip to Vietnam, followed closely by the end of a four-year relationship with a Harvard graduate student, to whom the hardback edition of this 1994 novel is dedicated. These accumulating events took their emotional and physical toll on O'Brien and may have contributed to the visceral and confessional quality of the novel. O'Brien also made a significant last-minute change in the book's final chapter (after a bound galley version had been distributed to some reviewers prior to the late October publication date). An added passage lessens the likelihood that readers will give greater credence to one possible ending (John Wade murdered his wife) than to the others (Kaplan 1995, 218).[3]

Since its publication, the book has received generally favorable reviews, with critics familiar with O'Brien's previous works praising the experimental narrative structure, the metafictional elements, the inconclusive portrait of the central character's heart and mind, and the novel's moral themes. A few critics note the book's appeal to a broad audience through its popular subjects of marriage, murder, politics, and war. Other comments about the book and author include "O'Brien's bleakest novel to date," "as gripping as a thriller," "admirably ambitious," "an epistemological adventure," and "a master evoker of shadowy psychological states." Some of the negative comments focus on the fragmented nature of the book (really three novels in one—murder mystery, politics, and My Lai); the "narrative pyrotechnics that never pay off"; the inconclusive ending, which seems like a "curious hedging of bets on the author's part"; the lack of character development for the female protagonist; and the absence of a "distinctive" presence to the book's central character, a criticism also leveled at O'Brien's characterization of William Cowling in *The Nuclear Age*. Even so, all the reviewers praise the passages and chapters in the novel devoted to the My Lai massacre. They note that O'Brien's use of reconstructed events, historical evidence, and individual psychological responses to the incident leads to an ambitious, powerful, and incriminatory treatment of a shameful episode in the Vietnam War, one that artists tend to avoid. "O'Brien's fictionalized use of that compacted atrocity of the war results here in some of the finest, hardest writing imaginable on the subject. Pop culture may be sucking the larger truths out of Vietnam by making it an entertainment vehicle, but in O'Brien's hands, the war is still deep, immediate and irredeemable."[4]

Unfortunately, some critics narrowly view the novel as simply one more piece of O'Brien's war fiction, with Minnesota's lakes and woods serving as a metaphor for the jungles of Vietnam.[5] A few others reduce the novel's multiple themes to one: "[N]o human project can survive the contamination of exposure to the Vietnam War."[6] This book, however, is much more than O'Brien's attempt at writing a Vietnam aftermath novel in the mode of Larry Heinemann's *Paco's Story,* Philip Caputo's *Indian Country,* or Bobbie Ann Mason's *In Country.* These novels focus on Vietnam veterans struggling with Post-Traumatic Stress Disorder (PTSD) brought on by their participation in the Vietnam War. Such a description is much too limiting for *In the Lake of the Woods,* as O'Brien traverses a broader moral, psychological, and experiential terrain.

On the surface, the plot, as is true with O'Brien's best works, is relatively simple. The story is told by an unnamed narrator, a Vietnam veteran, who has become obsessed with the disappearance in the fall of 1986 of a wife and husband: Kathy Wade and John Wade, a Vietnam veteran and defeated candidate for the U.S. Senate. They disappeared about a month apart in the Lake of the Woods, a 1,485-square-mile body of water located in north central Minnesota and southwest Ontario, Canada (a place where O'Brien and his family frequently spent summer vacations). Embarking on almost five years (1989–1994) of "hard labor" involving interviews, research, and consideration of possibilities, the narrator, a self-described "biographer, historian, medium" (*Lake,* 30), attempts the difficult task of reconstructing the lives of John and Kathy Wade. He also speculates about the circumstances related to their disappearances.

The known facts in this story are relatively few. Near the end of a 1986 Democratic primary campaign in Minnesota for the U.S. Senate, one candidate leaks information to the press that John Wade, the front-runner in the contest, participated in the My Lai massacre (16 March 1968). According to the story, Wade was a member of Lieutenant William Calley's company that under Calley's direct orders killed civilians, perhaps as many as 500, at the subhamlet of Thuan Yen, Viet Nam, designated on American military maps as My Lai (4).[7] This information, which proves to be true, devastates Wade's political fortunes and further undermines his already shaky marriage. After losing the election in a landslide, John and Kathy escape the media scrutiny by traveling to a cottage located on Lake of the Woods. After a few days of sorting through their marriage, emotional states, and future, Wade wakes up one September morning to find that Kathy has mysteriously vanished. This disappearance has occurred after John Wade's night of nightmares, "electric sizzle," and bizarre behavior. An extensive search by local authorities is unsuccessful. About a month later, as suspicion grows among local townspeople and authorities that John Wade may have murdered his wife, Wade also leaves the cottage, navigating a motorboat due north on the Lake of the Woods. After delivering a rambling monologue over a shortwave radio, he dumps the radio into the lake and disappears without a trace.

Suicide, flight, or rendezvous with Kathy—the narrator's story ends with many unanswered questions and various possibilities. But as is true in his other novels, O'Brien moves beyond the novel's simple plot and skillfully crafts a complex integrated novel containing several prominent features: material from O'Brien's related writings; a complicated narrative structure mixing fiction with historical details about My Lai and subsequent military investigations; an intriguing autobiographical relationship involving author O'Brien, the narrator, and John Wade; and O'Brien's ongoing consideration of the art of storytelling.

Related Writings

A short story, two earlier O'Brien characters, and a few short articles written by O'Brien become helpful background for readers of *In the Lake of the Woods*. First, "Loon Point," a 1993 *Esquire* magazine short story, depicts love, a passionless marriage, marital infidelity, and lies—subjects and situations that O'Brien borrows from the story and introduces into the novel as prominent features of John and Kathy Wade's marriage. Next, although O'Brien claims on most occasions to have had few of the typical postwar adjustment problems experienced by some Vietnam veterans, throughout his writing career he has been interested in the plight of these troubled veterans, with his characters Harvey Perry *(Northern Lights)* and Norman Bowker *(The Things They Carried)* falling into this category. Finally, in a series of articles about veterans, O'Brien also explores issues relevant to Vietnam veterans. In "Prisoners of Peace," a 1974 article for *Penthouse* magazine, O'Brien anticipates the form of *In the Lake of the Woods* by combining fictional scenes from basic training and combat with facts and interviews related to Vietnam veterans' adjustment problems, especially those involving PTSD, drugs, alcohol, unemployment, and crime. In this sympathetic piece, O'Brien paints a depressing portrait of Vietnam veterans as "loners in war, we are loners in peace."[8]

In "The Violent Vet," a more optimistic and radically different 1979 essay for *Esquire,* O'Brien criticizes the television and movie industries' widely presented stereotypes of Vietnam veterans as unemployable, suicidal, violent, and addicted to drugs. After arguing that the absence of reliable data about Vietnam veterans clouds the debate over adjustment problems, he suggests that "typical" Vietnam veterans, including himself, may be adapting better than originally believed: "What about the human capacity for renewal and self-repair? What about those—like me—who came home from war psychologically intact?"[9] Again in 1981, O'Brien published an essay about Vietnam veterans ("We've Adjusted Too Well") in *The Wounded Generation* (a study of post-Vietnam America), where he continues to refute notions that an abnormally high number of Vietnam veterans suffer adjustment problems. In this article, however, O'Brien laments that these veterans have forgotten too easily the harsh lessons of war that Vietnam taught.[10] Such issues of veterans' responsibility for their actions, failure of their memory, opportunities for renewal, and their emotional and psychological assimilation clearly influence key portions of *In the Lake of the Woods,* especially as they relate to John Wade's post-Vietnam adjustment.

The most intriguing background piece for this novel, however, is O'Brien's widely read account of his 1994 return to Viet Nam, "The Vietnam in Me," for the *New York Times Magazine.* As described by O'Brien, this article is a companion piece to *In the Lake of the Woods,* with portions of the book prefiguring passages in this confessional essay. The novel "was pretty much finished by the time I went to Viet Nam. And so the structure of the article, the focus of the article, relied heavily on work I had already done on *In the Lake of the Woods.* I borrowed phrases from the book, for example, and plunked them into the article" (Herzog, Interview). The result is a highly personal and shocking article that, like the novel, combines personal and historical facts with an exploration of an individual's heart and mind—O'Brien's. Along the way, O'Brien briefly recounts the My Lai massacre and testimony from participants and victims. He also comments on America's willful forgetfulness, or indifference, about this evil, and he criticizes the "narcissism" of American policy related to American MIAs at the expense of Viet Nam's missing soldiers. In addition, O'Brien chronicles two events in his own life. The first of these is the author's return in February 1994 to places within Quang Ngai Province, Viet Nam (including My Lai), where he served his tour of duty. Such a return, anticipated in the fictional story "Field Trip" *(The Things They Carried),* resurrects memories of dead friends, especially Chip Merricks; feelings of fear, guilt, hatred, and "black, fierce, hurting anger"; and a flashback to an experience in a flooded rice paddy that appears to be the basis for his fictional story "In the Field" in *Things.*

The second event O'Brien relates is the subsequent end of his relationship with girlfriend Kate, who encouraged the reluctant O'Brien to visit

Viet Nam and accompanied him on this 25th anniversary return. These two intertwined events have, according to O'Brien, a thematic connection to events in *In the Lake of the Woods:* "It [the article] was confessional about going to a war I hated. It was confessional about doing bad things for love, which is one of the essential themes both of the book and of the article—things we do in the name of love" (Herzog, Interview). Finally, in this article, O'Brien also reveals in a "little blunt human truth" the current pain in his life. Among other things, these revelations, in contrast with comments in some interviews about a relatively smooth postwar adjustment, suggest that O'Brien's Vietnam aftermath has not been as uncomplicated as he has frequently described: "For too many years I've lived in paralysis—guilt, depression, terror, and shame" ("Vietnam," 56).[11] Included in these bits of truth are glimpses into O'Brien's current "war of the living": "suicide on his mind," treatment for depression, memories of "some pretty painful feelings of rejection as a child," and the central source of his guilt and pain as described in words also appearing in *If I Die* and *The Things They Carried:* "I have written some of this before, but I must write it again. I was a coward. I went to war" ("Vietnam," 52). Like his central character from *In the Lake of the Woods,* O'Brien went to war out of a need for love, to be loved by his family and his country, a choice that has become the principal source of his own version of Vietnam PTSD. Thus, as a glimpse into the soul of O'Brien the soldier and author, this *Times* article is also a window into the hearts and minds of John Wade and the narrator of his story.

The My Lai Massacre

One question interviewers and readers pose to O'Brien about *In the Lake of the Woods* involves his inclusion of the My Lai massacre as the central episode in John Wade's Vietnam War experience. As noted earlier, although episodes involving atrocities by American soldiers in Viet Nam frequently appear in novels about the war, fiction writers, to date, have avoided the events during the four hours of American activity at My Lai (4) on 16 March 1968. After much deliberation, O'Brien took a big risk and decided to make this event and its aftermath a key moral touchstone in this novel. To accomplish this, O'Brien emphasizes historical accuracy (including names and sworn testimony of actual participants) with a minimum amount of fictionalization (minor alterations in events, a few additional characters, and invented dialogue).

From a literary perspective, O'Brien's reconstructing this despicable episode of American involvement in Viet Nam makes storytelling sense. The actions at My Lai and the subsequent military cover-up are evil events at the core of a book exploring the nature of evil, dark secrets, and lies. Thus, the incident provides author O'Brien with an instant dramatic moral issue. From a historical perspective, O'Brien's including this incident also seems appropriate because of its widespread social and political significance. Once the story of My Lai was reported to the American public, culminating in a series of reports in the *New York Times* (November 1969), the information further undercut America's innocence about the whole Vietnam experience. Subsequent testimony during military hearings and the trials of participants fueled already heated public debates about the morality of American involvement in this war; American military strategies of attrition and body counts; the culpability of the military chain of command for incidents at My Lai; conditioned savagery; and individual moral issues of courage, cowardice, responsibility, and restraint. Consequently, with such moral and historical importance, this incident becomes a perfect crucible for examining the character of a participant—the protagonist in O'Brien's novel. As O'Brien notes about his choice of using My Lai, "It is one of the choices I really am pleased with myself for having made. . . . If I was going to have an atrocity or have an act of real evil, the My Lai thing presents itself with such rich possibilities and such rich unresolved possibilities in the national psyche and in the human psyche" (Herzog, Interview).

Another obvious explanation for the presence of My Lai in this novel is that the author has a soldier's connection to the area. Since O'Brien's unit operated in My Lai one year after the massacre (although at the time soldiers were unaware of what had transpired earlier), the veteran-author has carried with him throughout his writing career strong memories and feelings about this infamous place. Even in 1969, Son My village (of which My Lai is a subhamlet) and the surrounding area of Quang Ngai Province, which was heavily populated with Vietcong and communist sympathizers, held a particular terror for O'Brien. One year after the incident at My Lai, O'Brien's unit was still patrolling the area that American troops called Pinkville. They faced villagers' hostility, endured hostile fire from an unseen enemy, and lost friends to mines. In this place, O'Brien was slightly wounded, and close friend Chip Merricks (Chip in *If I Die* and Curt Lemon in *Things*) stepped on a mine and died. For O'Brien such experiences engendered feelings of terror, helplessness, hatred, revenge, and combat numbness described in *If I Die in a Combat Zone*.

In his chapter "My Lai in May" from this war autobiography, O'Brien also tentatively explores the nature of conditioned savagery and evil, important issues related to the incidents at My Lai. Using his own unit's feelings and reactions as a guide as he writes about atrocities, he does not justify the My Lai massacre but suggests how the special features of guerrilla warfare in Viet Nam and the resulting emotional and psychological factors contributed to such abhorrent acts on both sides. Almost 20 years later in his *New York Times* article, O'Brien reiterates his feelings as a scared soldier patrolling the area of My Lai: "I more or less understand what happened on that day in March 1968, how it happened, the wickedness that soaks into your blood and heats up and starts to sizzle. I know the boil that precedes butchery" ("Vietnam," 53). Nevertheless, as O'Brien notes in this article, the men in his company, unlike those in Lieutenant Calley's, did exercise moral restraint. The same cannot be said for John Wade in *In the Lake of the Woods*. Overall, such issues of evil and control become important moral themes in the My Lai sections within this novel and obviously connect with similar themes examined from different angles in earlier works.

Finally, O'Brien includes the My Lai episode for two additional reasons. First, in preparing for his return trip to that area in 1994, he spent considerable time in the U.S. National Archives researching the after-action reports of American military units in Viet Nam. He also reviewed testimony from the Peers Commission (Department of the Army's 1970 preliminary investigation of My Lai) for inclusion in *In the Lake of the Woods*. As a result of his research, O'Brien became outraged at the descriptions of the savage acts of brutality and murder perpetrated by American soldiers on the Vietnamese civilians. He felt that he could not allow the My Lai incident to fade from America's conscience. To keep the memory of this event alive, he chose to adopt a primarily historical perspective, with some minor changes and additions, rather than a fictionalized view. Such a decision led to his use of participants' real names and their actual testimony: " 'There was a revenge factor in keeping those names alive. . . . The naming of names became increasingly important to me as I went along. I'd go through the Peers Report and find a man confessing to multiple murders listening to Meat Loaf tapes. The lengths these guys went to justify what they did and somehow keep themselves alive as human beings.' " (Kahn, Interview, 69). O'Brien's other rationale for using the My Lai episode in his novel is his most personal and painful. As O'Brien continues to work through his own guilt about the war and the horrors visited upon the Vietnamese, John Wade's guilt for his presence and actions at My Lai becomes a surrogate for O'Brien's own "abiding-to-my-grave" guilt for his participation in the Vietnam War, an "act of real evil": "And the My Lai thing, in its grotesque, monstrous, obscene evil, seems a fitting corollary. It seems to fit the sense of evil that I live with day by day and the guilt I feel day by day" (Herzog, Interview).

Structure

In addition to taking a risk with the content of this novel, O'Brien also experiments with the form. Readers of his previous works will, however, find in this book's structure some similarities to his previous novels, in particular shifting time sequences among past, present, and future, as well as interwoven chapters grouped according to distinct content and functions. The thematic links among these three groups are O'Brien's recurring tensions between fact and fiction, happening-truth and story-truth, and the failure of memory versus the power of imagination.

The controlling voice in the novel is that of an unnamed author-narrator who, several years after the Wades' mysterious disappearances, tells his speculative story containing biographical facts, reconstructed events, evidence, and possibilities. At the heart of the narrative are the 16 chapters in the book devoted to the narrator's factual and speculative reconstruction of the days immediately preceding and following the disappearances in the fall of 1986. Also within these chapters is the narrator's similar reconstruction, through flashbacks, of the history of the Wades' lives and marriage up to this point. Interspersed among these sections are seven chapters titled "Evidence" and eight chapters titled "Hypothesis." The evidence chapters contain the results of the narrator's background research (the historical present of the novel). Among a variety of materials, he includes transcripts of interviews with fictional characters (for example, Richard Thinbill), excerpts from biographies and memoirs of American presidents (Wilson, Johnson, and Nixon), actual testimony from the Peers Commission's investigation, instructions from magic handbooks, passages from books on psychiatric disorders among war veterans, and quotes related to military massacres in U.S. history.[12] Also included in one of the evidence chapters is a glossary of real magic tricks and one trick that author O'Brien invented just for the occasion. It foreshadows magician John Wade's disappearance (Herzog, Interview): *"Causal transportation:* A technical term for an effect in which the causal agent is itself made to vanish; i.e., the magician performs a vanish on himself" (*Lake,* 192). Another curious piece of important evidence is a quote from Crossan's *Historical Jesus* that seems to be indirect advice from the narrator to his audience: "If you cannot believe in something produced by reconstruction, you may have nothing left to believe in", (*Lake,* 294). In these evidence chapters and one hypothesis chapter are footnotes, in many of which the narrator documents the real and also the fictional sources of information he cites. Within the 133 footnotes themselves are 12 introspective or analytical footnotes in which the narrator speaks to readers about himself, his characters, his writings, a trip to My Lai in 1994, and the mysteries of love and the human heart.[13]

Since the narrator's story about the Wades ends without a definitive explanation of their mysterious disappearances, the third group of chapters ("Hypothesis") contains the narrator's possible explanations. Most of these focus on Kathy's disappearance: She meets a secret lover, panics and walks away along a dirt path, accidentally drowns in the Lake of the Woods after her boat hits a sandbar, loses her way on the lake, commits suicide, is murdered by her husband, or is part of an elaborate scheme culminating in the reunion of John and Kathy after their separate disappearances. These chapters are similar to the daydream sections of *Going After Cacciato.* Like Paul Berlin beginning with the fact of Cacciato's disappearance, the narrator starts with one of the last known facts about the Wades' disappearances—Kathy is gone—and the last known fact, "John Wade was a pro. He did his magic; then walked away. Everything else is conjecture" (*Lake,* 266). The narrator proceeds to imagine what might have happened (future time of this novel), but, unlike Berlin, he envisions several possibilities ranging from the romantic (both are alive and together) to the bleak (Wade murdered his wife).

As is true with O'Brien's integrated sections in all of his previous works, the author deftly interconnects the three major chapter groupings and the footnotes. For example, using his familiar technique of iteration, O'Brien presents the same important information and significant incidents from different perspectives within the different sections, thus creating new angles of interpretation. Equally important, each section becomes a commentary on the others or a source of information integrated into the other sections. Thus, the hypothesis chapters are logical extensions of clues about the Wades and their disappearances presented in the other two sections. Furthermore, the evidence chapters provide knowledge crucial to the narrator's reconstruction of the Wades' history and to his creation of logical hypotheses about their ultimate fates. In addition, these evidence chapters, with a preponderance of material taken from real sources, establish tensions between happening-truth and story-truth, the real world and a fictional world. These chapters lend a trial-like atmosphere to the novel as readers use the circumstantial evidence and new perspectives to judge the characters and select the hypothesis best fitting readers' interpretations of the evidence. Finally, the footnotes—bibliographical and autobiographical—further heighten the tension between fact and possibility throughout the sections and closely link the narrator to John Wade. As a result of this connection, the evidence, hypothesis, and story sections, which focus on Wade, have another connecting thread as they offer possible insights into the heart and mind of the unnamed author-narrator and—possibly—into O'Brien himself.

The Author-Narrator

Who is telling the story of John and Kathy Wade, the "I" of the footnotes in this novel? Is he, like the author-narrator of *The Things They Carried,* a fictional voice who reveals some details about his life and writing that coincidentally parallel those of the real Tim O'Brien? Or, despite some obvious fictional details, is this primarily the voice of the real Tim O'Brien of the nonfictional *If I Die in a Combat Zone,* the Tim O'Brien of numerous interviews with critics and reviewers, and the Tim O'Brien of the confessional article in the *New York Times Magazine?* Is author O'Brien engaged in more elaborate game playing with his unnamed narrator, or is he speaking directly to his readers? As one might expect, answers to these questions can be debated, but a reasonable response seems to be that the narrator is a combination of the real Tim O'Brien and a fictional character who might even be an extension of the narrator in *The Things They Carried.*

As noted earlier, O'Brien in an interview admits to using "footnotes from my own life," and several of these passages seem easy to spot. For example, footnote number 67 describes the narrator's trip to Viet Nam in 1994 with stops at the Son My Memorial and a visit to Thuan Yen (My Lai 4). Such a description parallels the details of O'Brien's return to Viet Nam described in the *New York Times Magazine.* Also, footnotes 88 and 127, which describe the narrator's own Vietnam War experiences and feelings, echo similar material found in *If I Die in a Combat Zone,* the magazine article, and interviews where O'Brien confesses how his combat experiences led to rage and guilt. For example, compare the narrator's remembered feelings about warfare presented in *In the Lake of the Woods* with those articulated by O'Brien in a 1994 interview. The first is from the novel: "Twenty-five years ago, as a terrified PFC, I too could taste the sunlight. I could smell the sin. I could feel the butchery sizzling like the grease just under my eyeballs" (*Lake,* 199). The second is from a 1994 interview: " 'I still feel that sizzle inside me sometimes,' O'Brien continues . . . 'The sins I committed over there . . . which were not murder. . . . Mostly sins of keeping my mouth shut. Of not saying, "Hey, stop doing that" ' " (Kahn, Interview, 69). In another footnote (#127) enumerating key scenes also described in O'Brien's war autobiography, the narrator mentions the death of Chip Merricks, who is the Chip from *If I Die* and Curt Lemon in *The Things They Carried.* Consequently, readers might feel comfortable in concluding that the narrator's other personal observations in some of these footnotes are also the words of author Tim O'Brien speaking directly to readers about the content of this novel and the writing process: "My heart tells me to stop right here, to offer some quiet benediction and call it the end. But truth won't allow it. Because there *is* no end, happy or otherwise" (*Lake,* 301).

Perhaps other passages also contain the words of son, soldier, and veteran Tim O'Brien engaging in confession and self-analysis: "One way or another, it seems, we all perform vanishing tricks, effacing history, locking up our lives and slipping day by day into the graying shadows" (*Lake,* 301). O'Brien, however, does not want readers to arrive at a comfortable resolution of this tension between the actual worlds of soldier-author O'Brien mixed with the following invented words of an unnamed soldier-author: "And so I lose sleep over mute facts and frayed ends and missing witnesses" (*Lake,* 266). Nevertheless, he does want readers to analyze carefully the heart and mind of this narrator-author, who becomes the second most important character in the novel.

From the footnotes, it is clear that the narrator is a Vietnam veteran turned author who served from 1969–1970 in Quang Ngai Province and walked the land of Pinkville and My Lai. From that experience, he is left in 1994 with a "handful of splotchy images," the "mystery of evil," and knowledge of how and why the My Lai massacre occurred. While researching for over four years his story of the Wades' disappearances, he has become obsessed with his task and fascinated as well as frustrated by the inherent conflict in this quest: "The human desire for certainty collides with our love of enigma" (*Lake,* 266). His exhaustive research involving libraries, archives, and interviews has produced "twelve notebooks worth" of information (biography, history, and speculation) and more to come. Moreover, as two characters in the evidence chapters indicate, this research has led to the narrator's emotional and intellectual preoccupation with the Wades' story: " 'She was my *sister*—why can't you [narrator] just leave her alone? It's like you're obsessed' " (*Lake*, 191); " 'You should think about getting back to your *own* life' " (*Lake*, 295). But the narrator finds himself on an epistemological quest that he cannot abandon, one that can lead to ultimate control and power—knowledge of an "other." Like soldier Paul Berlin who wishes to unlock the secrets of his own heart—"somehow working his way into that secret chamber of the human heart, where, in tangles lay the circuitry for all that was possible, the full range of what a man might be" (*Cacciato*, 73)—so this narrator wishes to move beyond the surface details of John Wade's life and into his buried life. He is preoccupied with unlocking the secrets and evil of John Wade's soul: "What drives me on, I realize, is a craving to force entry into another heart, to trick the tumblers of natural law, to perform miracles of knowing" (*Lake*, 101).

Ultimately, like Paul Berlin, the narrator of *The Things They Carried*, and even Marlow in *Heart of Darkness*, this author-narrator is also on a quest to know himself (Kaplan 1995, 198). He wishes to unlock the secrets of his own heart and mind and to confront his own acts of evil: "In a peculiar way, even at this very instant, the ordeal of John Wade—the long decades of silence and lies and secrecy—all this has a vivid, living clarity that seems far more authentic than my own faraway experience. Maybe that's what this book is for. To remind me. To give me back my vanished life" (*Lake*, 298). The narrator ultimately fails in his quest to know definitively "the implacable otherness" (*Lake*, 101) of John Wade and to discover the answers to the disappearances, but the narrator confronts some of the dark secrets in his own life: "I have my own secrets, my own trapdoors. I know something about deceit. Far too much. How it corrodes and corrupts" (*Lake*, 295).

For the narrator, the ultimate fascination of John Wade's life is that in Wade's experiences and character the narrator sees so much of himself, including sins of inaction and deceit, as well as a failure of memory. Finally, for author Tim O'Brien the fascination of both John Wade and the unnamed narrator is his connection to them. To some degree in this book, author O'Brien, through the souls of Wade and the narrator, confronts his own secrets about family, love, war, guilt, courage, and deception: "That dynamic of withholding [in O'Brien's life] was at the center of the book [*Lake*]. And I magnified it radically in the book, so that huge things were being withheld. Nonetheless, it [the book] was confessional in the way that it was extremely personal" (Herzog, Interview).

John Wade

Similar to moral choices O'Brien has made in his own life, choices involving courage, love, and deceit also shape the life of John Wade. In addition, details from O'Brien's life make their way into Wade's character: a Minnesota upbringing, the turmoil and loneliness of growing up with an alcoholic father, magic and politics as means of gaining acceptance, choices driven by a need for love, and the psychological fallout from Vietnam War experiences. In commenting on these connections, O'Brien notes that "I wake up the way John Wade wakes up, screaming ugly, desperate, obscene things. . . . That 'Kill Jesus' refrain [Wade's mantra] that goes throughout the book, that sense of self-hatred to the point of where's God, comes from my own soul. It isn't a made-up refrain; it is a real one out of my own life" (Herzog, Interview).

But Wade, nicknamed "Sorcerer" in Viet Nam because of his magic tricks, is much more than a surrogate for Tim O'Brien. Wade becomes a complex fictional character who can be viewed from many angles—victim, villain, coward, enigma, soldier, veteran, politician, husband, son, and magician. Like the novel's symbolic settings of water and woods, Wade's heart and mind are mysterious, dark, and deep: "Beyond the dock the big lake opened northward into Canada, where the water was everything, vast and very cold, and where there were secret channels and portages and bays and tangled forests and islands without names" (*Lake*, 1). In the biographical sections of Wade's story, the narrator attempts to navigate this uncharted territory.

As the characteristics of John Wade unfold, readers discover he shares some key traits with central characters in O'Brien's other novels, but he is also very different. Like Paul Perry, the adult John Wade carries with him the memories and emotional trauma from his childhood relationship with an overbearing father. Like Paul Berlin, Wade has a powerful imagination, one that since childhood he has used to dream and to escape the pressures of the real world. Also like Berlin the soldier, Wade is a "barely competent" soldier borne along by the war. Like William Cowling, Wade obsessively fears the loss of love; like the fictional Tim O'Brien of *The Things They Carried,* the civilian Wade struggles with the memories of his war experiences. Finally, like all of O'Brien's central characters, Wade is a control freak striving to establish order and

authority in a chaotic life punctuated by significant decisions. All the
while, he grapples with competing tugs of memory and imagination.

Yet Wade differs from O'Brien's other male characters in his aggres-
siveness, plans for his life, and an initial optimism about the future—all
symbolized by "a huge white mountain" described in the first chapter.
Unlike Paul Perry, Paul Berlin, and William Cowling, who often act out
of "sleepwalking default," Wade is ambitious to a fault and decisive in
making many decisions: "He had the sequence mapped out; he knew
what he wanted" (*Lake,* 34). Consequently, he is a successful public figure: three years as a legislative liaison in Minnesota, six years as a state
senator, lieutenant governor at age 37, and Democratic candidate for
the United States Senate at age 40. Much of Wade's drive and character
has been fueled by incidents in childhood, the Vietnam War, and marriage: " 'It wasn't just the war that made him what he was. That's too
easy. It was everything—his whole *nature*' " (*Lake,* 27). As a result, he
acts in response to shame, guilt, a fear of loss, a desire to be virtuous,
and an "electric sizzle" present at an early age. Most of all, like author
Tim O'Brien and his other central characters, John Wade acts out of a
need for love: "At times, too, John imagined loving himself. And never
risking the loss of love. And winning forever the love of some secret
invisible audience—the people he might meet someday, the people he
had already met. Sometimes he did bad things just to be loved, and
sometimes he hated himself for needing love so badly" (*Lake,* 60).
Accordingly this character displays intense love and noble intentions,
along with moments of manipulation, deception, humiliation, and rage.
Such a combination ultimately leads to "Loser by landslide at forty-one"
(*Lake,* 5) and two missing persons.

Wade's public and private lives are defined by four important relationships, with each providing readers with a slightly different outlook on
Wade's life: relationships with his father, the Vietnam War in general and
the My Lai massacre in particular, politics, and his wife. The first of these,
a new angle on O'Brien's recurring examination of father-son relationships, involves some prominent details from O'Brien's own life. When
John Wade is 14, his father, Paul, commits suicide by hanging himself in
the garage (not a fact from O'Brien's life). Up to this point, Paul Wade, an
alcoholic institutionalized on a few occasions, made John's childhood very
difficult with taunts about John's weight, his grades, and his magic. The
father could at times also be very witty, smart, and attentive to his son.

To escape these moments of rejection and his feelings of inadequacy
and to establish some command over his life, the young John Wade

often retreated into his imagination. These tricks of the mind—"mirrors"—enabled him to create pleasant images of his father and a happy relationship filled with love. Wade also became a magician. He practiced tricks for long hours in front of a mirror in the basement in order to master the gestures, the posture, and his style. Magic became an extension of the mirrors in his mind, as he conjured up illusions and manipulated an imaginary audience. After his father's death, the young boy attempts, through the imaginary mirrors, to assuage his anger at this loss (the first instance of the "sizzle in his blood" and the mantra "Kill Jesus") and to hold on to his father. Thus, like the narrator of "The Lives of the Dead" in *The Things They Carried,* Wade keeps his dead father alive by carrying on imaginary conversations or imaginary searches for his father. For the young Wade, these mirrors and magic serve as means for escape, knowledge, control, power, and possibilities of happiness in his life. Later, as an adult, Wade becomes even more obsessed with control as he attempts to hide parts of his character, protect his secrets, and manipulate others. He again retreats into tricks of the mind and into real tricks as ways of sustaining his sanity during difficult moments and of erasing unpleasant memories, "The mirror made things better" (*Lake,* 66). The adult Wade also holds on to the tumultuous relationship with his dead father, who still influences his choices: "More than anything else John Wade wanted to be loved and to make his father proud" (*Lake,* 208).

The second important relationship in Wade's life is his involvement with the Vietnam War. He goes to war because it is unavoidable (something that cannot be manipulated) and out of love (a desire to be loved by his dead father). Once in the war, his magic tricks, mental and physical, keep him sane in a chaotic, aimless existence, and they give him status among his fellow soldiers. In fact, Sorcerer finds himself "in his element," completing two tours (1968 and 1969) in a place where secrets abound and "magic was everyone's hobby and where elaborate props were always on hand" (*Lake,* 72). But along the way, Wade journeys deep into a metaphysical heart of darkness (evil magic) as he confronts evil in his own heart and in those of others.

The depravity in others appears at My Lai as Sorcerer's company, under the command of Lieutenant Calley, conducts a search-and-destroy mission that degenerates into four hours of unrestrained murder of the subhamlet's inhabitants—old men, women, and children. Wade looks on silently, passively, helplessly, "This was not madness, Sorcerer understood. This was sin" (*Lake,* 107). At one point during the killing, the terrified Wade runs away, only to shoot an old man with a hoe. And as the dazed Wade lies in an irrigation ditch filled with bodies, he shoots fellow soldier PFC Weatherby. The immediate and long-term fallout from these four hours of murder and Wade's failure to stop or report the incident complete Wade's heart-of-darkness journey. If shooting the old man and Weatherby is purely reflex, as Wade believes, his retreat afterward into mirrors and tricks of the mind damns him. Wade gives himself over to "mind-cleansing" tricks, as the mirrors allow his memory to fade, his culpability to disappear, and his plans for his life to become paramount: "He gave himself over to forgetfulness. 'Go away,' he murmured. . . . and the little village began to vanish inside its own rosy glow. Here he reasoned, was the most majestic trick of all. . . . This could not have happened. Therefore it did not. Already he felt better" (*Lake,* 108–9). Later, before leaving Viet Nam at the end of his second tour, Wade performs one more magic trick. This time, he revises the past and preserves his future by removing all evidence from the military files that he was present at the massacre.

Once out of the army, Wade turns to politics, a natural career path for a magician and someone seeking love, acceptance, and control: "Politics *was* manipulation. Like a magic show: invisible wires and secret trapdoors" (*Lake,* 35). He also views the political arena as a place for doing good and "salvaging something in himself." But guided by Tony Carbo, his cynical and opportunistic campaign manager, John soon replaces altruistic notions with a win-at-all-costs strategy. Magic replaces substance, and the secrets of Wade's past once again disappear behind the mirrors, self-delusion, and one more magic trick of reinventing himself for the voters: "The intent was never evil. Deceit, maybe, but the intent was purely virtuous" (*Lake,* 234). Soon, however, the dark secret of My Lai, revealed by Wade's opponent near the end of the campaign, leads to disorder and the end of the political tricks. Wade flees, not behind the mirrors in his mind, but with Kathy into the water and forests of Lake of the Woods—a different mirror: "[T]he wilderness was all one thing, like a great curving mirror, infinitely blue and beautiful, always the same" (*Lake,* 1).

The third important relationship in Wade's life, which becomes the principal subject of the story, is Wade's 20-year relationship with Kathy, including 17 years of marriage. Despite other parallels among the lives of the narrator, Tim O'Brien, and John Wade, nothing in the novel directly suggests that features from this marriage have an autobiographical connection for either the narrator or O'Brien. This marriage, domi-

nated by Wade, displays the same tensions of love, loss, control, manipulation, and deception characterizing Wade's other relationships. Without question, Wade is the central character developed in this novel, but
through analyzing this marriage, O'Brien begins to develop Kathy's
character, more so than with any of his female characters in the other
novels. For the most part, O'Brien presents Kathy's life in relationship
to Wade's, but moments occur, especially within the hypothesis and evidence chapters, when Kathy's inner life, independent of her husband,
emerges. She is variously described as being "private," "passionate," and
"independent" and having secrets of her own, including an affair with a
dentist and a penchant for occasionally vanishing. She also is a dreamer
who desires a life away from politics. After 20 years with Wade, Kathy
still loves her husband; yet she, like the central character in O'Brien's
short story "Loon Point," finds herself in a marriage lacking energy,
spontaneity, passion, and happiness: "Maybe, in the end, she blamed
herself. Not for the affair so much, but for the waning of energy, the
slow year-by-year fatigue that had finally worn her down. She had
stopped trying" (*Lake,* 253).

Unquestionably, the blame for this exhausted marriage lies with John
Wade, and certainly O'Brien fails to carry through in fully developing
Kathy's strength and independence, as well as her mind and heart. Consequently, O'Brien allows her to submit rather easily to Wade's plans for
their lives, including an abortion when she becomes pregnant at a key
point in her husband's political career. Occasionally, Kathy, like the spiritual guides of O'Brien's other novels (Grace Perry, Sarkin Aung Wan,
and Sarah Strouch), offers her husband other paths for his life: children;
romance symbolized by talk of a trip to Verona, the city of Romeo and
Juliet; and honesty. She also is a voice of reality after the election—"We
lost. That's the truth—we lost" (*Lake,* 21). Although Wade deeply loves
his wife, he rejects such options and assessments and tries to avoid the
realities of his life and marriage. Hence, he desperately holds on to this
relationship forged by incongruous elements of love, deceit, and tricks.

From the first days in 1966 of the Wades' relationship, John spies on
Kathy. At first, the activity is a game for Wade, one that he played earlier with his father. Later, although Kathy is aware of the spying, the
trick creates for Wade some mystery in their relationship as he enters a
hidden world with new angles of literal and figurative perspectives. Soon
the spying becomes an obsession for Wade, satisfying his need to have
absolute knowledge of this other person, manipulate her, control their
relationship, and prevent his losing her as he has his father. In the early

years of their relationship, before and after marriage, Wade believes they have become lost in each other's love like two snakes John sees in Viet Nam, "each snake eating the other's tail, a bizarre circle of appetites that brought the heads closer and closer until one of the men in Charlie Company used a machete to end it" (*Lake*, 61). After the war, as the white mountain of ambition, redemption, and acceptance beckons, Wade loses himself even more in the magic of politics. In doing so, he becomes oblivious to his wife's needs (a life away from politics) and finds himself in a relationship out of control. For John Wade, the trip to Lake of the Woods after the election is not only an escape from the public humiliation but also one last opportunity to restore happiness and order to his marriage. He wants to escape into imagination as he and Kathy plan, or pretend, the future.

After finishing this story of John Wade's various relationships, read-ers–like the unnamed author-narrator—are left with "supposition and possibility" about Wade's character and the outcome of his association with Kathy. Could a man who, in the narrator's own words, "was crazy about her [Kathy]" (*Lake*, 301) murder her in a moment of temporary insanity, or did he perform the ultimate magic trick of causal transporta-tion for both him and his wife, "one plus one will always come to zero" (*Lake*, 76)? Is Wade a helpless victim of life's trapdoors—choices deter-mined by a personality shaped by his life experiences? Is he an evil agent of his own demise, or does the narrator suggest a more sympathetic judgment: "Can we believe that he was not a monster but a man? That he was innocent of everything except his life" (*Lake*, 303)? In this novel of possibilities, many things are likely depending on the readers' inter-pretation of the facts, clues, and suppositions: "The angle makes the dream" (*Lake*, 286). And, as O'Brien fully intends, readers paying close attention to the narrator's story of Wade's life, along with significant citations in the evidence chapters, can engage in popular psychological analysis to excuse some of his contemptible thoughts, desires, and actions: son of an alcoholic; poorly trained soldier; veteran suffering from post-traumatic stress disorder; and a son engaging in a pathologi-cal search for a father, acceptance, and love. Other excuses include the ambiguity about the extent of Wade's participation in the events at My Lai—participant or onlooker? As Wade is about to disappear into Lake of the Woods, readers even encounter his rambling observations on his life and his argument that humans have limited choices in controlling outcomes in their lives: " 'We give ourselves over to possibility, to whim and fancy, to the bed, the pillow, the tiny white tablet. And these choose for us. Gravity has a hand. Bear in mind trapdoors. We fall in love, yes? Tumble, in fact. Is it *choice*? Enough said' " (*Lake*, 283–84).

Still, within the moral landscape of O'Brien's writings, despite the unexpected trapdoors, individuals have choices—opportunities to adjudicate competing moral values and to choose virtuous action (see the epigraph to *If I Die*). Accordingly, O'Brien's intentional ambiguity has a purpose. He wants readers to be cautious before labeling Wade a helpless victim of his childhood and adult experiences and glibly excusing his actions and deceit. Collaterally, O'Brien does not want readers to absolve American soldiers of their actions during the My Lai massacre because of their youth, the war environment, or the special character of the Vietnam War.

In directly assessing Wade's character and indirectly commenting on some traditional explanations for evil in war, O'Brien observes that Wade certainly has "a lot [misfortunes] to overcome in his life." Nevertheless, "all that material about his childhood, his love for Kathy, his background as a magician, and so on, those were the ordinary armchair psychology causal agents that we will point to. I put that stuff in, but at the same time, I went out of my way in that book to sort of denigrate it all. . . . The man had clearly, despite everything, the capacity to choose otherwise in his life, to choose well in his life" (Herzog, Interview). Consequently, as is true for O'Brien's central characters in his other novels, the moral measure of this soldier, husband, and politician emerges through John Wade's several difficult flee-or-fight decisions. As presented in the narrator's words, Wade's evaluation of his choices in these situations is that "the horror was partly Thuan Yen, partly secrecy itself, the silence and betrayal" (*Lake*, 272). Such a statement, similar to Marlow's narration of Kurtz's final estimation of his actions ("The horror! The horror!"), is the closest Wade comes to pronouncing self-judgment.

In the arenas of war, politics, and love, he has had opportunities to choose courageously. During the actual events at My Lai, Wade does not intervene, allowing the killings to continue. Soon after, when given the opportunity to act on the fictional Thinbill's pleas that they report the incidents at My Lai to the military authorities (an important moment representing the "inconvenient squeeze of moral choice": *Lake*, 214), Wade remains silent, tries to forget the occurrence through tricks of the mind, and attempts to deny his own culpability. Much later, in responding to Tony Carbo's questions about damaging secrets in the candidate's background, Wade simply lies. Perhaps the most damaging evasion of responsibility and honesty occurs in Wade's link with his wife. Wade has opportunities to act virtuously by confessing his sins—spying, My Lai, and the bad things done for love. On one occasion with Kathy he comes close to telling all, " 'I've *done* things' " (*Lake*, 74). Yet once again, Wade lacks the courage to act. Instead, he retreats into mind-numbing surface details of life, into political magic, into the mirrors in his mind, and finally into Lake of the Woods.

Two pieces of evidence in the novel suggest that the narrator and O'Brien believe Wade's greatest sins are his lying to others and to himself. The first passage from Dostoyevsky's *Notes from the Underground* appears in an evidence chapter and according to O'Brien (Herzog, Interview) is the "key quote" in those chapters:

> Every man has some reminiscences which he would not tell to everyone, but only to his friends. He has others which he would not reveal even to his friends, but only to himself, and that in secret. But finally there are still others which a man is even afraid to tell himself, and every decent man has a considerable number of such things stored away . . . Man is bound to lie about himself. (*Lake*, 145)

The second passage is from Wade's rambling monologue near the end of the novel and includes an intriguing pun: " 'Did I choose this life of illusion? Don't be mad. My bed was made, I just lied in it' " (*Lake*, 284).

Perhaps Wade's greatest lie is his claim that he does not recall what happened during the hours immediately preceding his wife's disappearance. The narrator in the final chapter suggests, however, that this failure of Wade's memory is indeed real, and Claude Rasmussen, who becomes a father figure for Wade, also believes this to be true. Of course, in this novel of magic and deception, anything is possible: victim or agent, murderer or grieving husband? As one might expect in assessing an O'Brien character, the answer is complicated. As O'Brien intends for all of his major characters, neither readers nor the narrator can gain full access into the human heart of John Wade. Mystery and ambiguity persist. Yet Wade, as portrayed by the narrator, appears to be a decent person who has made some evil choices in his life, all in the quest for love and all contributing to a life of deceit. Confession would have been the brave act for Wade and might have soothed his soul. Perhaps such a possibility is the motivation in this novel for the author-narrator and even for O'Brien to confess their sins.

The Magic of Storytelling

If *In the Lake of the Woods* recapitulates and extends the form and content present in O'Brien's previous works, then readers should anticipate that

in this novel O'Brien not only tells a story but also comments on the art
of storytelling. Appropriately, in this last novel, O'Brien—who appears
as a panelist at numerous writing conferences, teaches writing at various
workshops, and analyzes in essays and interviews the nature of fiction
and his own craft—extensively explores the nature and purposes of storytelling. As he has done so artfully in *Going After Cacciato* and *The Things
They Carried*, he once again examines storytelling with fresh insight.
O'Brien's observations emerge in this novel indirectly through his use of
magic as an extended metaphor for storytelling and directly through the
narrator's comments in the footnotes on the writing process and on the
contents of his story. To appreciate O'Brien's ideas about fiction presented in this novel, readers should first turn to his essay entitled "The
Magic Show," appearing in *Writers on Writing*. In this 1991 piece, O'Brien
compares the hobby of his youth—performing magic—with his "current
hobby"—writing fiction. He finds striking similarities between these two
art forms, including preparation, craft, purposes, "new realities and
truths," and relationships with the audience. Most of all, he links magic
and storytelling through the performers' and audiences' shared desire to
enter into the "mystery of things." O'Brien goes on to assert that for the
storyteller this interest means exploring the mystery of otherness as the
writer enters characters' minds and hearts. Also, according to O'Brien,
like the magician, "the writer of fiction . . . serves as a medium of sorts
between two different worlds—the world of ordinary reality and the
extraordinary world of the imagination" ("Magic," 178).[14]

In his novel, O'Brien takes these observations about the magic of storytelling and weaves them throughout the work. Consequently, metafictional passages appear in the evidence chapters and in a few of the footnotes, and O'Brien directly applies the principles of magic and mystery
in creating the novel's plot and characterizations. For example, throughout the evidence chapters instructional passages appear from an actual
1944 handbook written for novice magicians (Robert Parrish's *The
Magician's Handbook*). These sections explain the attractions of magic for
the performer ("a considerable feeling of personal power": *Lake,* 27) and
for audiences ("It is a paradox, a riddle, a half-fulfillment of an ancient
desire, a puzzle, a torment, a cheat and a truth": *Lake,* 96.).

The passages also describe the nature of magic tricks ("In every trick
there are two carefully thought out lines—the way it looks and the way
it is": *Lake,* 97.); and they advise the would-be magician ("You will
never explain your tricks [to an audience], for no matter how clever the
means, the explanation disappoints the desire to believe in something

beyond natural causes": *Lake,* 191.). Such observations about magicians, tricks, and audiences also suggest the relationships among author, story, and audience. Furthermore, within the footnotes, the author-narrator muses on the relationships among facts, fiction, imaginative reconstruction, truth, and lies. He also reiterates author O'Brien's notions of mystery, implacable otherness, and uncertainty as sources of both delight and frustration for storyteller and audience: "Nothing is fixed, nothing is solved. The facts, such as they are, finally spin off into the void of things missing, the inconclusiveness of conclusion. Mystery finally claims us" (*Lake,* 301).

With the narrator's closing phrase in the final footnote ("there is only maybe"—a typical O'Brien ending) and with the concluding sentence in John Wade's story (a question), Tim O'Brien ends this novel, as he has all of his other books, with possibilities. His own sleight-of-hand storytelling in the novel has been an intriguing parallel to John Wade's own tricks of the hand, mind, and heart throughout his life. And like the magician-politician John Wade, author Tim O'Brien has manipulated his readers with lies, "invisible wires and secret trapdoors" (*Lake,* 35). O'Brien maintains that "As a fiction writer, you live a life of fiction, deceit" (Herzog, Interview). But unlike Wade's evil magic, O'Brien's wizardry has been filled with entertainment, wonder, and instruction. Conjuring has become one more angle for O'Brien's ongoing exploration of the creative act: its foundation in experience, its synthesis of memory and imagination, its relationship to happening-truth versus story-truth, and the author's and characters' quests for knowledge of self and others.

O'Brien succeeds as a novelist because his writing is rooted in wonder and possibility that lead to important questions about the human heart and mind. In pondering these questions, he arrives at some truths along the way, but not the answers. "Absolute knowledge is absolute closure" (*Lake,* 266), a closure that for author O'Brien undercuts the purpose and attraction of storytelling for both the teller and the audience. In a similar way, absolute knowledge of Tim O'Brien and his writing is neither possible nor desirable. This critical examination of O'Brien's life and writings—angles of art and life—has provided some facts, a few truths, various perspectives, and numerous possibilities. Readers of this book, like the readers of *In the Lake of the Woods,* can now draw their own conclusions based on the evidence and their perspective: "The angle shapes reality."

Notes and References

Preface

1. As is now often common in Southeast Asian studies and in some dictionaries, I will be using the following spellings throughout this book to distinguish a country from a war experience. As stated in editor Robert Slabey's *The United States and Viet Nam: From War to Peace* (McFarland, 1996), *"Viet Nam* is an independent nation in Southeast Asia with its own people, language, and culture. *Vietnam* is an American formulaic identifying a continuing 'experience' in Southeast Asia (including Laos and Cambodia), in the United States, and elsewhere" (ix).

Chapter One

1. Don Ringnalda in a chapter of his book tells of a similar performance by O'Brien involving "On the Rainy River" in one of Ringnalda's classes on the Vietnam War at the University of Saint Thomas. Don Ringnalda, *Fighting and Writing the Vietnam War* (Jackson, Miss.: University Press of Mississippi, 1994), 102–3.

2. Martin Naparsteck, "An Interview with Tim O'Brien," *Contemporary Literature* 32 (Spring 1991): 7–8; hereafter cited in text.

3. Bruce Bawer, "Confession or Fiction? Stories from Vietnam," *Wall Street Journal* (23 March 1990): A13.

4. Tim O'Brien, *The Things They Carried* (1990; reprint, New York: Penguin, 1991), 38; hereafter cited in text as *Things.*

5. Tim O'Brien (unpublished interview with O'Brien conducted by Tobey Herzog on 11 and 12 July 1995 in Cambridge, Mass., at O'Brien's apartment); hereafter cited in text as Herzog, Interview. Unless specifically documented, general biographical information about O'Brien comes from this interview.

6. Brian C. McNerney, "Responsibly Inventing History: An Interview with Tim O'Brien," *War, Literature, and the Arts* 6 (Fall/Winter 1994): 5; hereafter cited in text.

7. Tim O'Brien, *If I Die in a Combat Zone, Box Me Up and Ship Me Home* (1973; reprint, New York: Dell, 1987), 20; hereafter cited in text as *Die.*

8. In a 1994 autobiographical article about his return trip to Viet Nam, O'Brien recalls "some pretty painful feelings of rejection as a child," and he describes himself at this age as being "chubby." Tim O'Brien, "The Vietnam

in Me," *New York Times Magazine* (2 October 1994): 52; hereafter cited in text as "Vietnam."

9. D. J. R. Bruckner, "A Storyteller for the War that Won't End," *New York Times* (3 April 1990): C15+; hereafter cited in text.

10. O'Brien notes that Erik Hansen, who is now employed in the Vermont educational system, has been involved to various degrees in editing all of O'Brien's books—except *In the Lake of the Woods*. What O'Brien values about Hansen's input is his friend's "philosophical responses," "textual responses," and his "attention to detail" (Herzog, Interview).

11. Barth Healey, "Flashes from the Foliage," *New York Times Book Review* (11 March 1990): 8.

12. Gail Caldwell, "Staying True to Vietnam," *Boston Globe* (29 March 1990): 75; hereafter cited in text.

13. A bit of interesting trivia to emerge from O'Brien's time as an intern for the *Washington Post* is his minor involvement in reporting the first event in what would become the Watergate scandal (and precipitate President Nixon's resignation in August 1994). O'Brien was the first *Post* reporter on the scene of what, at the time, was a minor story—the burglary (June 1972) at the Watergate Hotel and Office Complex in Washington, D.C. "When the call came in, they sent me [O'Brien] over to check it out. I think it was a Saturday. I was in the newsroom, and an editor came up and said, 'Go over to the Democratic National Committee Headquarters.' I was only there for an hour." "Bulletin Board," *St. Paul Pioneer Press Dispatch* (4 April 1990): 2D.

14. Larry McCaffery, "Interview with Tim O'Brien," *Chicago Review* 33 (1982): 136; hereafter cited in text.

15. Tim O'Brien, "The Magic Show," in *Writers on Writing,* ed. Robert Pack and Jay Parini (London: University Press of New England, 1991), 182; hereafter cited in text as "Magic."

16. Tim O'Brien, *In the Lake of the Woods* (1994; reprint, New York: Penguin, 1995), 288; hereafter cited in text as *Lake.*

17. Steven Kaplan, *Understanding Tim O'Brien* (Columbia, S.C.: University of South Carolina Press, 1995), 12–18; hereafter cited in text.

18. Gene Lyons, "No More Bugles, No More Drums," *Entertainment Weekly* (23 February 1990): 51; hereafter cited in text.

19. Catherine Calloway, "Pluralities of Vision: *Going After Cacciato* and Tim O'Brien's Short Fiction," in *America Rediscovered: Critical Essays on Literature and Film of the Vietnam War,* ed. Owen Gilman and Lorrie Smith (New York: Garland, 1990), 213; hereafter cited in text.

20. Tim O'Brien, *Going After Cacciato* (1978; reprint, New York: Dell, 1989), 1; hereafter cited in text as *Cacciato.*

21. Catherine Calloway, " 'How to Tell a True War Story': Metafiction in *The Things They Carried," Critique* 36 (Summer 1995): 249–50; hereafter cited in text.

22.   In Calloway's 1995 article on metafiction, she notes that "O'Brien draws the reader into the text [*Things*], calling the reader's attention to the process of invention and challenging him to determine which, if any, of the war stories are true" (249). Calloway also cites Patricia Waugh's definition of metafiction as a " 'term given to fictional writing which self-consciously and systematically draws attention to its status as an artifact in order to pose questions about the relationship between fiction and reality' " (250).

23.   Tim O'Brien, "Loon Point," *Esquire* (January 1993): 91–94. As I discuss in chapter 5, O'Brien incorporates elements of this story into the relationship between John and Kathy Wade in *In the Lake of the Woods*.

Chapter Two

1.   Eric James Schroeder, "Two Interviews: Talks with Tim O'Brien and Robert Stone," *Modern Fiction Studies* 30 (Spring 1984): 148; hereafter cited in text.

2.   O'Brien's letters sent home from Viet Nam were saved by his parents, but they were later lost in a flood in Worthington (Herzog, Interview).

3.   "Tale of Battle," *Times Literary Supplement* (19 October 1973): 1269.

4.   Chris Waters, "Everyman-at-Arms," *New Statesman* (4 January 1974): 24.

5.   Chester Eisinger, *Fiction of the Forties* (Chicago: University of Chicago Press, 1963), 21.

6.   Sandra M. Wittman, *Writing about Vietnam: A Bibliography of the Literature of the Vietnam Conflict* (Boston: G. K. Hall, 1989). Other helpful bibliographies of Vietnam War literature are John Newman's *Vietnam War Literature: An Annotated Bibliography of Imaginative Works about Americans Fighting in Vietnam*, 2d ed. (Metuchen, N.J.: Scarecrow Press, 1988) and Deborah Butler's *American Women Writers on Vietnam, Unheard Voices: A Selected Annotated Bibliography* (New York: Garland, 1990).

7.   Paul Fussell, *The Great War and Modern Memory* (1975; reprint, New York: Oxford University Press, 1989), 92; hereafter cited in text.

8.   Phillipe Lejeune, *On Autobiography*, trans. Katherine Leary (Minneapolis, Minn.: University of Minnesota Press, 1989), 4; hereafter cited in text.

9.   For a discussion of the roots, definitions, and some critical disagreements related to autobiography, see Robert Olney's "Autos*Bios*Graphein: The Study of Autobiographical Literature," *South Atlantic Quarterly* 77 (1978): 113–23.

10.   For a helpful discussion of narratives written by "Vietnamese exile writers," including Hayslip's and Tang's books, see the second chapter in Renny Christopher's *The Viet Nam War: The American War* (Amherst, Mass.: University of Massachusetts Press, 1995); hereafter cited in text.

11.   Thomas Myers, *Walking Point: American Narratives of Vietnam* (New York: Oxford University Press, 1988), 71; hereafter cited in text.

12.   Steven Kaplan, "An Interview with Tim O'Brien," *Missouri Review* 14, no. 3 (1991): 102; hereafter cited in text.

13.   Walter Capps, "The War's Transformation," *Center Magazine* 11, no. 4 (1978): 20.

14.   Phillip Caputo, *A Rumor of War* (1977; reprint, New York: Ballantine, 1978), xx.

15.   For a more in-depth discussion of American authors' portrayals of the Vietnamese, see my third chapter and also note #16 for chapter 3. Robert Olen Butler, who spent considerable time with the Vietnamese as an American military intelligence officer in Viet Nam and who speaks the language, has written novels and short stories that are some of the best American narratives presenting Vietnamese views and voices about the war, its aftermath, and Vietnamese communities in the United States.

16.   J. C. Levenson, Foreword, *The Works of Stephen Crane,* vol. 2 (Charlottesville, Va.: University of Virginia Press, 1975), xxxv.

17.   For a further discussion of O'Brien's narrative style in *If I Die*, see Eric James Schroeder's "The Past and the Possible: Tim O'Brien's Dialectic of Memory and Imagination," in *Search and Clear: Critical Responses to Selected Literature and Films of the Vietnam War*, ed. William J. Searle (Bowling Green, Ohio: Bowling Green State University Popular Press, 1988), 116–34.

18.   Roger Sale, "Fathers and Fathers and Sons," *New York Review of Books* (13 November 1975): 31; hereafter cited in text.

19.   J. A. Appleyard, *Commonweal* (5 December 1975): 597.

20.   Tim O'Brien, *Northern Lights* (New York: Delacorte/Seymour Lawrence, 1975), 45; hereafter cited in text as *Lights*.

21.   For an extensive discussion of this tripartite pattern in war novels, see my chapter 4.

22.   The Cuban missile crisis is remembered as one of the most potentially volatile confrontations in Cold War history. In mid-October 1962, American U-2 spy planes confirmed that the Soviet Union was installing nuclear missile sites in Cuba, just 90 miles off the southern coast of Florida. President Kennedy considered using preemptive air strikes to destroy the missile sites, but on Wednesday, 22 October, he announced that the United States would implement a naval blockade of Cuba to prevent Soviet ships from reaching the island. The President warned that any ship attempting to break the blockade would come under fire. The following day the blockade was activated. From that time until Sunday morning, 26 October, the United States and the Soviet Union entered into some of the most crucial negotiations in history. Fears of nuclear war increased each day. Eventually the Soviet Union agreed to remove the missiles. This event will also have a prominent role in O'Brien's 1985 novel *The Nuclear Age.*

23. Milton J. Bates, "Tim O'Brien's Myth of Courage," *Modern Fiction Studies* 33 (Summer 1987): 268–72.

24. Marie Nelson, "Two Consciences: A Reading of Tim O'Brien's Vietnam Trilogy: *If I Die in a Combat Zone, Going After Cacciato,* and *Northern Lights,*" in *Third Force Psychology and the Study of Literature,* ed. Bernard Paris (London/Toronto: Associated University Presses, 1986), 264–65.

Chapter Three

1. Michael Coffey, "Tim O'Brien," *Publishers Weekly* (16 February 1990): 61; hereafter cited in text.

2. For a discussion of these stories and O'Brien's changes before including them in *Going After Cacciato,* see Catherine Calloway's "Pluralities of Vision: *Going After Cacciato* and Tim O'Brien's Short Fiction."

3. Richard Freedman, "A Separate Peace," *New York Times Book Review* (12 February 1978): 1; hereafter cited in text.

4. Christopher Lehmann-Haupt, "Books of the Times," *New York Times* (2 February 1978): C17.

5. Philip D. Beidler, *Re-writing America: Vietnam Authors in Their Generation* (Athens, Ga.: University of Georgia Press, 1991), 11; hereafter cited in text.

6. For a list and discussion of which chapters fall into each category of fact, observation post, and daydream, see Dean McWilliams's "Time in O'Brien's *Going After Cacciato,*" *Critique* 29 (Summer 1988): 245–55.

7. See the following chapters: 14 (Frenchie Tucker and Bernie Lynn); 16 (Rudy Chassler); 20 (Pederson); 22 (Ready Mix); 31 (Billy Boy); 35–36 (Sidney Martin); 41 (Buff).

8. James Webb, *Fields of Fire* (Englewood Cliffs, N.J.: Prentice Hall, 1978), 201.

9. John Updike, "Layers of Ambiguity," *New Yorker* (28 March 1978): 130.

10. John M. Jakaitis, "Two Versions of an Unfinished War: *Dispatches* and *Going After Cacciato,*" *Cultural Critique* 3 (Spring 1986): 207.

11. Kali Tal, "The Mind at War: Images of Women in Vietnam Novels by Combat Veterans," *Contemporary Literature* 31 (Spring 1990): 84, 77; hereafter cited in text.

12. Arthur M. Saltzman, "The Betrayal of the Imagination: Paul Brodeur's *The Stunt Man* and Tim O'Brien's *Going After Cacciato,*" *Critique* 22 (Fall 1980): 36.

13. Robert M. Slabey, "*Going After Cacciato*: Tim O'Brien's 'Separate Peace,'" in *America Rediscovered: Critical Essays on Literature and Film of the Vietnam War,* ed. Owen W. Gilman Jr., and Lorrie Smith (New York: Garland, 1990), 210.

14. Maria S. Bonn, "Can Stories Save Us? Tim O'Brien and the Efficacy of the Text," *Critique* 36 (Fall 1994): 11.

15. For discussions of O'Brien's writing, editing, and publication patterns for *The Things They Carried*, especially differences between stories published in magazines and in chapters of the novel based on these stories, see Calloway's "How to Tell a True War Story"; Lorrie Smith's " 'The Things Men Do': The Gendered Subtext in Tim O'Brien's *Esquire* Stories," *Critique* 36 (Fall 1994), 16–39, hereafter cited in text; and Mark Taylor's "Tim O'Brien's War," *Centennial Review* 29 (Spring 1995), 213–29.

16. Renny Christopher's *The Viet Nam War, The American War* explores the issues of ethnocentricity and cultural awareness in American literature usually labeled "Vietnam War literature." Christopher argues that a vast majority of Vietnam War literature published in the United States contains only American, ethnocentric, narrow-minded portrayals of Viet Nam (she distinguishes "Viet Nam" the country from "Vietnam" the experience) and the Vietnamese.

Christopher asserts that O'Brien's *Going After Cacciato* is a typical example of what is wrong with American literature written by American authors about the Vietnam experience. Her criticism of *Cacciato* points to three major flaws. First and foremost is O'Brien's flawed portrayal of Vietnamese characters, such as Sarkin Aung Wan and Major Li Van Hgoc. According to Christopher, O'Brien upholds cliched American attitudes toward the Vietnamese by writing only from an American perspective, thus denying the Vietnamese characters the unique depth of voice they deserve. O'Brien substitutes for this authentic voice a limited, paternal, occasionally flawed American version of a Vietnamese perspective. Second, Christopher cites O'Brien's all-too-common portrayal of the Vietnam War as primarily an "internal war": "the United States versus the United States, . . . the squad . . . battling with Lieutenant Martin." She says that this limiting perspective removes any notion of the Vietnamese role in the war. Finally, Christopher accuses O'Brien of writing a "first-reaction response to the war," citing his failure "to look beyond simple dichotomies" into larger political and cultural issues (229–35) related to both Viet Nam and the Vietnam experience.

17. For a helpful presentation of a theoretical base for feminist criticism of literary representations of the Vietnam War, see Susan Jeffords's *The Remasculinization of America: Gender and the Vietnam War* (Bloomington, Ind.: Indiana University Press, 1989). In analyzing "the gendered structure of representations of the Vietnam War in America," Jeffords discusses how wars and the Vietnam War in particular are characterized by battlefields of "gender in which enemies are depicted as feminine, wives and mothers and girlfriends are justification for fighting, and vocabularies are sexually motivated." She goes on to note that narratives about the Vietnam War, most of which are written by males, are written "primarily to reinforce the interests of masculinity and patriarchy" (xi).

18. Lorrie N. Smith, "Back Against the Wall: Anti-Feminist Backlash in Vietnam War Literature," *Vietnam Generation* 1 (Summer/Fall 1989): 123; hereafter cited in text.

19. In an interview, O'Brien notes that "Sweetheart of the Song Tra Bong" is "one of the few cases in the book that is based on reality. A woman did in fact come to Vietnam, an ex-cheerleader just out of high school, pretty much as I described it. But the rest of the story I invented." Debra Shostak, *"Artful Dodge* Interviews Tim O'Brien," *Artful Dodge* 22/23 (1991): 89.

20. In an article on *The Things They Carried,* Steven Kaplan argues that the tensions between story-truth and happening-truth represent the ambiguity and uncertainty related to soldiers' and the United States's experiences in the Vietnam War: "The Undying Uncertainty of the Narrator in Tim O'Brien's *The Things They Carried," Critique* 35 (Fall 1993): 43–52).

21. Norman Maclean, *A River Runs Through It* (Chicago: University of Chicago Press, 1976), 104.

Chapter Four

1. Bruce Weber, "War and Peace," *Esquire* (September 1985): 269; hereafter cited in text.

2. For a fascinating discussion of publishing decisions and dollar amounts related to publication rights for this novel, see Weber's article.

3. Paul E. Hutchison, *Library Journal* 110 (1 October 1985): 114.

4. Michiko Kakutani, "Prophet of Doom," *New York Times* (28 September 1985): 12.

5. David Montrose, "Paranoia, American-style," *Times Literary Supplement* (28 March 1986): 342.

6. Grace Paley, "Digging a Shelter and a Grave," *New York Times Book Review* (17 November 1985): 7.

7. Tim O'Brien, "Darkness on the Edge of Town," *Feature* (January 1979): 42; hereafter cited in text as "Darkness."

8. Marc Leepson, "Interview: Tim O'Brien," *Gallery* (August 1986): 28; hereafter cited in text.

9. Tim O'Brien, *The Nuclear Age* (1985; reprint, New York: Dell, 1993), 13; hereafter cited in text as *Nuclear.*

10. For a discussion of the significance of these section and chapter titles see Lee Schweninger's "Ecofeminism, Nuclearism, and O'Brien's *The Nuclear Age,"* in *The Nightmare Considered: Critical Essays on Nuclear War Literature,* ed. Nancy Anisfield (Bowling Green, Ohio: Bowling Green State University Popular Press, 1991), 177–85.

11. For further discussion of this paradigmatic structure in modern war literature, see Tobey Herzog's *Vietnam War Stories: Innocence Lost* (New York: Routledge, 1992), 13–16.

Chapter Five

1. Although lacking any connection to the Vietnam War, O'Brien's most recently published short story, "Faith," in the *New Yorker* (12 February

1996) does contain O'Brien's familiar themes of childhood, love, marriage, and deceit with a dark, at times bizarre, vision and a Faulknerian influence. Such content suggests that O'Brien may not be moving in an entirely new direction with his fiction. He also writes in a January 1997 letter to me that this new story is part of a novel in progress.

2. Joseph P. Kahn, "The Things He Carries," *Boston Globe* (19 October 1994): 69; hereafter cited in text.

3. In comparing this galley version (last chapter labeled "Author's Note") to the published version of the last chapter (31: "Hypothesis"), one finds throughout the section only a few changes in words, minor additions and deletions, and some rearrangement of passages. But on page 302 of the published paperback version (305 in hardback) appears the following portion of a lengthy, added section:

> His tone was confessional. At times he cried. At dawn, just before signing off, he seemed to break down entirely. Not his mind—his heart. There were garbled prayers, convulsive pleas directed to Kathy and to God. . . . "Because you asked once, What is sacred? and because the answer was always you. Sacred? Now you know . . . Where *are* you?" A Murderer? A man who could boil? At no point in this discourse did John Wade admit to the slightest knowledge of Kathy's whereabouts, nor indicate that he was withholding information. (*Lake,* 302)

4. Gail Caldwell, "At Home in the Inferno of Memory," *Boston Globe* (9 October 1994): B15.

5. See Michael Kerrigan's review, "Memories of War," *Times Literary Supplement* (21 April 1995): 20.

6. Richard Elder, "Vanishing Act," *Los Angeles Times* (2 October 1994): 3.

7. First Lieutenant William Calley was one of 30 soldiers (enlisted and officers) charged with war crimes related to the My Lai massacre. He was, however, the only soldier found guilty and was sentenced to life at hard labor for the premeditated murder of "not less than 22 civilians." His sentence was subsequently reduced, first by the reviewing authority to 20 years and then by the Secretary of the Army to 10 years. After legal appeals and further reductions, Calley served about 3 years under house arrest. See William Wilson's "I Had Prayed to God That This Was Fiction," *American Heritage* (February 1990): 44–53.

8. Tim O'Brien, "The Vietnam Veteran: Prisoners of Peace," *Penthouse* (March 1974): 44.

9. Tim O'Brien, "The Violent Vet," *Esquire* (December 1979): 99.

10. Tim O'Brien, "We've Adjusted Too Well," in *The Wounded Generation: America after Vietnam,* ed. A. D. Horne (Englewood Cliffs, N.J.: Prentice Hall, 1981), 205–7.

11.   In a 1994 interview with *Newsday*, O'Brien supports this possibility of a difficult post-Vietnam adjustment by confessing that "Vietnam means for me having done twenty-five years of lies, twenty-five years of shame, twenty-five years of guilt." Dan Cryer, "Talking With Tim O'Brien," *Newsday* (16 October 1994): 32.

12.   According to O'Brien, this impressive array of research and quotes appearing in the "Evidence" chapters came from his extensive reading over many years of his life in diverse subjects. As a result, he was quickly able to compile the information for these chapters from this general reading: "I didn't have to research much of anything. I just had to go find the books and the pages. The only systematic research was on the My Lai Massacre" (Herzog, Interview).

13.   See the following footnotes: #21 (p. 30), #36 (p. 101), #67 (p. 146), #71 (p. 191), #88 (p. 199), #117 (p. 266), #124 (p. 295), #127 (p. 298), #128 (p. 299), #131 (p. 300), #132 (p. 300), and #133 (p. 301).

14.   In a 1979 interview, O'Brien notes that "books can also work as magic acts. You go into a magic theater and . . . you know the outcome, the story, but the mystery isn't so much in what's going to happen as it is in seeing it happen" (McCaffery, Interview, 144).

Selected Bibliography

PRIMARY SOURCES

Novels

Northern Lights. New York: Delacorte/Seymour Lawrence, 1975.
If I Die in a Combat Zone, Box Me up and Ship Me Home. 1973. Reprint, New York: Dell, 1983.
Going After Cacciato. 1978. Reprint, New York: Dell, 1989.
The Things They Carried. 1990. Reprint, New York: Penguin, 1991.
The Nuclear Age. 1985. Reprint, New York: Dell, 1993.
In the Lake of the Woods. 1994. Reprint, New York: Penguin, 1995.

Selected Essays and Short Fiction

"The Vietnam Veteran: Prisoners of Peace. *Penthouse* (March 1974): 44+.
"Darkness on the Edge of Town." *Feature* (January 1979): 42–49.
"The Violent Vet." *Esquire* (December 1979): 96–104.
"We've Adjusted Too Well." In *The Wounded Generation: America after Vietnam*, ed. A. D. Horne, 205–7. Englewood Cliffs, N.J.: Prentice Hall, 1981.
"The Magic Show." In *Writers on Writing*, ed. Robert Pack and Jay Parini, 175–83. London: University Press of New England, 1991.
"Loon Point." *Esquire* (January 1993): 91–94.
"The Vietnam in Me." *New York Times Magazine* (2 October 1994): 48–57.
"Faith." *New Yorker* (12 February 1996): 62–67.

SECONDARY SOURCES

Books and Parts of Books about O'Brien

Beidler, Philip D. *American Literature and the Experience of Vietnam*. Athens, Ga.: University of Georgia Press, 1982. 99–105 and 172–79+.
———. *Re-writing America: Vietnam Writers in Their Generation*. Athens, Ga.: University of Georgia Press, 1991. 28–37+.
Christopher, Renny. *The Viet Nam War, The American War*. Amherst, Mass.: University Press of Massachusetts, 1995. 229–35+.
Hellmann, John. *American Myth and the Legacy of Vietnam*. New York: Columbia University Press, 1986. 160–67+.
Herzog, Tobey. *Vietnam War Stories: Innocence Lost*. New York: Routledge, 1992. 139–66.

Kaplan, Stephen. *Understanding Tim O'Brien*. Columbia, S.C.: University of South Carolina Press, 1995.

Melling, Philip H. *Vietnam in American Literature*. Boston: Twayne, 1990.

Myers, Thomas Robert. *Walking Point: American Narratives of Vietnam*. New York: Oxford University Press. 1988. 76–89 and 171–85+.

Ringnalda, Don. *Fighting and Writing the Vietnam War*. Jackson, Miss.: University Press of Mississippi, 1994. 90–114

Articles and Reviews

Anisfield, Nancy. "Words and Fragments: Narrative Style in Vietnam War Novels." In *Search and Clear: Critical Responses to Selected Literature and Films of the Vietnam War*, ed. William J. Searle, 56–61. Bowling Green, Ohio: Bowling Green State University Popular Press, 1988.

Bates, Milton J. "Men, Women, and Vietnam." In *America Rediscovered: Critical Essays on the Literature and Film of the Vietnam War,* ed. Owen Gilman Jr., and Lorrie Smith, 27–63. New York: Garland, 1990.

————. "Tim O'Brien's Myth of Courage." *Modern Fiction Studies* 33 (Summer 1987): 263–79.

Bonn, Maria S. "Can Stories Save Us? Tim O'Brien and the Efficacy of the Text." *Critique* 36 (Fall 1994): 11–15.

Bowie, Thomas G. "Reconciling Vietnam: Tim O'Brien's Narrative Journey." In *The United States and Viet Nam: From War to Peace,* ed. Robert M. Slabey, 184–97. Jefferson, N.C.: McFarland, 1996.

Caldwell, Gail. "At Home in the Inferno of Memory." *Boston Globe* (9 October 1994): B15.

Calloway, Catherine. " 'How to Tell a True War Story': Metafiction in *The Things They Carried*." *Critique* 36 (Summer 1995): 249–57.

————. "Pluralities of Vision: *Going After Cacciato* and Tim O'Brien's Short Fiction." In *America Rediscovered: Critical Essays on the Literature and Film of the Vietnam War,* ed. Owen Gilman Jr., and Lorrie Smith, 213–24. New York: Garland, 1990.

Couser, G. Thomas. "*Going After Cacciato*: The Romance and the Real War." *Journal of Narrative Technique* 13 (Winter 1983): 1–10.

Freedman, Richard. "A Separate Peace." *New York Times Book Review* (12 February 1978): 1.

Griffith, James. "A Walk through History: Tim O'Brien's *Going After Cacciato*." *War, Literature, and the Arts* 3 (Spring 1991): 1–33.

Herzog, Tobey C. "*Going After Cacciato*: The Soldier-Author-Character Seeking Control." *Critique* 24 (Winter 1983): 88–96.

Jakaitis, John M. "Two Versions of an Unfinished War: *Dispatches* and *Going After Cacciato*." *Cultural Critique* 3 (Spring 1986): 191–210.

Jones, Dale W. "The Vietnams of Michael Herr and Tim O'Brien: Tales of Disintegration and Integration." *Canadian Review of American Studies* 13 (Winter 1982): 309–20.

Kaplan, Steven. "The Undying Uncertainty of the Narrator in Tim O'Brien's *The Things They Carried*. *Critique* 35 (Fall 1993): 43–52.

Kinney, Katherine. "American Exceptionalism and Empire in Tim O'Brien's *Going After Cacciato*." *American Literary History* 7 (Winter 1995): 633–53.

Klinkenborg, Verlyn. Review of *In the Lake of the Woods*: "A Self-Made Man." *New York Times Book Review* (9 October 1994): 1+.

Loeb, Jeff. "Childhood's End: Self-Recovery in the Autobiography of the Vietnam War." *American Studies* 37 (Spring 1996): 95–116.

McWilliams, Dean. "Time in Tim O'Brien's *Going After Cacciato*." *Critique* 29 (Summer 1988): 245–55.

Nelson, Marie. "Two Consciences: A Reading of Tim O'Brien's Vietnam Trilogy: *If I Die in a Combat Zone, Going After Cacciato,* and *Northern Lights*." In *Third Force Psychology and the Study of Literature,* ed. Bernard J. Paris, 262–79. Rutherford, N.J.: Fairleigh Dickinson University Press, 1986.

Paley, Grace. "Digging a Shelter and a Grave." *New York Times Book Review* (17 November 1985): 7.

Palm, Major Edward F. "Falling in and Out: Military Idiom as Metamorphic Motif in *Going After Cacciato*." *Notes on Contemporary Literature* 22 (November 1992): 8.

Raymond, Michael W. "Imagined Responses to Vietnam: Tim O'Brien's *Going After Cacciato*." *Critique* 24 (Winter 1983): 97–104.

Sale, Roger. "Fathers and Fathers and Sons." *New York Review of Books* (13 November 1975): 31–32.

Saltzman, Arthur M. "The Betrayal of the Imagination: Paul Brodeur's *The Stunt Man* and Tim O'Brien's *Going after Cacciato*." *Critique* 22 (Fall 1980): 32–38.

Schroeder, Eric James. "The Past and Possible: Tim O'Brien's Dialectic of Memory and Imagination." In *Search and Clear: Critical Responses to Selected Literature and Films of the Vietnam War,* ed. William J. Searle, 116–34. Bowling Green, Ohio: Bowling Green State University Popular Press, 1988.

Schweninger, Lee. "Ecofeminism, Nuclearism, and O'Brien's *The Nuclear Age*." In *The Nightmare Considered: Critical Essays on Nuclear War Literature,* ed. Nancy Anisfield, 177–85. Bowling Green, Ohio: Bowling Green State University Popular Press, 1991.

Slabey, Robert M. "*Going After Cacciato*: Tim O'Brien's 'Separate Piece.' " In *America Rediscovered: Critical Essays on the Literature and Film of the Vietnam War,* ed. Owen Gilman Jr., and Lorrie Smith, 205–12. New York: Garland, 1990.

Smith, Lorrie. "Back against the Wall: Anti-Feminist Backlash in Vietnam War Literature." *Vietnam Generation* 1 (Summer/Fall 1989): 115–26.

———. " 'The Things Men Do': Gendered Subtext in Tim O'Brien's *Esquire* Stories." *Critique* 36 (Fall 1994): 16–39.

Tal, Kali. "The Mind at War: Images of Women in Vietnam Novels by Combat Veterans." *Contemporary Literature* 31 (Spring 1990): 76–96.

Taylor, Mark. "Tim O'Brien's War." *Centennial Review* 29 (Spring 1995): 213–29.

Vannatta, Dennis. "Theme and Structure in Tim O'Brien's *Going After Caciato.*" *Modern Fiction Studies* 28 (Summer 1982): 242–46.

Weber, Bruce. "War and Peace." *Esquire* (September 1985): 269.

Wiedemann, Barbara. "American War Novels: Strategies for Survival." In *War and Peace: Perspectives in the Nuclear Age,* ed. Ulrich Goebel and Otto Nelson, 137–44. Lubbock, Tex.: Texas Tech University Press, 1988.

Zins, Daniel L. "Imagining the Real: The Fiction of Tim O'Brien." *Hollins Critic* 23 (June 1986): 1–12.

Bibliographies

Calloway, Catherine. "Tim O'Brien: A Checklist." *Bulletin of Bibliography* 48 (March 1991): 6–11.

———. "Tim O'Brien: A Primary and Secondary Bibliography." *Bulletin of Bibliography* 50 (September 1993): 223–29.

Jason, Philip K. *The Vietnam War in Literature: An Annotated Bibliography of Criticism.* Pasadena, Calif.: Salem Press, 1992.

Interviews

Bruckner, D. J. R. "A Storyteller For the War That Won't End." *New York Times* (3 April 1990): C15+.

Caldwell, Gail. "Staying True to Vietnam." *The Boston Globe* (29 March 1990): 69+.

Coffey, Michael. "Tim O'Brien." *Publishers Weekly* (16 February 1990): 60–61.

Cryer, Dan. "Talking with Tim O'Brien." *Newsday* (16 October 1994): 32.

Herzog, Tobey C. Unpublished interview with Tim O'Brien. Cambridge, Mass., 11–12 July 1995.

Kahn, Joseph. "The Things He Carries." *Boston Globe* (19 October 1994): 69+.

Kaplan, Steven. "An Interview with Tim O'Brien." *The Missouri Review* 14, no. 3 (1991): 95–108.

Leepson, Marc. "Interview: Tim O'Brien." *Gallery* (August 1986): 27–30.

Lyons, Gene. "No More Bugles, No More Drums." *Entertainment Weekly* (23 February 1990): 50–52.

McCaffery, Larry. "Interview With Tim O'Brien." *Chicago Review* 33 (1982): 129–149.

McNerney, Brian C. "Responsibly Inventing History: An Interview with Tim O'Brien." *War, Literature, and the Arts* 6 (Fall/Winter 1994): 1–26.

Naparsteck, Martin. "An Interview with Tim O'Brien." *Contemporary Literature* 32 (Spring 1991): 1–11.

Schroeder, Eric James. "Two Interviews: Talks with Tim O'Brien and Robert Stone." *Modern Fiction Studies* 30 (Spring 1984): 135–64.

Schumacher, Michael. "Writing Short Stories from Life." *Writer's Digest* 71 (April 1991): 34–39.

Shostak, Debra. "*Artful Dodge* Interviews Tim O'Brien." *Artful Dodge* 22/23 (1991): 74–90.

Index

The Author

Tobey C. Herzog is a professor of English and chair of the English Department at Wabash College in Crawfordsville, Indiana. He has a Ph.D. in English literature from Purdue University. He is the author of the book *Vietnam War Stories: Innocence Lost,* a cultural and literary study of American narratives on the Vietnam experience, and of several papers and articles on the war and its literature. His interest in the Vietnam War, its literature, and its soldier-authors emerges from his experiences as a teacher of modern war literature and as a veteran who served in Vietnam from 1969 to 1970.

The Editor

Frank Day is a professor of English and head of the English Department at Clemson University. He is the author of *Sir William Empson: An Annotated Bibliography* (1984) and *Arthur Koestler: A Guide to Research* (1985). He was a Fulbright lecturer in American literature in Romania (1980–1981) and in Bangladesh (1986–1987).